Education for Social Change

Also available from Bloomsbury

Comparative and International Education: An Introduction to Theory, Method, and Practice, David Phillips and Michele Schweisfurth
Educating for Peace and Human Rights: An Introduction, Maria Hantzopoulos and Monisha Bajaj
Education and International Development: An Introduction, edited by Tristan McCowan and Elaine Unterhalter
Global Citizenship Education: A Critical Introduction to Key Concepts and Debates, Edda Sant, Ian Davies, Karen Pashby and Lynette Shultz
Schooling as Uncertainty: An Ethnographic Memoir in Comparative Education, Frances Vavrus
The Bloomsbury Handbook of Global Education and Learning, edited by Douglas Bourn
The Bloomsbury Handbook of Theory in Comparative and International Education, edited by Tavis D. Jules, Robin Shields and Matthew A. M. Thomas
The Bloomsbury Handbook of the Internationalization of Higher Education in the Global South, edited by Juliet Thondhlana, Evelyn Chiyevo Garwe, Hans de Wit, Jocelyne Gacel-Ávila, Futao Huang and Wondwosen Tamrat

Education for Social Change

Perspectives on Global Learning

Douglas Bourn

BLOOMSBURY ACADEMIC
LONDON • NEW YORK • OXFORD • NEW DELHI • SYDNEY

BLOOMSBURY ACADEMIC
Bloomsbury Publishing Plc
50 Bedford Square, London, WC1B 3DP, UK
1385 Broadway, New York, NY 10018, USA
29 Earlsfort Terrace, Dublin 2, Ireland

BLOOMSBURY, BLOOMSBURY ACADEMIC and the Diana logo are trademarks of
Bloomsbury Publishing Plc

First published in Great Britain, 2022

A catalogue record for this book is available from the British Library.

A catalog record for this book is available from the Library of Congress.

ISBN: HB: 978-1-3501-9283-6
PB: 978-1-3501-9284-3
ePDF: 978-1-3501-9285-0
eBook: 978-1-3501-9286-7

Typeset by Deanta Global Publishing Services, Chennai, India
Printed and bound in Great Britain

To find out more about our authors and books visit www.bloomsbury.com and
sign up for our newsletters.

Contents

Foreword

In 2017, Roxane de la Sablonnière of the University of Montreal acknowledged the great interest of contemporary scholars in the question – "What leads to social change?" She examined numerous abstracts of peer-reviewed articles in the social sciences and psychology, seeking to develop a better typology of social change and highlighting the importance of continuing the efforts to understand its impact. Douglas Bourn's new book, *Education and Social Change*, makes a solid contribution to the field. His mapping of theories and practices in education intended to affect social change represents an effort in social cartography, a method the social sciences and education have borrowed from geography. It helps scholars to organize fields of knowledge as they identify and connect a variety of relevant works representing diverse actors' voices and actions.

Bourn starts out by situating himself in a lifelong web of professional development opportunities. From examining the educational ideas of the British Labor Party for his doctoral research, through employment in organizations dedicated to bringing about local and global social change through education, participation in the founding and directing of the British Development Education Association, and, lastly, bringing this experience to academia as author, professor and director of the Development Education Research Centre at the Institute of Education of the University College London, Bourn built a career responsive to issues relative to the advancement and dissemination of knowledge about the relationship between education and social change in an increasingly globalized context.

In terms of the value-laden term 'social change', Bourn is clear about its direction, the attainment of a more just and sustainable world, with education playing a historical central role. Here, educational access is an obvious given, as schools must first be available to students everywhere. The more complex question of educational forms – curricular and instructional practices – must be focused on the requirements: a global perspective; a recognition of social inequality and a belief in equity and the justice-seeking efforts to redress it; and the privileging of processes of reflection and dialogue that lead to personal transformation. Bourn stands clearly in the camp of critical global social justice education.

On a global scale, the largest organization to nurture theories and political guidelines for education as vehicle for social change is the branch of the United Nations in charge of science, culture and education, UNESCO. Bourn discusses UNESCO's role and historical documents offering principles and guidelines for education policies. These regard individual and collective human rights, most especially for oppressed groups. More recently, they have focused on the interconnected ideas about education for global citizenship and education for a sustainable future. In addition, Bourn also identifies issues concerning state-provided education, touching on enduring questions of education as a reproducer of the status quo as well as ability to act as change agent.

Western thought from the Global North has offered enduring – and interrelated – educational themes with social change in mind, such as the relationship between education and democracy, education for a new socialist order and education for liberation. Intentions to educate the young through and for democratic life have been current since the nineteenth century, as have ideas about education for socialism, both utopian and Marxist.

Bourn situates such questions and their proponents. He underscores the enduring belief in the relationship between education and democracy, as spelled out historically by American philosopher John Dewey. He discusses the relationship between education and socialism through the works of Robert Owen and R. H. Tawney, and of communists such as Nadezhda Krupskaya. Furthermore, he entertains the connection of education and liberation, which has come primarily from the Global South. Amongst its thinkers is the Brazilian Paulo Freire, whose work has led to the critical pedagogy of Henry Giroux, Michael Apple, Antonia Darder and others in the United States. Julius Nyerere, from Tanzania, marked the educational thought of African independence movements. Mohandas Gandhi, from India, brought ideas of resistance and liberation to the world.

Numerous scholar activists for social change since the turn of the twenty-first century have been addressing education in relation to issues relevant to environmental, economic and social-political sustainability, most especially catastrophic climate change. Neoliberal capitalist globalization has indeed created a new global system. Globalized societies now face glocal consequences of libertine market actions to generate profit and accumulate capital, leading to even greater social inequality, instability and environmental degradation.

Education for a global society; education through global social movements and for global social justice; education for global citizenship; education for sustainability – each has proponents and critics with designs for formal and informal curriculums and educational practices to move human consciousness and action towards necessary individual and social change. Bourn maps them, including those inspired in the experience of indigenous peoples that support the idea of *buen vivir* (to live well), setting quality of life for all above accumulation of wealth for a few.

Social change ultimately comes from agents acting in their everyday work. Bourn concerns his quest with the role of school teachers, university professors (academic tutors), youth leaders and agencies of civil society organizations, including the World Social Forum, to fashion social change. He brings a great deal of complexity, phenomenal networks of people labouring to create a different, a more humane and, as Paulo Freire would underscore, a more beautiful world. This is an indication that underneath Bourn's herculean effort as a scholar lies a man with the soul of a poet, who also understands the power of emotion in personal and societal change.

The artistry of the author manifests in ideas he has continued to propose for education: the educated person in our times must understand what happens in their surroundings as interconnected to what happens elsewhere in the world; must recognize life in a global society and the value of others' perspectives and experiences; must understand the impact of global forces through critical reflection on data and information; must nurture attitudes and skills of critical reflection and dialogue about self and society, including assumptions about the world examination of data and information; must have the ability to engage and work co-operatively with diverse others; and must be confident in the belief that another world is possible.

Bourn's *Education for Social Change* brings the reader into many paths of social change to achieve these outlined aims, both historically and contemporarily, involving a wealth of authors, movements and actual projects from around the globe. These will certainly be inspiring to academics, educators, leaders (young and older) of civil society organizations and of particular projects, and students of change from many backgrounds. May Bourn's mapping inspires the making of other maps of social change through education, as needed for deepening our knowledge and actions in the re/construction of global societies.

Tania Ramalho
State University of New York, USA

Acknowledgements

I would like to thank the following people for their help and comments on this publication: Hilary Alcock, Jacquie Ayre, Alison Bellwood, Nicole Blum, Emiliano Bosio, Jessica Bowl, Maureen Ellis, Son Gyoh, Sarah Hamilton, Fran Hunt, Susan Kambalu, Kyoungwon Lee, Ameet Mehta, Hannah Nixon, Katherine Pugh, Barry Rawlings, Dave Richards, Massimiliano Tarozzi, Momodou Sallah, Namrata Sharma and Liam Wegimont.

Thanks also to all those who participated in the webinar organized by the Development Education Research Centre at UCL for their observations on the themes I outlined for this book.

Thanks also to Moira Jenkins for her help with editing this volume.

Special thanks to Tania Ramalho for not only commenting on the draft but in providing the foreword.

This volume brings together many of the ideas, experiences and thoughts from my over forty years involved in promoting education for social change from my PhD, working for the Woodcraft Folk, founding the Development Education Association and setting up the Development Education Research Centre. None of these achievements would have been possible without the dedication, enthusiasm and, above all, commitment from many people who all shared a vision of wanting to see a more just and sustainable world. It is to them this book is dedicated.

I hope the themes outlined in this volume will inspire future generations of students and researchers to continue the struggle for an approach to education that can inspire people for social change.

Abbreviations

CAFOD	Catholic Agency for Overseas Development
CPD	Continuing Professional Development
CSOs	Civil Society Organizations
DEA	Development Education Association
DEC	Development Education Centre
ESI	Eco-Social Innovation
ESD	Education for Sustainable Development
ESR	Education for Self-Reliance
GCE	Global Citizenship Education
IBE	International Bureau of Education
ILP	Independent Labour Party
LHU	Liverpool Hope University
MDGs	Millennium Development Goals
NGOs	Non-Governmental Organizations
NYA	National Youth Agency
OECD	Organisation for Economic Co-operation and Development
RISC	Reading International Solidarity Centre
SDGs	Sustainable Development Goals
SUA	Slovakia University of Agriculture
UCL	University College London
UCLA	University of California at Los Angeles

UKSCN   United Kingdom Student Climate Network

UN   United Nations

UNESCO   United Nations Education, Scientific and Cultural Organisation

UNICEF   United Nations Children's Fund

WPE   Wider Perspectives in Education programme

Introduction

In many schools and educational institutions around the world, quotations from famous figures such as Nelson Mandela, Malala Yousafzai, Gandhi and Martin Luther King can be seen that suggest the importance of education as a means to make a better world and seek social change. A well-used quote from Malala, for example, states, '*One book, one pen, one child, and one teacher, can change the world.*' They are there to inspire learners to see the value of education and to realize that they, the learners, can make a difference. Behind such quotes and many other similar ones, there is an assumption that education can play a major role in securing social change. This belief is not something new. One can see elements of this belief in quotations from ancient philosophers from both the West and the East. As education has become more accepted as an integral element of the needs of all societies, its relative importance and role have increased. Today, international initiatives such as the Sustainable Development Goals put education as one of their top priorities.

Personal Journey

My own professional career has in many ways aimed to put some of these quotes into practice. The idea for this volume came from the professorial lecture I gave at the University College London Institute of Education in December 2018, where I shared a personal rationale for my approach to work and research which has been based on the potential role of education to secure social change.[1]

In that lecture I summarized my personal career including my doctoral research, my work for educational charities and my research and current post at the Institute. I mentioned that I had been fortunate in that my professional career had enabled me to put into practice ideas that I learnt from my doctoral research on the Development of Labour Party Ideas on Education (Bourn 1978). Following the completion of my thesis, I then worked for a radical national voluntary youth organization, the Woodcraft Folk, that put education for social change as one of its main aims and principles. After a brief interlude working for Friends of the Earth, in 1993 I was responsible for helping to launch, and was the founding director, of the Development Education Association (DEA). It was here that I learnt about the ways in which many organizations were bringing an understanding of the wider world to an approach to learning that encouraged social transformation. Finally, in 2006 I came to the Institute of Education, now part of University College London, bringing with me the ideas and learning experiences I had gained from the DEA to establish the first ever research centre specifically focused on development education and related terms such as 'global learning' and 'global education'.

Throughout this volume, reference will be made to some of the organizations referred to earlier and the learning I gained from my work with them. But this volume is not an autobiographical one, more an attempt to show that we can all make a difference and contribute to changing the world.

The world of the third decade of the twenty-first century is an unequal one with major social and economic divisions within and between nations. This book does not attempt to outline this in any detail because numerous volumes have shown how unequal the world is. It is assumed in this volume that the reader has either some existing knowledge and understanding of this inequality or is supportive of wanting to achieve a more just and sustainable world.

Aims of Volume

This volume aims to introduce the reader, be they students at undergraduate or postgraduate level, academics and researchers or practising educationalists in schools, informal or higher education, to the ways in which education for social change can be understood, interpreted and put into practice.

Underpinning the themes raised in this volume is the belief that in order to secure this more just world, education has to play a central role. This means not only access to education but to a different form of education than that which tends to dominate policies and practices around the world. The form of education I am promoting is what I would call a 'pedagogy of global social justice', and it has four main elements:

- Promotion of a global outlook
- Recognition of power and inequality in the world
- Belief in social justice and equity
- Commitment to reflection, dialogue and personal transformation (Bourn 2015).

This approach, which I have called Development Education or Global Learning, or what some people call Global Citizenship Education or Global Education, has as its underlying theme the potential power of education to bring about social change.

The themes addressed in the volume and the evidence referred to are influenced by and reflect some of my own experiences. This means that whilst there are references in the volume to influences from postcolonialism, critical pedagogy, authors and practices from the Global South, it reflects the perspectives of a UK educationalist, and therefore a number of the examples come from Great Britain. However, I try wherever possible to bring in perspectives from other regions of the world but it is not a volume that aims to bring in a global overview of what Education for Social Change means.

'Education for social change' is a term used by many radical educationalists, but what does it mean?

A major influence on my thinking for developing this approach has been the ideas and works of the Brazilian educationalist Paulo Freire. I had the privilege to meet him briefly in the United Kingdom during the 1970s, and I have continued to find his critique of education and its potential transformative role very compelling. His influence will be seen in several chapters including in particular the one on education for liberation.

Also influential in this volume is one of the disciples of Freire's work, the American educationalist Henry Giroux and his concept of 'critical pedagogy'. What I have found particularly powerful in his work is that, whilst being consistently critical of education in all of its forms, he believes that education can play a major role in changing the world.

A lot of my own personal theoretical influences came initially from aspects of Marxism. Whilst at university, I had been particularly influenced by the work of the French philosopher Louis Althusser, but increasingly found his thinking too structural; also, it ignored the power of individuals and groups to secure social change. I found instead the thinking of the Italian Marxist, Antonio Gramsci, more relevant and appropriate, particularly his concept of hegemony and the importance of culture.

One well-known phrase from Gramsci has continued to stay with me throughout my career, the 'pessimism of the intellect, the optimism of the world'. This to me has meant that it is in the hands of all of us to secure change the world, but we have to believe we can make a difference regardless of the many daily challenges we may face.

Alongside these figures, other names from education in the past will be referred to. These include the American philosopher and educationalist John

Dewey, who had a major influence on twentieth-century education not only in his home country, the United States, but throughout the world. Another figure is the British academic who played a major role in influencing socialist thinking in the United Kingdom on education and that was R. H. Tawney. He was no revolutionary, and consciously took a very different approach to education to that of Marxists, but his belief in the importance of education and directly engaging in policymaking has an important place in this narrative on social change.

This engagement in policy change has always been important to me, and was the main focus of my work within the DEA from 1993 to 2006. Here I learnt that regardless of who was in political power, educational changes could be made, or, perhaps more importantly, spaces could be created that enabled radical and progressive practices to nurture and grow.

This theme of 'creative spaces', of opportunities for educationalists to develop their own ideas and practices, is an important prerequisite of social change. That is why I have always been a strong proponent of resourcing educational and social groups to develop projects that can test out new ideas and resources and assess their value and possible replicability.

This is where and why I would suggest that supporting young people to explore and test out their own ideas and practices, to gain new skills and to have the opportunity to promote their voice to the wider world is so important. I learnt the potential that young people have from my work for the Woodcraft Folk, and it has been reinforced for me by the actions of thousands of young people around the world with regards to the climate emergency.

Theories of Change

Before discussing what is meant by social change and the role of education therein, it is relevant to address the concept of 'theories of change' and its relevance to the themes in this volume. Within organizational management theory, the concept of theory of change has emerged as a major influence on how businesses, public sector bodies and voluntary organizations monitor, assess and evaluate the success and impact of their programmes. There are various examples of theories of change including Kurt Lewin's change model, Kotter's eight-step approach and Prosci's ADKAR model.[2]

All of the models make reference to creating a climate for change within the organization, desire for change, processes of change and the evidence of impact.

Their relevance to the themes in this volume is twofold. Firstly, by merely posing the question of change, organizations and bodies have to rethink their role and purpose, consider long-term impacts, processes and movements, and explore the engagement of relevant stakeholders (Vogel 2012). Secondly – and this is more problematic – is that theories of change can often result in a linear process of learning and engagement, that as a result of one activity there is an inevitable next step. This can mean either ignoring processes of learning or reducing education to a mechanistic process of transmitting information leading to some form of behaviour change.

A theme in many chapters of this volume is that change is not mechanistic and rarely linear. But what is meant by social change also needs to be clarified before discussions begin on the role of education.

What Is Meant by Social Change?

Social change takes place when there is a desire for change by people. Sometimes this may be imposed by the state or other national bodies, but lasting change can only be effective if it has the goodwill and involvement of the populace. As Sharma and Monteiro (2016: 72) have commented, 'social change leads to transformation in thinking which in turn influences behaviour patterns in society.' The extent to which these changes emerge out of the desires or needs of communities and peoples and the impact on the changes on behaviour patterns will always be open to debate and will depend on the specific social and political context at a local and a national level. For example, the ways in which social change has taken place in China since the beginning of the twenty-first century is very different to how change has taken place in say South Africa or India. What is evident is that social change has become closely linked to economic change, the influences of globalization and, in many societies, the dominance of neoliberal thinking. This means that the processes and forms of change are likely to vary in different types of societies. A particularly important influence on forms of social change in the twenty-first century to date has been the power of social media and access to global forms of technology. The extent to which they are accessible to all, and the degree of digital media literacy, have become important factors in framing social change.

Social change also implies changes in beliefs, customs, cultural traditions, values and forms of behaviour. Whilst this volume will focus more on wider societal and political changes and the influence of specific ideologies, these more specific individual cultural influences have had a direct impact on education. It needs also to be noted that there is a wide body of literature that focuses more on the psychological, management and more personal forms of change (Have et al. 2018; Drury and Reicher 2009).

Whilst the two are obviously closely connected, there is one approach that is worth noting at this introductory stage. This is the Presencing model developed by Otto Scharmer from the Massachusetts Institute of Technology (MIT) and his Theory U. This theory, by using the shape of the letter U, suggests a process of change that moves from Co-Initiating through Co-Sensing, Co-Presencing to Co-Creating and, finally, Co-Evolving (Scharmer 2018). His work and model are relevant to the themes of this volume because they refer to moving people from an individual or ego-system to one of eco-system awareness; also, for their inclusion of systems thinking, dialogic learning and the concept of co-creating a future. Later chapters in this volume will pick up some of these themes, most notably systems thinking in relation to education for sustainable development, and dialogic thinking in terms of global citizenship and global learning.

The Power and Role of Education

If change is seen in terms of changes in attitude and outlook alongside structural changes in society, then education clearly has a central role to play. If education is seen as more than the imparting of information and knowledge acquisition, and includes forms of internalization by the learner in terms of their thinking and views on the wider world, then it clearly has a transformative role. Sharma and Monteiro (2016: 72) suggest:

> Transformational change of personal thoughts, attitudes, values and practices ultimately leads to social responsibility that broadens minds and creates a better society.

The extent to which education in itself leads to change and that it is a linear process may be subject to some debate, as later chapters will discuss, but there is no doubt that increased knowledge and learning can enrich communities and societies and broaden horizons and worldviews.

Later chapters will review the relationship of education to improving democracies and posing alternative forms of societies, but there is a general agreement around the world that all states have a responsibility within education.

Literature on Education for Social Change

Whilst the theme of education as a means of changing society can be seen in the writings of many educationalists, social thinkers and political leaders, there has been relatively little academic debate and key publications that look specifically at this topic.

One of the few that does is the edited volume by Elliott, Fourali and Issler (2012). The Introduction to this volume includes the following:

> As argued by many educationalists, education can either be part of the solution or the problem to world issues. If it wants to be part of the solution, education has to find ways of addressing real social issues and help the learner face new and future challenges with an attitude that values inclusiveness and sustainability and, ultimately, values the individual, society, humanity and the environment at large. (Elliott, Fourali and Issler 2012: 1)

This quotation poses some key questions about how education does engage in social change. It suggests that putting social justice and sustainability at the heart of this process is key, and these are themes and approaches that will be developed further in this volume.

A perennial debate is the extent to which the approach should be interventionist with explicit learning outcomes related to forms of social action or whether the power of education is important in itself. For example, there has been the argument that access to education would by itself lead to a more informed and engaged citizenry and a healthier democracy. It could be argued that a continuation of this approach can be seen in the United Nations' rights-based education initiatives which propose that every child should have the right to access good-quality education. Human rights are therefore seen as underpinning this approach.

Some, however, might argue that to achieve this rights-based model a more interventionist approach is needed. This links to an approach to education which sees learning as intervening to address inequalities and forms of social injustice and seeks the development of skills to secure societal change. These themes are covered particularly in the more historical-based discussions.

Any discussion on the role of education for social change has therefore to take account of the ways in which societies around the world have developed their own policies and programmes in this area. Within Western-based societies, the growth in the importance of education went alongside greater democratic engagement in political decision-making.

There has, however, been the contrary view that education has in itself been a tool of the state and has therefore reproduced the dominant ideological views. This was the view in the 1920s and 1930s in the United Kingdom, for example, of some radical political and social thinkers. But it has also been a view reflected from the 1960s onwards through the perspectives of Louis Althusser (1971), Bowles and Gintis (2011) and, to a certain extent, Pierre Bourdieu (1990). Whilst there are variations in their standpoints, they do suggest a close relationship between capitalism and the purpose of education.

Paulo Freire and Henry Giroux, whilst accepting the main tenets behind these perspectives, suggest that education can be equally a liberating as well as a repressive force. What Freire (1972) and Giroux (2011) also suggest is that this ideological domination is not inevitable and can be countered by counter-hegemonic perspectives and approaches.

Another important educational figure whose name will appear several times in this volume and who has written extensively around this subject is Michael Apple. His volume *Can Education Change Society?* (2013) includes discussion of the work of Freire and a range of American educationalists such as Counts, Du Bois and Woodson. Apple notes that education can be, and has been, an important site for changing and envisioning a new society and testing out new possibilities.

Apple also recognizes the important contribution of social movements that influenced changes within education which have then had an impact on wider society.

This volume, as will be shown, suggests that this approach of Freire and Giroux and Apple is perhaps the most appropriate way of highlighting the value of education for social change. Key to this approach, as they suggest, and as I will outline further in later chapters, is the role, perspectives and spaces for intervention for the educator, the extent to which they can be a liberating force for challenging dominant orthodoxies and promoting approaches that can have an impact on society.

Finally, I would suggest that another important figure and someone who influenced the development of my own early thinking on education was the late Brian Simon, a UK academic who, whilst writing primarily on the history of education, stated that 'education is about the empowerment of individuals – but also . . . as the mode of development of human beings in society' (Simon 1994: 3). He noted that a crucial issue is the relation between education and social change:

> This affects teachers and all involved in education which . . . is essentially about human empowerment . . . it is through activity in a social setting that human powers are realised. And this necessarily involves social change. Further it may

be argued, human energy is likely to be more effective the more people believe in their power to effect change – to bend society more nearly to their aspirations. (ibid., 9)

Throughout this volume, there is an underlying theme that although recognizing that education can and does perpetuate existing social relations, it can also be a site of change often as a result of pressure from social movements. Simon supports this whilst at the same time recognizing that there is no guarantee of continual social advancement:

It seems clear that the English experience, at least, indicates that there have been periods of more or less educational advance, based on local, popular movements and implying a critique of existing social order together with its institutional support network – that is carrying with it the implication of perhaps even radical social change. (ibid., 13)

In a number of chapters, reference is made to the role of social movements and civil society organizations as motors for change through educational programmes. These bodies are particularly mentioned in many of the case studies and examples of practice as well as being the focus of a specific chapter.

Throughout all of the chapters, a common theme emerges: What is the purpose of an education that serves the interests of formal, informal or further and higher education? This volume can only introduce the reader to a range of views and ideas about this question. However, what will be evident is that any discussion on the purpose of education has to take account of relevant social, economic, cultural and political forces and the extent to which there are spaces for dissenting voices and a range of perspectives.

Structure of the Volume

The aims therefore of this volume are to show how, from an understanding of the key issues around education for social change, through examples from both policies and practices, significant progress can be made. Throughout the volume, reference will be made to case studies and examples of practice and evidence from research as well as reviewing the main themes from the literature. This is especially the case in Parts II and III of the volume where the chapters make particular use of doctoral-level research, an often-neglected area of evidence for the themes outlined in this volume. Most of the case studies are included because they provide good descriptions of what the aims of the relevant chapter mean in practice. Each of them deserves a more in-depth investigation and analysis which goes beyond the scope of this volume. The research, mainly from former doctoral students, comes primarily from the United Kingdom and North America, and they have been chosen because they give in-depth evidence of the value of an education for social change approach.

The volume is divided into three parts following this Introduction. Part I looks at key themes and terms that have influenced thinking on education for social change. Chapter 2 will review the relationship of education to society and the state and looks particularly at four key themes: education as a human right, as a promotion of universal values, as an instrument of the state and as a site of resistance to dominant ideologies.

The following three chapters then take the theme of social change through a review of historical and current debates involving three concepts: democracy, liberation and socialism and a new society. Each of these three chapters will, in addition to reviewing the current literature, pose some questions for wider debate and discussion and explore the extent to which much of these discourses are relevant in the third decade of the twenty-first century. Each chapter concludes with some key questions and key texts that the reader might wish to consider in taking the ideas explored further.

Part II of the volume looks more directly at educational and social concepts that have influenced the discourses on social change. These chapters also pose what could be the main themes for an approach of education for social change. Chapter 6 discusses the context of globalization and proposes that, today, any reference to education for social change has to note the influence of global forces. The importance of living and working in a global society is a key element of the chapter.

Chapter 7 addresses the relationship of the concept of social justice to social change particularly through outlining the need for a distinctive pedagogical approach. Reference will be made to the application of the ideas of Freire and Giroux with examples from North America and the United Kingdom.

The concluding chapter of this section, Chapter 8, brings together the relevance to the main argument of the book of the concepts of transformation, sustainable futures and global citizenship.

Part III of the volume looks at what social change means in relation to specific educational groups. It is here, particularly, that the evidence from research and case studies of practice are seen as features of each chapter. Chapter 9 looks specifically at the role of teachers and formal schooling. Chapter 10 is on young people and youth work, and Chapter 11 covers the role of the academic tutor and higher education. Finally, Chapter 12 looks at the role and influence of civil society organizations working within education.

The fourth and final part of the volume looks at the role of international bodies and the potential importance of the Sustainable Development Goals. A feature of Chapter 13 is the influence of UNESCO and the role it plays within both policies and practices around global citizenship and sustainable development. The final chapter is a short Conclusion which brings together the main themes of the book, suggesting that social change needs to be seen in terms of global social change and posing some final questions for further consideration by researchers, practitioners and students.

Questions for Further Consideration

- What does social change mean to you?
- To what extent can education be a vehicle for social change?
- What do you see as the role of the state in influencing what is taught within schools, colleges and universities?

Further Reading

Apple, M. (2013), *Can Education Change Society?*, Abingdon: Routledge.
Elliott, G., C. Fourali and S. Issler (eds) (2012), *Education and Social Change*, London: Continuum.
Scharmer, C. O. (2018), *The Essentials of Theory U: Core Principles and Applications*, Oakland, California: Berrett-Koehler Publishing.

Changing Role and Relationship of Education to Societal Change

The concept of education for social change poses a number of assumptions about the relationship between learning and the needs of societies. It also suggests that social change implies the need for a different values base and one that seeks a better society. This chapter reviews these assumptions through initially looking at the work of UNESCO in this area and related literature. It begins by focusing on two themes: education as a human right and the promotion of universal values. The chapter then reviews the ideological role of the state and the role education plays within this. The chapter concludes by suggesting that education can also be a site of resistance to dominant ideologies and provide counter-hegemonic approaches.

Education as a Human Right

Any discussion on education as a vehicle for social change has to start by addressing what is meant by it being a fundamental human right. If education is seen as an important vehicle for social change, then this implies there is a recognition of its value and importance. Whilst education has been a major demand of many social movements since the nineteenth century, it was only with the post-1945 international consensus that it became enshrined as a human right in international law. The United Nations (UN) General Assembly in 1948 adopted the UN Declaration of Human Rights. Since then, all countries in the world have adopted at least one human rights treaty which has guaranteed the right to education (UNESCO 2019). This rights-based approach to education has underpinned international legal policies on education over the past seventy years. But although education is accepted as part of the United Nations Convention on

Human Rights, this has not been easy to achieve in many societies. Only as a result of constant struggle has a near-universal acceptance of this been possible.

The Declaration in 1948 stated that in addition to everyone having the right to education, there was a broader social purpose:

> Education shall be directed to the full development of the human personality and to the strengthening of respect for human rights and fundamental freedoms. It shall promote understanding, tolerance and friendship among all nations, racial or religious groups, and shall further the activities of the United Nations for the maintenance of peace. (United Nations 1948)

Since then, there have been a plethora of further treaties and agreements either reinforcing or developing what education as a human right has meant. These have included specific initiatives on girls and women, people with disabilities, indigenous communities and the Convention on the Rights of the Child. The 1999 General Assembly of the UN emphasized that education is an empowerment right:

> the primary vehicle by which economically and socially marginalized adults and children can lift themselves out of poverty and obtain the means to participate fully in their communities. Education has a vital role in empowering women, safeguarding children from exploitative and hazardous labour and sexual exploitation, promoting human rights and democracy, protecting the environment, and controlling population growth. Increasingly, education is recognized as one of the best financial investments states can make. (United Nations Human Rights Office 1999)

This statement is making a clear claim about the relationship of education to social change. Education can play a major role in combating global poverty, in enabling the equal rights of men and women and in the promotion of democracy.

These international initiatives and others promoted by the UN and UNESCO have put the primary responsibility for ensuring education as a fundamental human right for all on the state. In some countries, this responsibility rests at the national level but in others it is at regional or provincial level. This rights-based approach to education has underpinned most international education policies over the past two decades. Education for All was central to the Millennium Development Goals and is now a central element of the UN Sustainable Development Goals (SDGs).

Nickel (2007) defines human rights as universal norms that describe standards of behaviour that protect people of all ages from all forms of abuse, be they social, economic, political or legal.

In discussing education as a human right, there needs first of all to be some clarity as to what is meant by human rights. Influenced by the work of Nickel, UNESCO identified human rights as having the following characteristics:

- *Human rights are rights*: Human rights are not promises, privileges, or goals, they are rights. Rights are entitlements. Human rights are usually 'claim rights', which means they impose mandatory obligations on duty-bearers.
- *Human rights are plural*: Human rights encompass a variety of protections, from the right to freedom of speech and the right to a fair trial to the right to health and the right to education.
- *Human rights are universal*: Human rights apply to everyone by virtue of their status as 'human'.
- *Human rights are high-priority*: Human rights cannot be ignored. They demand consideration and compete with other concerns (UNESCO 2019: 25).

Whilst there may be a degree of agreement on these points, there is perhaps less international agreement as to whether human rights are about legal frameworks and laws or something more. There is an argument that human rights are equally about moral rights, and the example often used is apartheid in South Africa and its denial of equality for all.

Education can also be seen in this context. Although education has been central to numerous international human rights treaties,[1] its importance goes beyond legal obligations and could be said to be fundamental to any policy initiatives and practices concerned with learning. For example, education should be seen as universal with everyone having the right to it without discrimination. It should also be seen as a key priority for all states, and can also be a key mechanism for ensuring the implementation of other human rights. Education is therefore seen as a 'multiplier right' and ensures greater understanding of and engagement with other human rights.

This right to education also implies a number of specific components that have been part of various UN initiatives and has been enshrined in both the Millennium Development Goals from 2000 and the SDGs from 2015. These include that education should be free and open to all, that teachers are trained to deliver quality learning, and that education is conducted in a free and transparent way.

The relationship between education and human rights is not only about the individual; it also implies a contribution to society. These wider purposes have been noted by UNESCO as:

- Promoting economic growth through an educated and skilled labour force.
- Foster democratic and peaceful societies, by teaching tolerance, mutual respect, and respect for human rights and encouraging participation and inclusion in decision-making processes.
- Encouraging a rich cultural life, by promoting the learning of languages, the arts, sports.
- Help build a national identity, by directing the curriculum to teach national values, history, and customs.
- Promote social justice aims.
- Overcome persistent and entrenched challenges, such as gender inequality (UNESCO 2019: 35).

Through a range of policy statements and initiatives, UNESCO has been conscious to reaffirm the role and importance of education to the public good – in contrast to more neoliberal perspectives that have emphasized the value of education to economic development and skills promotion.

Another more recent initiative by UNESCO has been to link human rights to sustainable development. This first began to be promoted within the UN Decade on Education for Sustainable Development from 2005 to 2014, and since then the two have become inextricably linked within the SDGs.

An emphasis on a rights-based approach to education could, however, lead to a neglect of key questions such as the aims and purposes of education, the content of the curriculum and approaches towards teaching and learning. There has also been concern that the focus on human rights could be interpreted as ensuring the dominance of Western values and norms. Whilst historically there may be some basis to this, all too often criticisms from this perspective have tended to promote specific cultural practices above universal and moral rights.

The approach suggested in this volume is that whilst having some common objectives such as free and quality education, the learning opportunities need to take account of relevant social and cultural norms.

As suggested earlier in this chapter, a possible criticism of the rights-based approach is that it could be interpreted as downplaying the importance of the aims and content of learning. One UN initiative that does bridge this potential divide is the UN Convention on the Rights of the Child, where they are perhaps most explicit. Article 29 of the Convention of the Rights of the Child states:

that the education of the child shall be directed to:

(a) The development of the child's personality, talents and mental and physical abilities to their fullest potential.

(b)   The development of respect for human rights and fundamental freedoms, and for the principles enshrined in the Charter of the United Nations.

(c)   The development of respect for the child's parents, his or her own cultural identity, language and values, for the national values of the country in which the child is living, the country from which he or she may originate, and for civilizations different from his or her own.

(d)   The preparation of the child for responsible life in a free society, in the spirit of understanding, peace, tolerance, equality of sexes, and friendship among all peoples, ethnic, national and religious groups and persons of indigenous origin.

(e)   The development of respect for the natural environment (UNICEF n.d.: 29).

Implicit in this article is an assumption of the value of a child-centred approach to learning, preparing the child for engaging in society and in a form that has a strong values base. This approach moreover suggests that the teaching methods used in schools should reflect the spirit of the Convention. This means that education should prepare children for life in which they can develop a healthy lifestyle and good social relationships, be creative and look at issues critically, and above all develop the ability to make well-balanced decisions.

What has also emerged as a way of consolidating this rights-based approach has been that not only should every child have the right to education, they 'also have the right to be equipped with the skills and knowledge that will ensure long-term recognition of and respect for all human rights' (UNICEF and UNESCO 2007: xii).

This has led to an approach to education called human rights education. Leading proponents of this approach have been Hugh Starkey and Audrey Osler.

Osler has rightly suggested that 'people need to know they have rights in order to claim them' (Osler 2016: 119). She goes on to state that rights are only won as a result of struggle. To her, rights are also about a vision of greater justice.[2]

This promotion of the linkage between education and human rights has been at the forefront of many initiatives by international bodies such as UNICEF that have seen the UN Convention on the Rights of the Child as an embodiment of this. Unfortunately, this Convention has not been ratified and supported by all countries, although it has underpinned popular educational initiatives such as UNICEF's Rights Respecting Schools Initiative in the United Kingdom which is discussed further in Chapter 7.

The SDGs have also provided an important new boost to the promotion of education as a human right. SDG4 of the Goals is on education, and has the following targets:

4.1 Ensure universal, free, equitable, and quality primary and secondary education.
4.2 Ensure universal access to quality pre-primary education.
4.3 Ensure equal access to quality technical, vocational, and tertiary education.
4.4 Increase the number of youth and adults who have relevant skills, including technical and vocational skills, for employment, decent jobs and entrepreneurship.
4.5 Ensure equal access to all levels of education particularly of marginalized groups.
4.6 Achieve full literacy of youths and substantially increase literacy of adults.
4.7 Ensure that all learners acquire the knowledge and skills needed to promote sustainable development, including, among others, through education for sustainable development and sustainable lifestyles, human rights, gender equality, promotion of a culture of peace and non-violence, global citizenship and appreciation of cultural diversity and of culture's contribution to sustainable development (United Nations 2016a).

Of these targets, perhaps the most important for the themes outlined in this volume is the last one because of the direct reference to key terms that imply social change such as sustainable living, rights, gender equality and peace. The inclusion also of the term 'global citizenship' is very significant because it is a recognition of the need to look beyond the nation state as a means of securing change.

However, unlike other aspects of UN Declarations on education, the SDGs have no legal obligations. The extent to which nation states are therefore taking seriously some of these commitments is already very variable around the world. This is particularly the case with Target 4.7. The issues these points raise are discussed later within the chapter that reviews the opportunities and challenges these international agreements and the work of bodies such as UNESCO provide for encouraging education for social change.

Education as Promotion of Universal Values

The second contextual theme of this chapter, and one that follows naturally from the previous section on human rights, is that of universal values. Not surprisingly, most of the initiatives around this theme have also come from the United Nations.

Kofi Annan (former Secretary General of the UN), for example, said in 2003:

Every society needs to be bound together by common values, so that its members know what to expect of each other and have some shared principles by which to manage their differences without resorting to violence.

That is true of local communities and of national communities. Today, as globalisation brings us all closer together, and our lives are affected almost instantly by things that people say and do on the far side of the world, we also feel the need to live as a global community. And we can do so only if we have global values to bind us together. (United Nations 2003)

Behind this quotation from Kofi Annan is a proposition that education is more than just a human right but is potentially a way of bringing people together from across the globe.

Over the past thirty years, UNESCO has been the leading international body promoting universal values through three specific initiatives. The first was their International Commission on Education for the Twenty-First Century chaired by Jacques Delors which led in 1996 to the publication of the report *Learning: The Treasure Within* (Delors 1996), usually known as the *Delors Report*. The second is their 2015 report *Rethinking Education Towards a global common good?* (UNESCO 2015). The third is their series of initiatives, in the second decade of the twenty-first century, against extremism and the role education can play.

A central theme in the Delors Report was the role of education in promoting a universal values-base message. The 'four pillars of education' are one of its key messages: learning to know, learning to do, learning to live together and learning to be (Delors 1996: 85-98). This approach reflected Delors' aim to promote a more humanistic approach to education rather than one of neoliberalism.

Rethinking Education, whilst continuing to reflect UNESCO's humanistic approach to education, aimed to take account of the importance of social challenges regarding inequality, the environment and the need for social justice. The foreword by the then director general of UNESCO, Irina Bokova, stated:

The world is changing – education must also change. Societies everywhere are undergoing deep transformation, and this calls for new forms of education to foster the competencies that societies and economies need, today and tomorrow. This means moving beyond literacy and numeracy, to focus on learning environments and on new approaches to learning for greater justice, social equity and global solidarity. Education must be about learning to live on a planet under pressure. It must be about cultural literacy, on the basis of respect and equal dignity, helping to weave together the social, economic and environmental dimensions of sustainable development. (UNESCO 2015: 3)

Bokova went on to suggest that 'there is no more powerful transformative force than education – to promote human rights and dignity, to eradicate poverty and deepen sustainability, to build a better future for all, founded on equal rights and social justice, respect for cultural diversity, and international solidarity and shared responsibility, all of which are fundamental aspects of our common humanity' (ibid., 4).

Reflecting the earlier Delors Report, *Rethinking Education* also promoted a humanistic approach with a now-greater emphasis on combating discrimination in all its forms. There was also a call for the promotion of education as a common good alongside a recognition of pluralistic voices:

> How can a plurality of worldviews be reconciled through a humanistic approach to education? How can such a humanistic approach be realised through educational policies and practices? What are the implications of globalisation for national policies and decision-making in education? . . . What are the implications for education of the distinction between the concepts of the private good, the public good, and the common good? (Ibid., 13)

The report concludes by recognizing these challenges: we must recognize the diversity of lived realities whilst reaffirming a common core of universal values. Reflecting ideas from Amartya Sen, the emphasis on humanistic values should be the foundation and purpose of education, including:

> respect for life and human dignity, equal rights and social justice, cultural and social diversity, and a sense of human solidarity and shared responsibility for our common future. (ibid., 39)

Education can, however, never be value-free. In all societies there have been cultural and ideological influences that affect behaviours, attitudes and approaches to learning. But whilst this promotion of values can help to provide a common international vision of education, it can also lead to the domination of certain more powerful voices such as those from the West. Values are an essential component of all education but there are clear dangers that the term has all too often been used without any sense of context.

The challenges about the use of universal values have in the past decade become a major issue of debate because of the desire by international bodies such as UNESCO to use them as a way of combating extremism and addressing intolerance (UNESCO-IBE n.d.: 5).

A possible way through these debates between the promotion of universal values and the recognition of specific national and cultural voices is the distinction made by the International Bureau of Education (IBE) within UNESCO. They view values as standards that apply to beliefs and actions, with implications for the well-being of the individual, especially in regard to relations with others. They suggest that 'universal values' refers to values that are – or ought to be – common to all people, regardless of time, location, personal characteristics and background. Another way of viewing universal values, then, is that they are 'common values' (ibid., 6).

Conscious of the potential challenges and criticisms of the term 'universal values', the IBE in addition suggests the term 'particularistic values'. This recognizes that values can differ along cultural, ethnic, religious, gender or age lines. Particularistic values are therefore seen as values that reinforce a sense of belonging to a particular grouping of people. The IBE further noted that a lack of awareness and understanding of these specific cultural values could lead to conflict and tensions within and between societies (ibid.).

To achieve some sense of commonality, the IBE in conclusion suggested instead a hybrid approach of what they termed 'qualified universality', which, whilst acknowledging different interpretations, suggested there was an argument for common values across cultures (ibid.).

Whilst this hybrid approach has some value, it still raises some questions about how they relate to changes in society and what form of society people should be striving for.

Another factor which needs to be brought into the debates on universal values is the way in which neoliberal forces have become particularly influential. Here values are equated with individualism and economic success.

The critique of UNESCO's position on Global Citizenship Education by Hatley, which is discussed in more detail in Chapter 13, is perhaps a more useful approach. She suggests that the values promoted by UNESCO are too abstract and disconnected from social reality (Hatley 2019).

Universal values may be well intentioned, and those such as justice, peace and sustainability are normatively considered a common good. In fact, the elevator effect applied to universal values may be positive in nations whose values may not currently align with mutual human well-being.

In her thesis, Hatley notes :

Universal values within UNESCO's Global Citizenship Education can be seen as a complementary vehicle for the imposition of western dominance. Values in society are said to act as social regulators of people's actions such that people act in a way that serves power. Values influence people's actions but can also be used by the powerful as an excuse for unjust acts which originate from a desire to dominate. (Hatley 2018: 51)

It is this failure to recognize the power and influence of ideology and cultural norms that can be said to be at the heart of criticisms of the promotion of universal values.

The tensions and possible contradictions between these different views on universal values can be seen in Vaughan and Walker (2012). They comment that:

communities might choose educational values that are not to the benefit of all (e. g. girls), so either there needs to be some core of universal values arising from the goal of 'human development', and/or a process that subjects a particular community's or society's reasoning about education to impartial scrutiny. (ibid., 497)

Perhaps a potential way forward, whilst recognizing the hegemonic influences of universal values, is to pose the question: Is there space for alternative perspectives and approaches? As Arkoun (2004: 48) states, 'Values must be constantly reflected upon and recreated in response to the actions of the powerful such that potential oppression is resisted.'

Finally, in this discussion on values there is a need to briefly discuss two examples of where and how this emphasis has had an impact on education. The first is what has been called 'values-based education', which aims to give higher prominence to values within the life of a school. Whilst this approach to education has many good intentions such as wanting to see values like respect, integrity, honesty and compassion having a higher prominence within the life of a school, there are dangers of promoting a specific ethos and approach (Values Based Education, n.d.).

An example of the dangers of a values-based approach can be seen in England after 2010 when the UK government introduced the promotion of 'Fundamental British Values' into the school curriculum. These values were seen as 'democracy, individual liberty, rule of law, and mutual respect and tolerance of those with different faiths and beliefs'. But behind them was a political and ideological agenda that saw education as addressing what were seen as extremist views emerging in British societies following a series of terrorist attacks.

As one of the United Kingdom's leading education trade unions has commented:

However, these values are certainly not unique to Britain. All of these values underpin the Universal Declaration of Human Rights, and in accordance with this, we have chosen to refer to them as 'Universal Values'. . . . Indeed, 193 countries are now members of the United Nations, which has adopted the declaration. Rethinking the values in this way prevents any conflation between British stereotypes and history, and values education and helps us to consider this duty in an inclusive fashion. (NAS/UWT n.d.)

Therefore, whilst the promotion of such values can be laudable, there is always the danger that this promotion of universal values can be a way of exerting state power over education. This has been noted by Vincent and Hunter-Henin (2018) in their study on British Values. Therefore, any discussion on education for social change needs to include consideration of the role and relationship of education to the nation state. It is to this area that this chapter now turns.

Education, Ideology and the State

In most Western societies, education only became related to the state from the late nineteenth century onwards. It was when education became seen more as a civic function and identified with the ideal of a national state. An observer on these changes was the philosopher Emile Durkheim, who became a major influence on early thinking on the sociology of education (see Leighton 2012: 60). He rejected the growing challenge to the potential transformative power of education and concluded in his Division of Labour in Society first published in 1893 that education was the mirror image of society and could only be reformed if society was reformed (Durkheim 1977).

Later writers on the sociology of education, such as Parsons, went further and suggested that education serves to integrate and produce conformity (Leighton 2012).

From a more radical political perspective, there was also the view that education was an instrument of the capitalist state, and therefore its potential independent role in changing society was always going to be limited until capitalism itself was overthrown. The relationship between education and the dominant capitalist ideologies of Western societies has been a theme particularly of Marxist-inspired academics in the twentieth century. For example, one can see this in the writings of Louis Althusser, who saw education as part of the Ideological State Apparatus, a means of the ruling class securing its own social and political domination over a society. To Althusser, schools served to mould children to fit into the ideological dominance of capitalism and that included conformity, deference to authority, respect for existing order and to be technically competent (Althusser 1971: 126–7).

The American academics Samuel Bowles and Herbert Gintis make similar assumptions in their influential text *Schooling in Capitalist America: Educational Reform and the Contradictions of Economic Life*, first published in 1976. A central theme of this volume is the idea that the norms and values pupils learn in school correspond to the norms and values which will make it easy for future capitalist employers to exploit them at work. Education provides knowledge of how to interact in the workplace and gives direct preparation for entry into the labour market. Although their ideas evolved, to Bowles and Gintis schools were still seen as reproducing existing inequalities, and they rejected the notion that there are equal opportunities for all. In this way, they argue that education explains social inequality (Bowles and Gintis 2002).

A slightly different perspective is that taken by the French philosopher Pierre Bourdieu, who used the terms 'cultural capital' and 'cultural reproduction'. Davison (2012: 239) sums up his thinking well as:

> Put simply cultural reproduction is the process through which existing cultural values and norms are transmitted from generation to generation thereby ensuring continuity of cultural experience across time. Bourdieu proposes that different social groups have different 'cultural capital', which may be seen as the knowledge, experience and connections an individual has, and develops, over time that enable a person to succeed more so than someone with knowledge, experience and connections that is seen in society as being of less value.

To Bourdieu, 'the education system reproduces all the more perfectly the structure of the distribution of cultural capital among classes . . . in that the culture which it transmits is closer to the dominant culture and that the mode of inculcation to which it has recourse is less removed from the mode of inculcation practised by the family' (Bourdieu 1973: 80).

The education system is therefore an agent of cultural reproduction biased towards those of higher social class.

Whilst the perspectives of Bourdieu again have some relevance in helping to understand the influences on education, they do not address the perspectives of those who wish to challenge these dominant orthodoxies.

The views on education suggested earlier can also lead to a sense of disempowerment amongst practising educationalists who have a belief in the value of learning to change society. Therefore, it is suggested here that what needs to be recognized within the discourses on the role and relationship of education to the state and society is that these areas are sites of ideological struggle.

Education as a Site of Resistance to the Ideological Dominance of the State

As suggested earlier, whilst both the perspectives of Althusser and Bowles and Gintis have some value in helping us to understand the relationship of education to capitalist societies, their perspectives – as various people have commented (Brown and Lauder 1991; Apple 1982) – are rather simplistic and ignore or give minimal consideration to the role of teachers and educationalists in general. Althusser makes a passing reference to 'heroic teachers' but, as critics have argued, education is a site of ideological struggle. Teachers and educators are not automatons of the state. They have ideas and perspectives of their own, and are willing to provide a range of viewpoints and perspectives. Educational practices are not solely determined by economic and dominant ideological factors.

In contrast to these theories of education being the reproducer of dominant capitalist modes and ideologies, there is the 'transformational approach' or critical pedagogy as it has often been called.

An important figure in posing a positive approach around education for social change, particularly in relation to the role of the state, is the American educationalist Michael Apple. He stated that an education system was not an instrument of the capitalist state but the product of conflict between the dominant and the dominated (Apple 1982). He went on, 'education is at once the result of contradictions and the source of new contradictions. It is an arena of conflict over the production of knowledge, ideology, and employment, a place where social movements try to meet their needs and business attempts to reproduce its hegemony' (ibid., 50). Apple, influenced by the writings of the Italian Marxist Antonio Gramsci, noted the influence of ideological and cultural formations, identifying three specific sites of resistance:

- The informal and hidden curriculum
- The formal curriculum
- Values and beliefs of teachers.

To Apple, therefore, it is when educationalists who wish to resist dominant ideological influences turn directly to the factors that address this hegemony, namely class and capitalism, that change can be forthcoming (Apple 2013).

He argues that the hegemony of the state and elites which dominate its workings are always fragile, always temporary and constantly subject to threat. There will always be openings for counter-hegemonic activity (Apple 2014: 10).

An understanding of the term 'hegemony' is important here. This term is most closely associated with the Italian Marxist Antonio Gramsci. To Gramsci, hegemony is when the dominant groupings in society, through civil society and the arms of the state, secure consent from the 'great masses of the population to the general direction imposed on social life' (Gramsci 1971: 12).

This in practice meant that there is a close relationship between how he sees the term 'hegemony' and that of education in its broadest sense. Hegemony, for Gramsci, is an ensemble of relations which are conceived as pedagogical relations:

> Every relationship of 'hegemony' is necessarily an educational relationship and occurs not only within a nation, between the various forces of which the nation is composed, but in the international and world-wide field, between complexes of national and continental civilisations. (Quoted in Mayo 2017: 37)

But as Gramsci further discussed, these dominant forces were always subject to contestation and challenge as a result of social, political and ideological struggle. It is here that the term 'counter-hegemonic' becomes valuable to use as providing an alternative to the dominant educational ideas.

As Giroux (1981: 26) has stated:

> Gramsci's notion that hegemony represents a pedagogical relationship through which the legitimacy of meaning and practice is struggled over makes it imperative that a theory of radical pedagogy takes as its central task an analysis of how both hegemony functions in schools and how various forms of resistance and opposition either challenge or help to sustain it.

Critical pedagogists such as Giroux, as a result of the influence of Gramsci, go beyond traditional Marxian notions regarding economic determination to one where culture is posed as a dynamic and lived reality contested through schooling institutions.

Counter-hegemony is therefore seen as the gap between dominant class interests and broader societal interests through which the dominant class establishes hegemony. As Tarlau noted in commenting on the influence of Gramsci:

> schools are both a part of the state's apparatus and a civil society institution where resistance can be organised. (Tarlau 2017: 121)

Influenced by Gramsci and his discussions on the role of intellectuals, Apple (1982) posed that as intellectuals framed the ideologies within schools, they could therefore be sites of alternative ideas and contestation. This led to Aronowitz and Giroux (1993) developing the idea of transformative intellectuals to describe teachers and other cultural workers who work inside and outside state institutions to challenge the dominant hegemony (Pizzolato and Holst 2017: 23).

Another influencer on the thinking of both Apple and Giroux was the Brazilian educationalist Paulo Freire. The ideas of Freire are discussed in more detail in later chapters, but, as Giroux indicates, his influence and importance can be seen in his promoting the use of the term 'pedagogy' as a way of addressing the opportunities education can provide in order to change society:

> For Freire, pedagogy was central to a formative culture that makes both critical consciousness and social action possible. Pedagogy in this sense connected learning to social change; it was a project and provocation that challenged students to critically engage with the world so they could act on it. (Giroux 2010: 2)

Therefore, if a pedagogical approach is taken within a counter-hegemonic form of education that promotes alternative values bases, then education can become a voice not only of resistance but one of seeking social change. It is this tension between seeing a more open-minded inquiry-based approach and that of alternative values bases that is often at the heart of much of the debates in this area.

In the early decades of the twentieth century, in both North America and Europe there were growing socialist-based movements that were challenging the domination of capitalist influences within education. Counter-hegemonic forms of education emerged, such as Socialist Sunday schools as well as other forms of radical schooling. In North America particularly, these movements also had a distinctly anti-racist element, giving space and voices to African Americans, very often women (Teitelbaum 1993).

The response to this is dealt with in later chapters but it is necessary at this stage to suggest that a way through this dilemma is to ensure that a range of voices and perspectives are included within learning. What needs to be encouraged and promoted more are the counter-hegemonic approaches because they are often the ones most marginalized and have least power and influence.

Education as a Means to Achieving a Better Society

What emerges from within much of the discussions around education as a site of resistance is its relationship to developing in learners the skills for active engagement in society. This means: What is the role of education in securing a more active and engaged citizenry?

Later chapters will outline in more detail how educationalists and policymakers have interpreted the role of education as a means of achieving a better society. Here the aim is just to introduce the question as to what extent education can help to achieve a better society and what have been the main mechanisms for doing this.

One approach that became popular in the later decades of the twentieth century was that outlined by Postman and Weingartner in their seminal work on *Teaching as A Subversive Activity* (1971). This slender volume critiqued the dominant form of education that was based on these principles:

- The concept of absolute, fixed, unchanging truth – particularly from a polarising good–bad perspective.
- The concept of certainty. There is always one and only one right answer.
- The concept of isolated identity – that A is A, once and for all.
- The concept of fixed states and things.
- The concept of mechanical causality.
- Differences only exist in parallel and opposing forms: good–bad, right–wrong.
- Knowledge emanates from a higher authority and is given.

They said that an answer to this was a new form of education which has as its purpose developing 'inquiring, flexible, creative, innovative, tolerant young people who can face uncertainty without disorientation, who can formulate viable and new meanings to meet changes to the environment which threaten survival' (ibid., 204).

These are very laudable phrases, but to what extent has this new approach to education had a direct relationship to securing social change? This has been a perennial issue within the field that I am most familiar with, development education and global learning. For example, funders of activities in this field have posed questions such as, in what ways can such projects help contribute to alleviating global poverty?

The difficulties of providing evidence to support such goals have resulted therefore in more sceptical policymakers using this as a basis for not funding projects in the field.

One of the main themes of this volume is instead to pose a distinctive pedagogical framework that encourages a sense of the value of global social justice. A key challenge therefore is building a constituency of engagement and support for social change within the educational community.

Conclusion

This chapter has introduced ideas about what can be meant by the term 'education for social change'. It has discussed a number of ways that education has been perceived in relation to the needs of society and the ways in which it can contribute to changing society.

The theme of education as a human right has underlined many educational policy initiatives since the latter decades of the twentieth century. The second theme of education in terms of the promotion of universal values, despite the leadership from UNESCO, has been much more controversial. This discussion on values then led onto considerations about the ideological role of education in relation to the state. Finally, the chapter has also introduced some of the issues about the extent to which education by its very nature can change society or whether it requires the input of counter-ideas to those that are dominant within the perspectives from the state.

In taking these discussions forward, it is necessary first of all to consider, from both a historical and a contemporary sense, the ways in which there has been a linkage between the promotion and expansion of education systems and securing a more democratic society.

Questions for Further Consideration

- To what extent is there a recognition from societies around the world that education is a human right, and what does this mean in practice?
- The promotion of universal values within education is clearly problematic. What are the best ways of ensuring that values-based perspectives are reflected within all forms of learning?
- Education is part of the state apparatus but it has also a degree of relative autonomy in many, if not all, societies. What should be the forms this autonomy and perhaps resistance to dominant ideological influences take?
- Can teaching really be a subversive activity?

Further Reading

Bourdieu, P. (1973), 'Cultural Reproduction and Social Reproduction', in Brown, R. (ed.) *Knowledge, Education and Cultural Change*, 71–112, London: Tavistock.

Bowles, S. and H. Gintis (2002), 'Schooling in Capitalist America Revisited', *Sociology of Education*, 75, no. 1 (January 2002): 1–18.

Delors, J. (1996), *Learning, the Treasure Within: Report to UNESCO of the International Commission*, Paris: UNESCO.

Hatley, J. (2019), 'Universal Values as a Barrier to the Effectiveness of Global Citizenship Education: A Multimodal Critical Discourse Analysis'. *Journal of Development Education and Global Learning*, 11, no. 1: 87–102.

Postman, N. and C. Weingartner (1971), *Teaching as a Subversive Activity*, London: Penguin.

Right to Education (n.d.), *Understanding Education As A Right*. Available online: https://www.right-to-education.org/page/understanding-education-right (accessed 23 November 2020).

UNESCO (2015), *Rethinking Education*, Paris: UNESCO.

UNICEF and UNESCO (2007), *A Human Rights Based Approach to Education for All*, New York: UNICEF. Available online: https://www.unicef.org/publications/files/A_H uman_Rights_Based_Approach_to_Education_for_All.pdf (accessed 20 November 2020).

2

Education for a Democratic Society

Introduction

The wider purposes of education and its contribution to societal change have been most closely associated with the goals of securing a more democratic society. This chapter will outline some examples of how education has been seen in this context. This includes the ways in which the labour movement in the United Kingdom, for example, played a major role in linking education for democracy to a vision of a new society. A key figure in the United States was John Dewey, who called for a new form of cosmopolitan democracy where education could break down social inequalities. In the 1930s, education became seen as a bulwark against fascism. In more recent decades, the linkages between education and democracy have been features of post-apartheid South Africa and the new liberal democracies in Central and Eastern Europe. Education and democracy have more recently been linked through increased calls for the teaching of civics and citizenship and the promotion of democratic schools. Finally, the chapter concludes by suggesting that the role of education for democracy needs to be reconsidered in the light of globalization, the instant access many people have to the internet and the ways in which communities around the world are now using forms of social media to call for social change.

Changing Role of Education within Industrial Societies

Up until the late nineteenth century in most evolving industrial societies, education was viewed as a personal affair and not the concern of the state. The schooling that did exist tended to be divided between the needs of the aspiring middle classes through grammar schools and voluntary-based schools for the poor and children of working-class families. But with the expansion of the

Industrial Revolution, there was an increasing need for a more skilled workforce. The child population was rapidly growing, and following the introduction of legislation preventing children from working down the mines and in many factories, there was increased pressure to provide more schooling. Amongst industrialists and politicians, there was still resistance to expanding education as it was feared it could lead to social upheaval. But to others such as Adam Smith, education could be a means of minimizing conflict and discord in society.

In the United Kingdom, as the nineteenth century progressed, there was grudging acceptance of the need to extend the school system, but it was seen primarily as a way of ensuring the continued status quo of the social order. Within the growing labour movement in the United Kingdom, however, there was not only a call for more education but an underlying assumption that if working-class communities had increased knowledge, then a better society would inevitably emerge. To the Chartists, for example, education was seen as a 'universal instrument for advancing the dignity of man and gladdening his existence' (Lovett 1876: 431).

The linkage between education and a more democratic society became the dominant theme of both those who wished to preserve the status quo and those who wished to see a more egalitarian society. For example, in England the passing of the 1870 Education Act, which secured elementary schooling for all children, followed on from the 1867 Reform Act, which had extended the franchise. Whilst there were further reforms at the turn of the century which provided free elementary education, there were still obstacles for further advancements for working-class children.

Although many in the British Labour Movement were by the beginning of the twentieth century calling for increased access to higher-grade schools, the Fabian Sidney Webb suggested a different approach, what became called the ladder approach to schooling. His ideas were to seek out the most able children in the interests of national efficiency and give them a training fit for a public elite. Webb's elitist approach and disdain for mass public education can be seen in this article in *Fabian News* in 1903:

> The really democratic purpose of public education was not to dole out elementary education to all and sundry, nor yet to develop a race of scholarship winners but to train up the most efficient and most civilized body of citizens, making the most of the brains for all in the interests of the community as a whole, developing each to the margin of cultivation. We must discard the old notion of education free of cost as a grant of charity to the poor; we no longer think that a free opening of all avenues to individual ability is the ideal. (Webb, quoted in McBriar 1962: 208)

Whilst the dominant views within the British Labour Movement at this time were less elitist, there remained well into the 1930s support for what could be called a ladder approach to schooling. As a scholarship system evolved, working-class children were increasingly given the opportunity to go onto secondary school education if they could pass the relevant examinations. This ladder approach was seen as a way of showing that 'what is good for the rich man's child should be within the reach of the worker's child'.[1]

Within the United Kingdom, however, as in many industrial societies in the early decades of the twentieth century, increased schooling for children became linked to seeing that increased knowledge would lead to a more democratic society.

Knowledge is Power

Throughout the late nineteenth century and well into the twentieth century in the United Kingdom, the promotion of education was seen to be of equal relevance and importance to adults as it was to children. Trade unions and various workers' movements such as the Clarion Clubs in the late nineteenth century had fostered and supported opportunities for working-class adults to further their learning through evening classes and day schools. But it was the foundation of the Workers' Educational Association (WEA) in the United Kingdom in 1903 that enabled a major expansion of educational provision for adults.

To many early leaders within the Association, there was an assumption of a close relationship between education, knowledge, democracy and political power. This can be best summed up by this observation from the head of the WEA in 1916, in the midst of a world war:

> Our educational ideal must fit in with our national ideal. Our national ideal is that of a democratic self-governing community which aims at giving the fullest scope to the expression of individuality. But the world is divided into nations whose interests are to some extent conflicting and most of who are not living in democratic institutions. Hence our educational ideal must provide for a people who are efficient in national competition, strong in national defence, yet free in thought, speech and action. (MacTavish 1916: 4)

This belief that the power of increased knowledge would lead to a better democracy gained increased support after the First World War with the introduction of universal male suffrage and limited female suffrage. There was an assumption amongst many Labour figures at the time that increasing knowledge and more educational opportunities would help the Labour Party achieve political power (see Bourn 1978).

There was also support for more education for two other reasons. For some trade unionists, education was seen as an answer to the influence of politicians. For others, this support for an 'educated democracy' was seen as the antidote to the rise of Bolshevism and the fear of revolution.

Throughout the interwar period, this view of an educated democracy grew in influence and importance within the British Labour Movement. Leading intellectual figures of the time such as Harold Laski, R. H. Tawney, A. D. Lindsay and G. D. H. Cole all spoke of the relationship between democracy and knowledge. Laski (1923), for example, suggested that education had a bearing upon the life of the state more than at any previous time.

These views of the relationship between education and a more democratic society tended, however, to be framed within the context of increased access and knowledge. Yet for many leading Labour figures at this time, this sense of optimism was dashed by the failure to secure mass political support for their party despite having two minority Labour governments during this period. There was a sense amongst some of the Labour leaders of working men and women being indoctrinated with capitalist ideas. Ramsay MacDonald referred to people being easily gullible. It was suggested that what was needed was a form of 'educative socialism', and this will be discussed more in Chapter 4.

These views by some of the Labour figures of the early decades of the twentieth century need to be understood within the context of the time, of a desire and thirst for knowledge by many working men and women. This belief in the value of education for both the betterment of the individual and for wider society became embedded within the culture of many working-class communities within the United Kingdom.

However, to reflect on the question of the relationship of education to democracy, the most important educational figure in the twentieth century was the American educationalist and philosopher John Dewey.

Relationship between Education and Democracy

Dewey saw a relationship between the growth of education, the emergence of more democratic forms of government and the nation state.

What is, however, significant about Dewey is that he saw democracy as more than a form of government; he had a vision of a cosmopolitan democracy, and saw it as a 'mode of associated living, of conjoint communicated experience . . . each has to refer to his own action to that of others, and to consider the action of others to give point and direction to his own' (Dewey quoted in Starkey 2017: 41–64).

Democracy, Dewey suggested, means breaking down the barriers of class, race and national territory. For Dewey, social justice would be realized when individuals were free to participate in occupations of their choice, whilst also contributing to the welfare of their fellow citizens and society in general. To Dewey, a more just society could emerge only when the individuals most burdened by injustice were involved in actively working for social change. It is here that Dewey's concept of a participative democracy can be seen through education encouraging people to engage in all aspects of societal life. With society having many injustices, Dewey held that schools were responsible not for reproducing the status quo, but for developing young people into active social beings (Boyles, Carusi and Attick 2009: 35).

To Dewey, democracy had to be closely related to education, for it was through giving people the knowledge, skills and values base to identify problems and find ways to solve them that societies would be more effective. It would also mean, as Dewey suggested, enabling people to play an active role in society (Dewey 1937; Harbour 2015; Biesta and Burbules 2003).

There was a clear linkage between Dewey's views on education and democracy; it was through dialogue and discussion that changes in society would emerge. Towards the end of his life, however, he gradually moved away from seeing education as the primary vehicle for political change to calling for more direct political activity. In 1937, reflecting the changing global context, there was the need to question democracy itself:

> The problem of education in its relation to direction of social change is all one with the problem of finding out what democracy means in its total range of concrete applications: economic, domestic, religious, cultural and political. (Dewey 1937: 416)

Education as a Means to Defend Democracy

Dewey's concerns about what was meant by democracy in the 1930s reflected concerns across not only North America but Europe as well. The rise of fascism and fears about what communism could mean led to calls for education for democracy taking on a new and more directly political meaning. Many politicians and academics of all persuasions began to re-evaluate their ideas on democracy. Its preservation became an important political objective. There was a growing view that educating children in citizenship and democratic ideals was one of the ways to defeat the threat which the new political crisis had created.

The trade union movement in the United Kingdom played a leading role in the promotion of the relationship between education and democracy. Their policy document on this subject in 1937 stated that 'the main purpose of modern education should be to preserve and extend liberty' (TUC 1937). Ernest Bevin, a leading trade union figure at the time, said that the defence of democracy was a political and educational demand (The Record, September 1939, quoted in Bourn 1978: 320). Some of the dilemmas and problems political figures had during this period were about what exactly was meant by a democratic society and what was the role of education therein. As J. H. Nicholson (1936: 38), a leading educationalist at the time, wrote:

> Until we know what kind of society we want, we cannot make a plan for the schools. What are the special features of a democratic society which must be reflected in its education?

The Emergence of Civics and Citizenship Education

What the debates on education for democracy also raised was to what extent was the school curriculum, for example, covering learning about political systems and ideas.

In 1934, the *New Statesman* in the United Kingdom published a supplement on education for citizenship which included articles from leading Labour figures such as G. D. H. Cole. The following year the Association for Education in Citizenship was formed with support from Labour and Liberal figures. In the past there had been some support in educational and labour circles for the idea of teaching civics, but it had been viewed within the concept of 'liberal education', of meeting the needs of the individual rather than those of society as a whole. Now the Association was calling for classes on citizenship which would make children aware of democratic principles including the values of tolerance and individual liberty (Association of Education for Citizenship 1939; Cohen and Travers 1939).

These themes increasingly dominated educational debates in the early years of the Second World War, and they became a major stimulus for ensuring that educational reform did take place in England with the 1944 Education Act. But as to what should be the content of that education and what sort of democracy was less clear. Even R. H. Tawney, one of the most influential of Labour thinkers on education during this period, said little apart from calling for a child's schooling to be 'broad and humane'. He did, however, state that education should not be simply based around subject areas and concluded that what was taught was less important that 'the angle from which it is approached and the spirit in which it is handled by the teacher' (Tawney Papers Box 24 23/1, quoted in Bourn 1978: 336).

This consensus of seeing a connection between education and democracy was noted in the *Times Educational Supplement*, which stated the 'future of democracy depends upon education' (Bourn 1978: 329).

But as to the content of education and the role of citizenship education, it was another fifty years in England before the subject came onto the political agenda with the return again of a landslide Labour government in 1997 and the appointment of David Blunkett as secretary of state for education.

In the United States, however, in the post-war period there were discussions about the relationship of education to democracy. For example, in Pennsylvania there was in the 1960s a course for schools entitled Problems of Democracy. Civics and social studies were part of the curriculum in many states but an area that had not been addressed was higher education. The Truman Commission Report understood that in a democratic nation education must be much more than a mechanism to prepare people for leisure, work and the voting booth. It must prepare everyone for life in a democracy. The authors of the report wrote:

> Democracy is much more than a set of political processes. It formulates and implements a philosophy of human relations. It is a way of life – a way of thinking, feeling, and acting, in regard to the associations of men and of groups, one with another. . . . To educate our citizens only in the structure and processes of the American government, therefore, is to fall far short of what is needed for the fuller realization of the democratic ideal. It is the responsibility of higher education to devise programs and methods which will make clear the ethical values and the concept of human relations upon which our political system rests. (President's Commission on Higher Education 1947: 11–12)

Although it took many years for most of these recommendations to be implemented, the aim provided a framework for higher education in the United States for the next fifty years including tackling racial and sexual inequality and the emergence of community colleges (Gilbert and Heller 2010).

From Citizenship Education to Learning Democracy and Democratic Education

The post-war growth and interest in civics and citizenship education on both sides of the Atlantic posed questions about whether the aim of the learning was more than an understanding of democratic institutions and the extent to which it should include the skills needed to ensure active engagement.

Manning and Edwards (2014), in their systematic review of the literature on citizenship education, noted that most of the policies on citizenship education pay scant regard to the socio-economic factors that influence young people's engagement. 'Civic education . . . is typically conceived in naive, mechanistic terms as a remedy for young people's apparent lack of knowledge and interest in electoral politics' (ibid., 5).

What is evident from various initiatives from Europe and North America about citizenship, civics and democracy is the emphasis on a deficit model; the more learners became aware of democratic institutions, the better democracy there would be.

One figure who has brought the debates back to the relationship of education to democracy is Biesta and his concept of the 'learning democracy'. He poses that teaching citizenship should be located within a broader context of learning for the individual. He also suggests the need to move from a deficit model of citizenship education, what the learner needs to know, to one that builds on their own experiences. Biesta also criticized the concept of citizenship education as being instrumental:

> The focus is mainly on the effective means to bring about 'good citizenship' rather on the question what 'good citizenship' actually is or might be. The idea of citizenship as an outcome is also problematic because it is fabricated on the assumption that citizenship is a status that is only achieved after one has success. Assumption is that young people lack the dispositions, knowledge and skills to be citizens and if they are given this knowledge and skills they will become 'good citizens'. (Biesta 2011: 6)

To Biesta, citizenship should be seen to be about what people do and the nature of their participation and engagement in society.

Similar comments could be made about the limitations of the term 'citizenship' in relation to higher education. Universities can and do make a contribution to encourage more informed and engaged citizens, but as Giroux suggests, they need to function as 'a vital public sphere for critical learning, ethical deliberation and civic engagement' (Giroux 2003: 196).

These debates pose questions about forms of democracy and how they relate to education, and a valuable summary of these questions can be seen in Sant's article on the review of the literature around democratic education (Sant 2019).

Her review identified seven distinctive forms of pro-democratic education (liberal, deliberative, participatory, multicultural, cosmopolitan, critical and agonistic) and two against (elitist, neoliberal).

The most common of these models is the *liberal* one in which freedom is seen as more important than any other democratic value. As Sant (ibid., 663) notes:

> Liberals assume that rational citizens will use their freedom to act for the common good. From this point of view, democracy is morally valuable: It functions as a political expression of the liberal value of self-fulfilment and it fosters (political) equality by providing equal rights to participate in political and social life.

In terms of education, this approach meant an emphasis on access to education with universalization being the goal.

The second approach is the *neoliberal* one with the emphasis on individualism and competition through market forces with learners being perceived as consumers with private interests and needs prevailing.

The third is that of *deliberative democratic education*, where decisions are made through public forums. The education element is seen as providing the skills and values for such public deliberations.

The fourth is *multicultural democratic education*, where the focus is on having a multiplicity of spaces where democratic practices could take place. The emphasis here is on diversity and ensuring plurality of voices are heard and to learn from others.

The fifth is that of *participatory democratic education*, where democratic values permeate all aspects of society. Here there is also an assumption of action. It is assumed that learners would participate in all educational activities and have their views heard and acted upon.

The sixth is *critical democratic education*, where the focus is on social transformation and critical engagement, with all learners having the opportunities for engagement for social change.

The seventh and final form of democratic education is that of *agnostic democratic education*, where there is no consensus but open dissent and where there is constant questioning of assumptions and approaches (ibid., 665–79).

In order to summarize these different approaches into what they mean for education for democracy, Sant, building on the work of Biesta, categorized them into three distinct groups:

education for democracy covering liberal, and aspects of critical, deliberative, and participatory approaches. 'This perspective interprets democracy as a universal normative imperative and education as an "instrument" for achieving this goal'. (ibid., 680)

The second approach is *education within democracy*, which is related to neoliberal and elitist approaches, where democracy and education are instrumental to securing a particular political and ideological approach (ibid., 682).

The third approach is what Biesta and Lawy (2006) define as *education through democracy*. This approach sees education and democracy as interlinked, and there is an emphasis on participatory, critical and multicultural approaches.

Many of these approaches are taken forward in later chapters through the discussions on education for sustainability and global citizenship. What the different approaches also pose, and this perhaps is not discussed sufficiently in Sant's article, is the influence of the forces of globalization. The extent to which global forces are shaping democratic structure and the nature and forms of learning have direct consequences upon participation in societies. It is relevant to note here that education for, within and through democracy poses questions about how schools are structured, their curriculum and the extent to which they have a wider social vision related to equipping learners with the knowledge, skills and values base to encourage a more just society. Examples of these approaches can be seen in the various movements and initiatives around the concept of 'democratic schools'.

Democratic Schools

During the twentieth century, inspired by the ideas of Dewey, and seeking an alternative model of schooling and learning, there have been numerous experiments and initiatives that put the concept of democracy at its heart. These have included, in the United Kingdom, A. S. Neil's Summerhill School which has, since its foundation in 1921, been seen as one of the leading independent progressive schools run on democratic principles.

Since then, many schools have been established around the world following similar principles. Many of them are part of the European Democratic Education Community (EUDEC), an international network of schools which fosters democratic schooling along the following principles:

Democratic education is education which most appropriately meets the needs of the learner, the community and society. It does this through developing reflective individuals who are collaborative problem-solvers and creative flexible thinkers. Just what the world of constant political turmoil and emergent technologies need. (European Democratic Education Community, n. d.)

In North America, Michael Apple has been a leading proponent of the concept of the democratic school and has said that all those directly involved in a school should be involved in its decision-making processes (Apple and Bean 1999).

In the United Kingdom, there is also the democratic education movement, co-ordinated by the Phoenix Educational Trust.[2]

For both of these networks, the UN Convention on the Rights of the Child, referred to in the previous chapter, is seen as their guiding principle.

Behind these movements is a belief in the power of education to encourage a sense of the value of engagement in society. Such an approach also suggests consideration of the themes of social justice, respecting views and ideas of others and a sense of critical reflection. Many of these themes are discussed in more detail in later chapters but what must underpin them is that education, the school or other relevant institution builds within its structures and ethos a sense of the value of participation, of openness to new ideas and social responsibility. Therefore, a democratic educational institution has to be an integral component of education for social change.

Education for Democracy in Central and Eastern Europe

Following the collapse of communism in Central and Eastern Europe, there were a range of initiatives about building new democratic societies and the role that education could play in this. In a number of countries, a form of civics education was seen as one of the main ways of developing a more 'educated democracy' (Slavkova and Korte 2019).

Poland, for example, introduced 'civics' into the curriculum, and from 2009 put more of a focus on skills and action than on acquiring knowledge of society and politics. But what did come to dominate debates between education policymakers was the tension between the nation state and wider world perspectives (Radiukiewicz and Grabowska-Lusinska 2007). This was heightened after 2010 with changes in the politics of Poland and the dominance of the Law and Justice Party, and a turn towards more conservative and nationalistic approaches. However, there was still an interest and support within civil society organizations for a broader and more global interpretation of education for democracy (Kuleta-Hulboj 2020).

A more progressive approach to citizenship and democracy in education could be seen in Estonia in their 'civic values' for the curriculum which included freedom, democracy, respect for the mother tongue and culture, cultural diversity, tolerance, environmental sustainability, respect for the law, co-operation, responsibility and gender equality. These values were expected to be seen within all subjects. For secondary schools, the curriculum further stated that school life should be organized 'as a model respecting human rights and democracy' based on equal treatment and gender equality (Hartmeyer, McAuley & Wegimont 2019: 46).

In some countries, the leadership and main drive for education for democracy has come from civil society organizations. One example of this is the Pontis Foundation in Slovakia, which has as its mission:

> Through our activities, we strive to contribute to transforming Slovakia into a better country, a place for free and responsible people who improve their lives and their surroundings. We want a prosperous and sustainable country, which is a good 'global citizen'. (Pontis Foundation n.d.)

The Pontis Foundation has played an important role in supporting projects and initiatives around education, democracy and global social change, and were one of the sponsors of the higher education example from Slovakia, discussed in more detail in Chapter 11.

Education for Democracy in South Africa

The other area of the world where there has been significant movement on what is meant by education for democracy is South Africa. Following the demise of apartheid, the ANC-led government called for education to have a transformative function and to promote a new values-based democracy. The *Manifesto on Values, Education, and Democracy* (MoE 2001) outlined values such as social justice, equality, non-racism, non-sexism, Ubuntu (human dignity), an open society, accountability and reconciliation. Curriculum materials made reference not only to civic responsibility but also to the promotion of human rights, challenging prejudices and preparing young people for responsibility at local, regional, national and global levels (Hunt 2007).

Implicit in this approach to the curriculum were significant differences to initiatives in Central and Eastern Europe. As Hunt (ibid.) has noted, there was an emphasis on education encouraging students to be responsible citizens and uphold the value of human rights.

This connection between education for democracy and citizenship has been a central theme of South African policies and programmes. For example, the Manifesto on Values, Education and Democracy makes reference to citizens' rights and responsibilities and to nurture a culture of participation within educational institutions.

But as Cappy (2016: 124) has shown, these aims put immense pressure on teachers, many of whom were ill-equipped to encourage a more transformative learning process. Most teachers viewed their role in promoting social change as teaching *about* values of the new democracy (such as respect and equality), rather than inspiring critical reflection on collective action that young people could take to transform the world around them (ibid., 124). The practice was narrative instruction – or *telling* students what to think and how to act.

Hunt (2007: 145) also noted that another challenge in putting the aims of the curriculum into practice was the lack of clarity as to how 'democracy' was interpreted. Citizenship goals could mean very different things depending on the nature of the school (Jansen 1997).

Democratic education within a South African context also poses engagement with a range of wider social, cultural and economic factors such as the use of different languages, access to resources and addressing historical differentiation based on ethnicity and class.

This South Africa example shows that education for democracy has to be much more than rhetoric and fine policies. There needs to be the infrastructure, support networks, resources and above all opportunities for the professional development of educators.

Conclusion

This chapter has aimed to show how the concept of democracy has been a theme of education policies and programmes in countries in Western and Eastern Europe, the United Kingdom, the United States and South Africa from the late nineteenth century onwards up until the present day. However, many of the initiatives have seen education as being central to promoting or securing a more democratic culture within the society, to instil democratic knowledge, values and skills within the learners. There has also been a recurring theme of an assumption of a democratic deficit within societies with education being seen as the saviour.

However, from the nineteenth century to the present day, it is clear that education has been seen as an essential component in advancing societies to be more democratic. This began with a focus on access to education, moved on to understanding how democracies work to more recently posing questions about what is meant by democracy.

What is, however, significant about a number of the initiatives on education for democracy has been that, whilst progressive in terms of learning principles, they tend on the whole to emphasize personal development and individual experiences. It could be argued therefore that even some of the examples outlined in the latter part of this chapter reinforce a wider concern Apple has about how democracy is perceived and that is as a form of possessive individualism (Apple 2005: 219). He further suggests that in many countries democracy has been turned into consumption practices, with the ideal citizen being the purchaser. As leading figures from Dewey to Tawney and Biesta have commented, the debates on education for democracy pose wider questions on what should be the form of society that this learning is working towards. These questions are discussed further in Chapter 5.

Questions for Further Consideration

- Dewey has been seen as a key figure in the role of education in achieving a more democratic society. What is particularly relevant about his ideas today?
- What models and forms of education for democracy exist in your own society today?
- What does democracy mean in practice for present-day educational institutions, be they schools, colleges or universities?
- What are the strengths and weaknesses of promoting an education for democracy model as an approach to education for social change?

Further Reading

Apple, M. and J. A. Bean (1999), *Democratic Schools*, Buckingham: Open University Press.

Biesta, G. (2011), *Learning Democracy in School and Society*, Rotterdam: Sense Publishers.

Cappy, C. L. (2016), 'Shifting the Future? Teachers as Agents of Social Change in South African Secondary Schools', *Education as Change*, 20, no. 3: 119–14.

Dewey, J. (1937), 'Education and Social Change', *Bulletin of the American Association of University Professors* (1915–1955), 23, no. 6: 472–4.

Mannings, N. and K. Edwards (2014), 'Does Civic Education for Young People Increase Political Participation? A Systematic Review', *Educational Review*, 66, no. 1: 1–24.

Radiukiewicz, A. and I. Grabowska-Lusinska (2007), 'Education for Democratic Citizenship in Poland', *Journal of Social Science Education*, 6, no. 2: 21–8.

Sant, E. (2019), 'Democratic Education: A Theoretical Review (2006–2017)', *Review of Educational Research*, 89, no. 5: 655–96.

3

Education for Liberation

Introduction

Within the discourses around 'education for social change', a term that occurs many times from both theorists and practitioners is that of liberation. The term 'education for liberation' is one that is closely associated with struggles for political freedom or to combat discrimination and oppression. It therefore has a clear political meaning and has been most closely associated with liberation struggles in Latin America, sub-Saharan Africa and South Asia, and with Black voices and communities in the United States. This chapter is therefore framed within a de-colonial context, and if we explore global social justice within education, then a central theme has to be combating oppression, removing the yoke of colonialism and liberating people to engage in meaningful social change.

The chapter addresses these themes through key anti-colonial figures: Mahatma Gandhi and Julius Nyerere and the great Brazilian educationalist Paulo Freire, who framed education for liberation with a more anti-capitalist perspective. The influence of these figures on a range of educational and political activists will be discussed. This includes the term 'critical pedagogy' and various movements for social change in Latin and North America and in Europe that have put 'education for liberation' as their main message.

Gandhi and Spiritual Liberation

One of the most influential liberation figures around the world has been the great Indian thinker Mahatma Gandhi. Although Gandhi experienced education and life as a lawyer in South Africa and England, his approach to education and societal change for a country to be free from colonialism was to emphasize traditional and home-based economies.

This approach to societal change could be seen in Gandhi's views on education. Gandhi's philosophy of education was thus part of his resistance against colonialism. Gandhi saw the influence of colonialism on education in India as a form of cultural imperialism. The emphasis on schooling being in English meant there was a disconnection of students from their community.

He was a great promoter of the potential value of education with an emphasis on character building, and on ethical and moral values. But reflecting his belief in the value of home-based industries, Gandhi encouraged schools to include handicrafts as a compulsory subject in the curriculum.

When it comes to linking education to liberation, Gandhi emphasized the more personal and spiritual side. This personal liberation came from increased knowledge, freedom from colonial enslavement and the close interplay of body, mind and soul. He also emphasized moral codes and character-building aspects, including areas such as truth, nonviolence and charity. This notion of liberation includes liberation of the individual soul (moksha); but to Gandhi, the self and other are inextricably linked. Sharma (2020) summarizes this as social and self-actualization.

Gandhi named his educational programme *Nai Talim* (new system of education). This meant an emphasis on education as preparation for life and not one based on textbooks. It also meant an emphasis on practical crafts in order to build up 'a non-violent, non-exploiting social order in which the ideals of freedom, equality, and brotherhood can be fully and universally realized' (Pyarelal, 1997: 332).

An important term that summarizes Gandhi's thinking on education is *Sarvodaya*, which means the welfare of all including a sense of spiritual enlightenment.

Gandhi's continued influence has been more in his vision of education rather than the specifics of the content of the curriculum.

Nyerere and African Liberation

Another major figure in the promotion of education for liberation was Julius Nyerere of Tanzania who led his country into independence from colonialism and was its first president. Although he was less influential than Gandhi and Freire, Nyerere's writings and practices demonstrate the close linkage between the promotion of education and national liberation. His importance also needs to be understood within the context of his time, as de-colonization began in

Africa in the 1960s when there was still a dominant assumption around the world that African perspectives on education and society were backward and antithetical to development. He developed an African approach to social change with a focus on the concept of *Ujamaa* ('familyhood' in Kiswahili), based on the notion of equality which Nyerere argued was an integral part of traditional African societies. Nyerere emphasized the promotion of traditional African ways of living, of co-operation and the central role of the family (Mulenga 2001; Nyerere 1976) because he believed it could help people feel more positive about their own place and contribution to society.

Education was seen by Nyerere as key to this self-advancement of people and the goal of a more egalitarian society. Liberation from the shackles of colonialism and from a sense of inferiority meant to Nyerere that education could help learners have a common purpose and aim to live and work in a co-operative manner. As Nyerere himself stated, 'The purpose of education is therefore liberation through the development of man as a member of society' (Nyerere 1976: 6).

On Nyerere's stance, Otunnu (2015: 20) has commented:

> Nyerere's educational philosophy, an integral part of the socialist project, focused largely on self-reliance, total liberation and empowerment of the person and society, and the active integration of education throughout one's life and in every aspect of human existence. The philosophy was represented through two broad policy positions: education for self-reliance and adult education. A closer examination of the philosophy demonstrates the universal relevance of this approach to education, especially in severely underdeveloped former colonial societies that desire to transform a colonial model of education by building a self-reliant, egalitarian, human-centered socialist project.

Nyerere, in summary, said that the central purpose of education:

> is the liberation of Man from the restraints and limitations of ignorance and dependency. . . . The ideas imparted by education, or released in the mind through education, should therefore be liberating ideas; the skills acquired by education should be liberating skills. (Nyerere cited in Hall and Kidd 1978: 27–8)

To Nyerere, teachers had a role in motivating learners, encouraging creativity and critical thinking. Mulenga (ibid., 453) suggested that Nyerere believed teaching ought to be democratic, and the teacher was best able to help the student by using a method that could be described as problem posing.

Putting his ideas into practice, however, proved to be problematic to Nyerere. Whilst there was an initial major expansion of all aspects of education with a focus on combating illiteracy and the promotion of gender equality in Tanzania, the pressures of external capitalist influences and weak internal infrastructures meant that many aspects of his vision were not realized. One area that Nyerere did make some progress on was his 1967 policy of Education for Self-Reliance. The goal of Education for Self-Reliance (ESR), as Mulenga (ibid., 453) has noted, was to:

> transform Tanzania from a colonial society into an egalitarian society based on equality and justice within the overall framework of *Ujamaa*. ESR was to introduce a type of education that would prepare the youth to play a constructive role in the development of a Tanzania in which all members shared in all things equally and fairly.

Nyerere's legacy is that his vision of education continued to have an influence throughout the continent. As Otunnu (2015: 31) has commented:

> no African leader in history has played a more important role in the practical liberation of Africa and for African unity than Nyerere. His commitment to global solidarity and eradication of poverty and inequality also made him the unrivalled voice of the global South for over three decades. In fact, his influence continues to shape the conversations about the North–South relations and the need for solidarity in the global South.

Mulenga (ibid., 453), in reviewing Nyerere's educational philosophy, notes that many African scholars have taken issue with Nyerere's argument that traditional African society was classless and casteless. Others also suggested that there was a sense of emotional nostalgia for a traditional African society that never existed (Mulenga 2001). There is clearly an element of essentialism within Nyerere's ideas (Fuss 1989: xi) but, as Cook-Lynn in Weaver (2000) notes, essentialism can be stated to downplay the value of the indigenous voice.

Paulo Freire and Liberation

The term 'education for liberation' is most closely associated with the Brazilian intellectual and political activist Paulo Freire. Although influenced and inspired by the revolutionary practices of Fidel Castro and Che Guevera, he looked for alternatives to guerilla warfare and armed struggle to secure social change via a sense of personal–political praxis developed through dialogue and literacy.

Dialogue was seen by Freire as a way of learners reflecting on their own life and experiences seeking those central concerns which became words to inform literacy and conscientization, creating praxis and thus developing agency. His most influential publication was *Pedagogy of the Oppressed* (Freire, 1972) but his whole life was based on putting his ideas into practice.

For Freire (1972), liberatory education brings together the act of knowing existing knowledge and the act of creating new knowledge. Liberatory education is based on dialogue and on active learning in a constant cycle of reflection and action to transform the world (Schugurensky 2014: 104–5). It includes not only recognition of oppression but also that those structures are historical and can be changed through human action.

To Freire, not only should education be transformative, it should foster transformation. As Cappy (2016: 122) notes, Freire:

> supported critical conscientisation through education, wherein people reflect upon their social situation so they may envision both individual and collective actions that can be pursued to improve their humanity and the humanity of those around them.

Dialogue and problem-posing were seen as key approaches by Freire to use education to secure social change. Underlying his approach to pedagogy is a belief in the goal of social justice and an understanding of poverty, oppression and capitalism. Freire saw 'the greatest humanistic and historical task of the oppressed: to liberate themselves' (Freire 1972: 21).

Later chapters will explore in more detail Freire's ideas and influence on pedagogy and social justice, but it is important at this stage to note that his approach had two distinct stages:

- The oppressed unveil the world of oppression and through praxis commit themselves to its transformation.
- In which the reality of oppressed has already been transformed, this pedagogy ceases to belong to the oppressed and becomes a pedagogy for all . . . in the process of permanent liberation (ibid., 31).

In terms of the emphasis on liberation, Freire saw conscientization through dialogue as being key (ibid.).

Education for liberation for Freire was also about praxis, a constant process of action and reflection (ibid., 52), with the goal of humanization and the creation of a more just society. His Christian faith was an important part of his philosophy, but this did not mean a passive acceptance of the status quo, rather a commitment to seek social and personal transformation. Freire's outlook was also clearly political in siding with the oppressed people for whom education for liberation was a means for them to achieve real power.

Freire himself said:

> Truly liberating education can only be put into practice outside the ordinary system, and even then with great cautiousness, by those who overcome their naiveness and commit themselves to authentic liberation. (Freire 1984: 528)

In his book *Politics of Education*, Freire (1985) develops the idea of liberation and says the future of the oppressed is the realization of their liberation. As Allman and Wallis (1997) state:

> Freire saw education as preparing people to 'liberate themselves from all oppressive conditions and to do so in collective solidarity with others. The liberation alternative involves learning "to read the world", our reality, critically and developing a will for and a commitment to social, economic and political transformations'. (Allman and Wallis 1997: 113)

The interpretation and application of Freire's concepts of education for liberation by Anne Ryan (2011) provide a very good summary of his thinking. She has written that education for liberation passes through three phases:

- Awakening awareness which means to make meaning of personal experience.
- Critical analysis to understand how the world works and where individual experience fits.
- Changing reality to actively engage in creating a more equitable society.

Whilst there have been numerous criticisms of Freire's writings for being too idealistic and not rooted in social reality,[1] his approach to education as a vehicle for liberation and social change has clearly been very influential. Leading intellectuals such as Henry Giroux and Peter McLaren have clearly been indebted to Freire. Their work is discussed in more detail in later chapters.

Freire's work and influence can be seen throughout many facets of education including adult learning, inspiring social movements in both North and South America, and being a leading influence on the fields of development education, global learning and global citizenship (Bourn, 2015). His influence can be particularly seen in approaches to what and how people learn. This has led to the development of the concept of critical pedagogy.

There are similarities in the ideas of Freire with those of Gandhi and Nyerere. Both Nyerere and Freire were promoters of adult education. For Nyerere (1978: 28–9), 'adult education should promote change, at the same time as it assists people to control both the change which they induce, and that which is forced upon them by the decisions of other men or the cataclysms of nature.' Both Freire and Nyerere were critical of the dominant forms of education and their ideological influences in reproducing dominant ideas of the time.

In terms of comparisons between Freire and Gandhi, both saw education as central to combating oppression; to Gandhi the focus was on colonialism, and to Freire it was more rooted in capitalism. They both, although in different ways, proposed alternative forms of education. To Gandhi the emphasis was on developing crafts and manual labour within the curriculum and use of indigenous languages as the basis of teaching. On the other hand, Freire emphasized more a pedagogy to combat oppression with a clear Marxist influence. What, however, is common to them both is their belief in education as a means for social transformation and the need to address both the content and approach to teaching

Education for Black Liberation

Within the civil rights movement in the United States from the 1960s onwards, there has been a reference to the term 'education for liberation'. There is evidence that the ideas of Freire can be seen within some of the discussions on the priorities of the Black American's struggles. Particularly influential was Freire's emphasis on challenging oppression and using education to empower the dispossessed (Darder 2015, 5–9). There was also amongst aspects of the Black liberation movement a reference back to African values as proposed by Nyerere. One can also see linkages between Martin Luther King's philosophy of nonviolence and the ideas of Gandhi.

It was from these influences that campaigns emerged to promote the stories of leading Black figures within the school curriculum (Payne 2003).

These debates on Black liberation reflect broader questions that have been posed around the emerging discourse particularly in North America of the term 'liberatory education'. Kristen Atkinson (2012: 15) has defined it as educational programming grounded in social justice and anti-oppressive praxis. She notes that a range of academics view liberatory pedagogy as a compelling method for developing peoples' critical consciousness and transforming their sense of moral integrity (Ginwright and Cammarota 2007; hooks 1994; Ladson-Billings 1995).

Influenced by ideas of Freire, a key figure in developing this liberatory education is bell hooks. To her, liberatory education is about teachers and learners working together (hooks 1994). For bell hooks, there were three key components of her educational philosophy:

- Education as resistance, teaching and learning as revolutionary acts.
- Engaged pedagogy.
- Learning as joy and ecstatic transformation.

Reflecting her political commitment, hooks saw education for liberation as promoting critical awareness in students. As Lanier (2001: 4) notes:

> It enables students to begin to question the prevailing paradigms of race, class and patriarchy found abundantly in schools . . . and gives students confidence in their authority to engage in such questioning.

Lanier further notes in reviewing hooks:

> Moral and cultural transformation, a central outgrowth of liberatory education, cannot be achieved however without dramatic reconfiguration of standard teaching practices in higher education classrooms; the prevailing paradigms of the academy and the professor must be overturned for transformational pedagogy to take root. (ibid., 6)

Reflecting themes outlined earlier and in the previous chapter, hooks saw securing participation and engagement of students as challenging but very important to education for liberation (Atkinson: 15).

For hooks, liberatory education was also part of her feminist outlook and she combines this with being a woman of colour to develop an 'engaged pedagogy', a 'transgressive pedagogy' (hooks 1994). Florence (1998: xvi), in commenting on this pedagogy, stated that it calls 'for a re-conceptualisation of the knowledge base, linking theory to practice, student empowerment, multiculturalism, and incorporation of passion, to make learning more engaging and meaningful'.

hooks' pedagogical approach resonates closely with ideas of Freire, Mezirow and Giroux, and is covered in more detail in the chapter on pedagogy for global social justice.

Liberation for Whom?

Whilst these views on education for liberation demonstrate there are a number of clear discourses around the term, particularly the influence of Freire, what they also show is their relationship to campaigns and calls for freedom from colonial and capitalist oppression. As Ira Shor (1990), a follower of Freire, said, in answer to what liberation means, it was from something and for something. To Shor, liberation, in addition to including freedom from oppression in society, meant also freedom from the pressures and restrictions of school life with testing, administration and emphasis on a narrow curriculum.

At a more individual sense, liberation can be seen, in the Gandhian sense, of a state of freedom of the mind where one can explore new ideas and thinking.

At a communal level, 'liberation' needs also to be recognized in terms of reaction to oppression, inequality and prejudice. The term was in the 1950s and 1960s associated with a distinctive Christian movement of Liberation Theology. The term was used in 1971 by the Peruvian priest Gustavo Gutiérrez, who wrote one of the movement's most famous books, *A Theology of Liberation*. Also since the 1960s there have been distinctive movements in support of women's liberation, Black communities and LGBTQ organizations.

These movements pose the extent to which education for liberation can and should be seen in an individualistic or communal way. As Hakken (1983: 17) has questioned:

> To what extent is liberation a personal and a social phenomenon?
> How do we know when a society or individual is liberated?

As suggested, to talk of a pedagogy for liberation is usually seen as a counter-hegemonic approach that advocates alternative forms of learning. As Sizemore (1973: 395) has intimated, 'the liberation curriculum needs be a "freedom for" and not a "freedom from" curriculum to promote creativity since creative acts produce new knowledge and 'break out of the determined chain of the world's energy'.

Putting Education for Liberation into Practice

There are numerous examples, in North America particularly, of educational movements that reflect these perspectives and traditions. These include the Rethinking Schools collective[2] and the Equity Literacy Framework.[3]

An example of a movement to put these ideas into practice is the Education for Liberation Network (ELN) in the United States,[4] a national coalition of teachers, community activists, researchers, youth and parents who 'believe a good education should teach people . . . how to understand and challenge the injustices their communities face' (Education for Liberation Network 2020).

The Network was founded by, and initially led by Black and indigenous people and People of Colour, and aims to connect people to learn from each other. It particularly focuses on supporting 'disenfranchized members of society'. They aim to do this through 'teaching young people the causes of inequalities and injustices in society and how communities have fought against them'. Reflecting other social movements around liberation, the Network sees a major role of their work to help young people believe in themselves so that they can challenge the injustices they see around them. The Network, also reflecting Freirean thinking, emphasizes dialogue and encourages the questioning of one's own assumptions and to imagine a better world.

A feature of the Network is to 'cultivate cultural knowledge and pride and encourage a positive sense of personal and collective identity'. Like other social movements around Black liberation, the Network puts all of its educational work within the context of combating social injustice:

> Across the country educators are increasingly frustrated with a system of education that disadvantages low-income youth and youth of color. Many are trying to fight back by developing their own curricula and methods that reflect both their care for young people and their ideas about justice and fairness. But these educators often find themselves isolated, with few resources, little support and limited connection to others who share their concerns. (ibid.)

Conclusion

This chapter has reviewed the perspectives of Freire, Nyerere and Gandhi in terms of education for 'liberation' and then reviewed more recent examples and practices of what the term means. The chapter has noted that there is a close association between the usage of the term with that of the voices and agendas of Black organizations in the United States.

The concept of education for liberation has been posed in recent years by the British writer Michael Rosen. He ask to what extent a vision of an education for liberation can be used as a way to challenge dominant orthodoxies of schooling. Rosen (n.d.) suggests, 'If we are serious about "education for liberation" we need to expose who controls education, we need to argue for democratic processes throughout . . . education.' This means, he suggests, promoting:

- Alternative principles based on how teachers and students can co-operate and enable learners to take control of how they learn and what they learn.
- Alternative principles on how education is organized, how schools are run, and what happens to power inside schools.
- Alternative principles in relation to cognition and democracy: that's to say, an education based on investigation, discovery, discussion, imagination and play.

In conclusion, Rosen said that there is a need to challenge who controls education and pose alternatives. These questions from Rosen also pose wider points for reflection as to what are the strengths and weaknesses of 'education for liberation' in the context of social change. An obvious criticism is that the term could be interpreted in an individualistic and not a collective sense. But as the example from the Network has shown in this chapter, the term can have a very popular relevance related to addressing inequality and oppression. There is clearly a linkage between how liberation is perceived with that of addressing the impact of colonialism.

Education for liberation from Gandhi and Nyerere through to Freire has clearly been a powerful call for social change. The writings of bell hooks are suggested as being of particular contemporary relevance at a time of increasing social injustices around the world. As this chapter has shown, the term is more than just rhetoric and has within its various interpretations an approach to learning that is rooted in social justice, combating oppression and seeking freedom for expression and independent voices.

Questions for Further Consideration

- To what extent can education for liberation be seen as an approach for both individual empowerment and collective-based social change?
- What do you see as the contemporary relevance of the ideas of Freire, Nyerere and Gandhi?
- How do you build the themes raised in this chapter into approaches within schools, colleges, universities and the wider community?
- In what ways can an initiative like Black Lives Matter become a driver for education for liberation?

Further Reading

Cappy, C. L. (2016), 'Shifting The Future? Teachers as Agents of Social Change in South African Secondary Schools', *University of South Africa Education as Change*, 20, no. 3: 119–40.

Freire, P. (1972), *Pedagogy of the Oppressed*, London: Penguin.

Freire, P. and I. Shor (1987), *A Pedagogy for Liberation*, London: MacMillan.

hooks, b. (1994), *Teaching to Transgress*, New York: Routledge.

Nyerere, J. (1976), 'Education and Liberation', *Africa Development*, 1, no. 3 (November): 5–12.

Sharma, N. (2008), *Makiguchi and Gandhi: Their Educational Relevance for the 21st Century*, Maryland: University Press of America.

4

Education for Socialism and a New Society

Introduction

The connection between education and society has often been seen in terms of promoting or aiming for a better or even a different world. In the nineteenth and twentieth centuries, this linkage between education and social change was often related to calls for different ways of living and working. The most popular manifestations of this have been the campaigns for a socialist society.

This chapter reviews some of the debates around education for socialism. In the United Kingdom, leading protagonists of education for socialism were Robert Owen and R. H. Tawney, who saw the goal of a new society based on egalitarian and co-operative principles. Another tradition was that which had a more directly Marxist influence, seeing education as being part of the class struggle for a new society. Various Marxist figures from Europe and Russia are discussed alongside the UK educationalist Beryl Pring and the concept of polytechnic education. The chapter then reviews how education is involved in Cuba's post-revolutionary period and the extent to which this could be located within the broader traditions around education for socialism. Finally, the chapter looks at two educational traditions which have relevance to socialist debates, the concept of popular education and, secondly, co-operative approaches to learning and co-operative schools.

The Ideas of Robert Owen

The obvious place to start in reviewing debates on education for socialism is with those who have been called the 'utopian socialists'. There were two leading figures from this political tradition in the late eighteenth and early nineteenth centuries, the UK entrepreneur Robert Owen and the French philosopher Charles Fourier. As Leopold has noted in commenting on them, both:

placed human nature at the centre of their educational views, and they both saw their educational views as forming an important and integral part of their wider project of radically transforming the social and political world. (Leopold 2011: 620)

Owen became manager of a large textile factory in New Lanark, Scotland, which he turned into a co-operative community. In 1813, he published *A New View of Society* which was broadly humanist in perspective. Central to his educational philosophy was a belief in the importance of the development of character and resilience. To Owen, knowledge was the basis of building a new society, 'by banishing ignorance and establishing the power of truth a national society would ensue' (quoted in Silver 1975: 52). Like many later thinkers, Owen saw the acquisition of knowledge as the key to building a new society.

Owen reflected many of the enlightenment traditions of the potential of human reason and believed that education was central to building a new society. In his co-operative communities in New Lanark in Scotland and New Harmony, Indiana, in the United States, he experimented with new forms of schooling influenced by these ideas.

As regards the content of the curriculum, whilst this was fairly traditional, it was co-educational. What was distinctive was the desire to make learning a pleasure and to have no scolding or punishment. Children were encouraged to seek dialogue with their teachers and lessons might be held indoors or outdoors (Leopold 2011: 626).

Similar views on education and a new society could be seen in the ideas of the French thinker, Charles Fourier, whose philosophy was based on the idea of harmony. To Fourier, education could liberate human nature and enable children and young people to develop their individual characteristics. What was particularly original and distinctive about his ideas was his concept of 'harmonian education', which should take place without schools and teachers and be run by the local community. There was also in his vision a connection between work and education including practical tasks as well as learning about music and cooking (Leopold 2011).

Whilst these figures were later criticized by Marx and others, they provided an important basis for later discussions on the direction of socialism with education being seen as a central component. Their influence can be seen in the United Kingdom in the Chartist movement and elsewhere in Europe on the goals of a new society.

British Labour Leaders and Education: Educative Socialism

Throughout the nineteenth century, numerous Labour figures across Europe saw a connection between increased learning opportunities and creating a new society. Whilst much of this interest in the importance of education was linked to the concept of self-improvement, towards the end of the century socialism and education became more closely linked through the ideas of William Morris. Knowledge and values based on aesthetics were seen as central to Morris:

> Intelligence enough to conceive, courage enough to will, power enough to compel. If our ideas of a new society are anything more than a dream, these three qualities must animate the due effective majority of the working people; and then, I say, the thing will be done. (Lecture on Communism in Morton 1973: 229)

Morris' ideas influenced many later British Labour figures including Keir Hardie, Bruce Glasier and, to some extent, Ramsay MacDonald (Morgan 1975; Marquand 1977). This can be seen in the early ideas of the Independent Labour Party (ILP), when they called for the objects of schools to be not based on fact cramming 'but the leading of children to observe and reason for themselves and to inculcate a love of knowledge for its own sake' (Education a Socialist Idea – ILP tract quoted in Bourn 1978: 16).

Although there was a strong moral and ethical basis to many of the ideas at the time, there was also a class identity and a recognition of the influence of capitalist ideas on schooling. The response was the creation of the Socialist Sunday Schools movement, which, using the format of church Sunday schools, set up socialist alternatives for children. By 1900, there were over a hundred of these schools, but they never became part of a mass movement, relying on local initiatives usually led by members of the Independent Labour Party (Reid 1966; Simon 1965). These schools reflected a clear alternative culture that would foster socialist ideals in working-class children. For many British socialists, working-class children were regarded as important groups in which to develop a commitment to socialism. As Gerrard states:

> the aim to instil socialist knowledge and critical capacities occurred alongside a strongly articulated conception of childhood, and respect for children's own political and intellectual development. (Gerrard 2011: 716)

A similar movement evolved in the United States but suffered from internal disagreements relating mainly to the balance between broader progressive educational goals and promoting socialism. There was a clear socialist endeavour in their aims:

> The system of public instruction prevalent in this country glorifies the competitive idea as applied to industry and all other walks of life. To prevent their children from being prejudiced against socialism, to make their children realise the class struggle and their own part in that struggle, Socialists are beginning to supplement the work of the public schools. (Quoted in Teitelbaum and Reese 1983: 438)

Between 1900 and 1920, at least ninety-four schools were established in sixty-five towns and cities across the United States. Whilst in both countries these Socialist Sunday schools clearly gained support from working-class communities, they suffered from political divisions during the First World War and the emergence of Communist parties which led to splits in the movement (Teitelbaum 1993).

For many Labour figures in the early decades of the twentieth century, an educated democracy was seen as virtually the same as education for socialism. However, there was a distinctive strand, for example, within the British Labour Party, of what could be called 'educative socialism'. Leading figures in this were Keir Hardie, Ramsay MacDonald and Philip Snowden. MacDonald, for example, believed that social change came through moral and intellectual development rather than economic conflict:

> Education was seen as the stepping stone towards and the foundation of a socialist state. (Schools and Citizenship – Leeds Weekly Citizen, 8 May 1925, quoted in Bourn 1978: 314)

Influenced by the positivists Herbert Spencer and Comte, MacDonald developed an 'evolutionary' theory of socialism based on social progress and changing the outlook of people. He saw the 'education of labour as the means of overcoming conflict in society' (MacDonald 1920: 65). Socialism was seen as the way forward through providing a different moral and social purpose to that of capitalism:

> Labour strives to transform through education, through raising the standards of mental and moral qualities, through the acceptance of programmes by reason of their justice, rationality and wisdom. (ibid., 103)

Fundamental to this conception of socialism was the belief that public opinion as opposed to class struggle was the vehicle for social change.

These ideas were influenced by religious ideas about the moralism of the working man. Perhaps the most influential Labour thinker on these moral perspectives of socialism was R. H. Tawney, whose approach came more from an Anglican than a nonconformist perspective. Conscious of the need to promote an alternative to a Marxist view of societal change, Tawney put the emphasis on moral exhortation:

> to persuade people how much could be accomplished by a movement of individual moral values. . . . In order to effect social change it was necessary to embrace certain moral ideas and to have the will to act upon them. (Wright 1987: 107)

To Tawney, the foundation of a new society could be built on the widest possible dissemination of education and culture, combined with personal liberty, social equality and co-operation.

Socialism for Tawney was envisaged as only being possible through a change in social relationships, the creation of a new manner of life based on co-operative relationships. Central to his conception of socialism was the ideal of fellowship, of a society of equal communal relationships and no class divisions. Tawney's biographer has suggested that he 'amongst British socialists has come nearest to providing a truly hegemonic philosophy transcending sectional claims, bidding to remake British society by democratic means' (Terrill 1974: 176).

Educational equality was key to his thinking and from this Tawney suggested that schools could become the germ for developing new social relationships for a better society. He proposed that, imaginatively handled, education could break down the possessive individualism of a capitalist culture. Through education, he wrote, 'men [could] transcend the limitations of their individual perspectives and become partners in a world of interests which they can share with their fellows' (quoted in Terrill 1974: 182).

Education for Tawney was fundamental to creating a new society, central to determining the character and attitudes of the future generation. He saw education as a symbol of social unity, a community of learning by co-operative experiments.

Education and socialism, to him, therefore became synonymous. Tawney (1924: 58) wrote:

> the greatest possible educational equality is one of the conditions indispensable to any socialism which is not the mere rule of a bureaucratic elite or an apathetic mass. The society based on the free co-operation of citizens, which is the ideal of the socialist, depends in short, on the widest possible diffusion of education. . . . We are working for the future, but the future is with us here and now. It is attending school.

This belief in the widest possible development of education was in reality Tawney's great contribution. His ideas on socialism can now appear to be rather naïve. They were clearly idealistic but there was clear linkage between his concept of socialism and education and the content and the nature of the teaching. Tawney was sympathetic to some of the ideas emerging around more progressive approaches to teaching but his main influence was in consistently calling for the expansion of secondary education.

Whilst Tawney was able to gain respect from across the labour movement, his ideas were clearly framed within a conscious desire to combat Marxian socialism.

Following the Second World War, education ideas and policies in the British Labour Party tended to focus on the issue of the nature of secondary education, and this continued right up to the 1960s and 1970s. For the Labour Party, like much of the left in Europe and beyond, education was no longer seen as the primary means of achieving a new society. There became more of a focus on economic development, health and reducing inequalities. Although Tony Blair, when he became Labour prime minister in 1997, said that his priority was education, education, education, in practice, despite some major investment in the sector, it did not lead to a radical change of direction. By this time, however, the term 'socialism' was not one that would be regularly used by him or other Labour leaders.

Marxist Education and Socialism

The second major tradition to review, which has influenced thinking and practices on education for socialism, has been Marxism and the assumption that the dominant influence on securing a better society is the nature of class divisions and their impact on culture and ways of living and working.

With the growing influence of Marxist thinking in the United Kingdom and in other countries after 1918, ideas and policies on education came to reflect this more directly class-based perspective. In the United Kingdom, this could be seen in the creation of the Labour College movement and the establishment of the Plebs League magazine. The Plebs' conception of education was political: 'to develop and increase the class consciousness of the workers in order to aid them to destroy wage slavery and to win power' (quoted in Macintyre 1980: 81).

The emphasis in this approach was that education, through a distinctive cultural approach, can free working people from the chains of capitalism. As Phillips and Putnam (1980: 19) have commented:

'Education for Emancipation' meant the creation of a proletarian intellectual culture which would allow the working class to shrug off the distortions of 'public opinion', 'educational uplift', and 'scientific objectivity'.

For many of the proponents of this approach, there was a strong emphasis on class consciousness with the focus mainly on education for adults:

> Unless the workers have in their minds the light of proper understanding – unless they possess the knowledge which will be termed the map of class consciousness – they are flotsam, tossed willy-nilly upon the seas of capitalist confusion. (NCLC, 1931, Education and the World Crisis, quoted in Bourn 1978: 319)

Whilst this movement had some influence within the labour movement in the United Kingdom between the wars, it increasingly suffered from internal conflicts and from an increasingly dogmatic and economically reductionist view of education and social change.

However, the movement did result in some insightful publications that looked at the class-based nature of the education system, including the content of textbooks and the promotion of imperialistic views. One noticeable example of this was Mark Starr's book *Lies and Hate in Education,* published in 1929.

Equally significant, but perhaps intellectually more coherent and developed, was Beryl Pring's book published in 1937 and called *Education: Capitalist and Socialist.* She was an active Labour educationalist, and the importance of this publication is that whilst believing in the class-based nature of societies, including the education system, she nevertheless believed there were emerging progressive ideas and traditions that could help in building a new society.

Pring, whilst accepting the limitations of the capitalist education system, said that there was a need to campaign for immediate reforms and to look towards more progressive forms of teaching and learning. She noted there were many 'courageous individual experiments in English schools to-day' (Pring 1937: 122) but the challenge was the values base of society. She said the ultimate goal of schools should be to turn out minds that are sensitive, self-reliant, responsible, reasonable, appreciative, well-informed and tolerant (ibid., 128). What was also unusual within the frame of a Marxian approach was her emphasis on the importance of the needs of the individual child. She was clearly influenced by a range of progressive educational thinking developing at the time including John Dewey, Dora Russell and the emerging Dalton Plan approach to the curriculum across Europe. This meant to her:

> I have said that socialist education should aim at being educational rather than primarily socialist. I have emphasised this aspect because I wish to conciliate the intense individualism of many educationalists, who are alarmed by certain aspects of the socialist doctrine. (ibid., 258)

She went further and said:

> The task of socialist education is not merely to make the plain man understand the workings of society around him, but to make him contemplate intelligently changes in that society. (ibid., 266)

What is also significant about Pring's approach, differing from other forms of socialist education then emerging most notably in the Soviet Union, was that in socialist schools there will be no teaching of 'truth', but only the presentation of opinions; the teacher must deny himself the satisfaction of one of the major desires of mankind, the wish to convert (ibid., 266).

Unfortunately, Pring's ideas do not appear to have had a major influence on the Labour Party or the wider British socialist movement at the time. However, the linkage she outlined to progressive educational thinking reflected similar trends emerging within the Labour Party at this time. For example, the New Education Fellowship, the leading progressive educational movement of the time, included well-known Labour figures such as R. H. Tawney. As Chapter 3 in this volume has shown, by the mid-1930s educational and political figures were becoming increasingly concerned about the threat of fascism and the need to defend the concept of democracy which was regarded as being of paramount importance.

Marxist Ideas on Polytechnic Education

Whilst Marx and Engels wrote few articles on education, there was an underlying assumption in much of their writing that, free from the shackles of capitalist drudgery, workers would be emancipated to become new individuals through education. From narrow forms of labour, working people could become rounded individuals, learning a range of skills and forms of vocation. This approach to Marxism tended to develop and have its greatest influence in Russia through the emphasis on technological education.

After the Russian revolution in 1917, N. K. Krupskaya, who was Lenin's wife, became the champion of this new form of education. It put a major emphasis on the natural sciences and preparing children for productive work. To Krupskaya, there was a need for all pupils to learn the sciences and to move beyond reading, writing and arithmetic (Skatkin and Cov'janov 1994). This approach was called polytechnic education. Another feature of her initial ideas was to encourage teaching methods that encouraged pupils to think independently, to be inquisitive and creative.

Krupskaya notes, however, that it would be wrong to conclude that the polytechnic approach is just one of acquiring an aggregate of knowledge and skills, of a number of crafts, or merely the study of modern engineering. The polytechnic is a whole system that studies the bases of production in their various forms, states of development and manifestations (ibid.).

There were other ideas on education emerging in the Soviet Union that to some extent built on Krupskaya's work, notably Lunarcharsky and Schatzky, but their views were deemed to be too individualistic for the now-emerging Stalinist Russia with its emphasis on obedience and discipline. Instead, it was the teacher and founder of the Gorky Colony, Makarenko, whose ideas gained greatest prominence. Influenced by his teaching of a group of young people, Makarenko put the emphasis on military training, productive work and accepting authority. What this led to eventually was a move away from the concept of polytechnic education to one based on traditional textbook-based forms of teaching (Makarenko 1973).

What this evidence from the Soviet Union shows is that despite attempts to promote a more enlightened and progressive approach to learning, education became the direct instrument of a very rigid state system. Unfortunately, this approach to education not only continued after 1945 in the Soviet Union but was reproduced in the new communist states of Central and Eastern Europe. In East Germany, there were attempts to use some of the rhetoric from Krupskaya; as Castles and Wusternberg (1979: 99) have noted:

> Instead of totally developed individuals capable of creatively transforming society, the aim is the well-trained, hard-working, conformist wage workers.

What became dominant with this approach to education was the linkage between the needs of the state and the aims of education. This, as Boughton (2013: 249) notes, became subsumed with the role of the Party, in this case the Communist Party:

> The revolutionary Marxist tradition teaches that the party and its line is of central importance to revolutionary practice and therefore to popular, i.e., political education. . . . Collective united class action, led by the party, creates class power which does not exist unless and until such action is taken. This

power, this action, drives social change, creating the experiences from which we learn. The party, in other words, educates the educator, through driving revolutionary practice.

Another feature of this communist influence was the emphasis on the connection between learning and productive work and this continued into some of the educational policies of liberation movements in the 1960s and 1970s, which had been heavily influenced by Soviet ideas (Alexander 1990). A consequence of this was that when these liberation movements came to power what tended to be missing from their educational policies was a consideration of some of the broader pedagogical approaches that had been suggested by earlier Marxist educationalists.

Education in Cuba

One country that demonstrates some of these contradictory traditions and influences has been Cuba, where, since its revolution in 1959, education has been seen as a cornerstone of its socialist programmes.

An important early influence on the development of its educational programme was one of its key revolutionary figures of the time, Che Guevara. To Che, socialism, including education, should be built upon moral principles with a focus on forms of social action (Breidlid 2007; Barteau and Webb 2019). Holst (2009: 158), quoting Guevara, summarized this approach:

> There exists neither trade nor profession that can be learned from books alone ... but [a student's] real graduation – as is the case with any professional – takes place in the practice of his profession.

Guevara identified the 'transformation of human consciousness' as key to revolutionary change, and this became embodied with the 'values' elements of the school curriculum (Gasperini 2000). This also led to an emphasis on the collective rather than the individual.

Influenced by Soviet ideas on education outlined earlier in this chapter, there was a strong emphasis in Cuba on vocational education. As Charon-Cardona (2013: 301) states:

> Parents and primary school students dreamt of gaining a place in the selective vocational schools. They were, and are still today, considered prestigious institutions, and credentials from them endow social status in Cuban society.

Whilst education was seen as a right for everyone in Cuba, it was also expected that all citizens would participate in society and contribute to the national good.

The Cuban government under Fidel Castro's leadership was successful in taking forward Guevara's ideas, which can be seen in its recognizing the need to invest in basic educational needs, particularly reading and writing. Another of the distinguishing features of Castro's educational programme was in bringing into closer alignment the education institutions and the community. Learning was a responsibility for all peoples within the community. As Barteau and Webb (2019: 106) have commented:

> When members of the community participated in the education of its youth, not only did it send the message that education was valued, but also that the students were not alone and that the community supported them in their endeavours. The benefits extended to the parents whose close ties with the teacher equated to accessibility providing a resource to help their children with their studies, and the close ties with the community provided joint effort in ensuring the child's future as a contributing member.

As a result of these successes, Cuba came to be regarded as one of the great success stories in education. Not only did it achieve high literacy rates, but the performance of its students compared favourably with others elsewhere in Latin America.

Cuban society emphasizes collective ethos rather than the individual which has had consequences for the nature and forms of education.

This success story, however, became challenged in the first two decades of the twenty-first century with the collapse of the Cuban economy as a result of the political changes in Russia and elsewhere in Eastern Europe, alongside continued embargo and hostility from the United States. Teachers' salaries did not keep pace with the needs of the time, and many of them left the profession. As a consequence, the quality of teaching declined (see Barteau and Webb 2019).

The Cuban education system, like the rest of its society, struggled in the light of economic pressures and increased tensions between its long-term socialist goals and the practicalities of everyday life. Blum (2011) noted these tensions and referred to them as double consciousness and double standards, having to operate differing and often contradictory values in order to survive. There has, however, in the past decade been a resurgence in attempts to promote a more values-based approach to education to address an increasingly disenchanted youth (Griffiths and Millei 2013).

What is evident from reviewing the vision of socialist education in Cuba is that there are a number of features which clearly make it distinctive from other ideas and practices under this banner. Firstly, there has been a strong values-based dimension to the curriculum. Although schooling emphasizes the collective, ideological and individual planes of values can be seen (Dawley-Carr 2015). What is less evident are the skills of enquiry, critical thinking and viewing issues from different perspectives (Blum 2011). But as Harnecker (2013: 119) has noted:

> the social imaginary of social justice and emancipation is still present. Although the grandchildren of the historic generation are less familiar with socialist and revolutionary ideals, they generally grasp the importance of dignity and justice and reject subordination.

Secondly, whilst there has been the emphasis on solidarity at local, national and global levels, there has at the same time been a strong nationalist trend, as can be seen from the research on civics and citizenship education by Dawley-Carr (2015).

Thirdly, and despite these negative trends, the Cuban education system has provided free schooling for all, and supplied school materials and a high-quality health system which has had knock-on effects in terms of ensuring engaged pupils (Charon-Cardona 2013).

Education for socialism in Cuba is therefore a work in progress, reflecting some of the contradictions but also opportunities from earlier movements in Europe and North America.

Finally, this chapter reviews two examples of educational approaches that have their intellectual origins in forms of socialism and also show linkages with themes discussed in earlier chapters.

Popular Education

The term 'popular education' can be first seen as education for the masses or the poor and as an alternative to education for the privileged. In the early decades of the twentieth century, the term became most closely associated with socialist and anarchist groups . A series of international popular education conferences were held but a split emerged between Catholic and secular groups (see Braster, Simon & Grosvenor, 2013).

After the Second World War, the term became linked to literacy projects and educational initiatives in the Global South, and is often closely associated with approaches to learning that have similarities to the ideas discussed in the previous chapter on education for liberation. But it is a term that has become linked to approaches to adult education that have a clear political focus and clearly have their roots in socialist ideas be they from Marx, Gramsci, Guevara or Freire. The term has been used within liberation and struggles for socialism in Latin America, Africa and the Pacific.

The term, as Crowther, Galloway and Martin (2005: 1), state:

is based on a clear analysis of the nature of inequality, exploitation and oppression, and is informed by an equally clear political purpose. . . . The implicit theoretical base is a materialist political economy . . . [it] seeks to take the side of and be in solidarity with particular collective identities and interests and it stands against others . . . popular education is essentially and fundamentally a political project.

What often distinguishes usage of popular education from broader liberation education approaches is its emphasis on class, as Carlo Nuñez has stated:

A process of education and training carried out politically from a class perspective that forms part of or is articulated with action organised by the people, by the masses, in order to achieve the objective of constructing a new society in accord with their interests. (Cited in Austin 1999: 43)

Within many of the liberation movements, popular education was seen as synonymous with creating a new society. This, for example, can be seen in the liberation movements in East Timor (Da Silva 2011).

However, there are major questions about who are the drivers for change within liberation movements who wish to see a socialist society and see education as one of its founding principles.

Boughton (2013: 251) suggests that there is a need to make less ambitious claims for popular education:

it requires us to develop a clearer account of the relationship between education and social change, one which does not leave itself open to the kind of naive formulations that permeate some writings about new social movements, which imply that there is a path to social justice and equality that does not pass through politics, that does not have to come to terms with the question of political power and how it is achieved and exercised and that does not have to deal with the central problem of socialist theory, the problem of the state.

Boughton (ibid., 253), like Holst (1999), suggests that what needs to be recognized is the role of revolutionary parties as the drivers and enablers of social change. They note that people liberally make reference to the Italian Marxist Gramsci but ignore his belief in the central role of a political party, in his case the Communist Party.

One of the most common examples used to outline what 'popular education' means in practice has been the work and practices of Augusto Boal and his 'Theatre of the Oppressed' (Boal, A) (2008). Boal was a Brazilian theatre director, writer and politician whose work Theatre of the Oppressed became famous throughout Latin America and beyond for bringing in themes of human rights and social justice into a participatory form of theatre using democratic and co-operative forms.

Another example of putting these ideas of social justice and calls for a new social order within education into action was the Highlander Folk School founded by Myles Horton, who later collaborated with Freire (Horton and Freire, 1990). The school was founded in the 1930s, and its purpose was to make people more powerful, to bring white and Black people together. At first its focus was on supporting workers from industrial trade unions but from the 1950s it linked racial justice to economic justice. It became a focal point for civil rights activists including Martin Luther King and Rosa Parks. One of the movements it created was the Citizenship Schools movement which focused on enabling Black people to read and write under the leadership of Septima Clark. This movement later became run by the Southern Christian Leadership Conference. The Highlander school supported a range of radical political struggles despite being labelled as a 'school for communists and subversives'. It continued until 1961 when the state of Tennessee revoked its licence. Since then it has continued its work under the name of the Highlander Research and Education Center and today continues to support movements in their fights for justice and equality particularly focusing on leadership development programmes. The Center sees itself as a catalyst for grassroots organising and movement building for the Appalachia area and more widely the South in the United States.[1]

Popular education in a variety of forms has continued into the twenty-first century through the continuation of initiatives such as Highlander Center, continued interest and influence in the ideas of Boal and through a series of international conferences co-ordinated by the Popular Education Network. This Network of primarily higher education academics, focusing on adult education still sees the purpose of the movement to be to support local activists and produce educational materials for social and political action (Crowther, 2013).

Co-operative Education

Another example is that of co-operative education, which brings us back to some of the ideas suggested in the work of Robert Owen and their potential contemporary relevance as a form of education for socialism.

Building on the early ideas of Owen and taken further into consumerism later in the nineteenth century, the co-operative movement has had strong links with socialist movements. In Britain and later elsewhere in the world, co-operative education, whilst based on mutual societies, has consistently supported learning and has been seen as a vehicle for social change.

Whilst there have been many examples of schools that have aimed to be linked to some of these networks outlined earlier, the Co-operative Schools movement, a UK network of schools sponsored by the co-operative movement, shows that some of the historical principles behind education for socialism continue to have contemporary relevance. This network began in 2009 and became an important network of state schools based on the co-operative values of self-help, self-responsibility, democracy, equality, equity, solidarity, honesty, openness, social responsibility and caring for others (Woodin 2015).

These schools have reflected a number of themes covered in this volume including what Woodin has called 'democratic experimentalism' and social justice. These schools emerged as successive governments sought to enable schools to be independent of local authorities and have external sources of funding. As Woodin (2019: 1165) noted:

> The application of co-operative values and principles have levered open arenas of debate on what an inclusive and mutual system of education might look like, now and in the future, with ownership, equality and democracy never being far from the surface.

But many others were much more cautious, and in recent years, from a high point of over six hundred co-operative schools, their numbers have dramatically reduced by 2020. This was due to a combination of external factors such as wider problems within the co-operative movement and the failure to clarify its role as a network of schools.

What, however, could be stated is that the most effective co-operative schools could be seen to offer a potential counter-hegemonic model for education, one which provided potential creative spaces for radical and transformative approaches to learning.

Co-operative models of learning, whilst being challenged by the influence of neoliberalism, have continued to exist in many regions around the world. Some models have relied on the influence of the traditional consumer movement, whilst other models have led to forms of workers' co-operatives.

Conclusion

This chapter has aimed to show that there have been many good intentions to promote a connection between education and building a socialist society. In the

United Kingdom, there were many creative ideas during the first few decades of the twentieth century, but they tended to be rather idealistic in tone and bore little relation to the immediate needs of the education system. The vision that an educated democracy would lead to a socialist society was seen to have its shortcomings, not least in ignoring the ideological role the state plays in reproducing dominant views about the value of existing societies. But within the ideas of Tawney and others, and their critique of capitalism from a moral standpoint, there is perhaps the elements of a relevant contemporary approach that questions the dominant neoliberal and individualistic cultures of the twenty-first century. The influence of Marxism, whilst providing a grounding for some excellent critiques of the nature of the education system, led to a more distorted form of socialism in the Soviet Union and Eastern Europe. Cuba, despite its ongoing economic and political difficulties, provides at least some positive elements of what a socialist vision of education can look like. There may be some shortcomings to the education system in Cuba, but it has provided examples around the tensions between individual and collective needs and a values-based curriculum that can inform other approaches and movements around the world in the future.

The references to popular and co-operative education show that the influences of socialist ideals can still be seen through a sense of social justice, solidarity and mutual co-operation. Above all, they provide a potential counter-hegemonic narrative to the dominance of neoliberalism, marketization and competitiveness that still pervades education around the world.

Whilst education for socialism may not appear in the curriculum of many schools, colleges and universities around the world, the movements and leading figures behind this goal have contributed considerably to social change. There are many examples in the United Kingdom and elsewhere in the world that ensure education for socialism is not lost. An excellent example in the United Kingdom is the People's History Museum in Manchester, which provides a wealth of resources and workshops for teachers and young people about socialist movements around the world.[2]

Questions for Further Consideration

- To what extent do some of the early ideas of education for socialism have contemporary relevance, particularly in terms of the desire to combat the 'possessive individualism of capitalism'?

- What is the relationship between education for a new society and the need to give greater resources to a more vocationally based approach to learning?
- What role can co-operation play in seeking a more just society through education?

Further Reading

Breidlid, A. (2007), 'Education in Cuba—An Alternative Educational Discourse: Lessons to be Learned?', *Compare: A Journal of Comparative and International Education*, 37, no. 5: 617–34.

Castles, S. and W. Wustenburg (1979), *The Education of the Future: An introduction to the Theory and Practice of Socialist Education*, London: Pluto Press.

Leopold, D. (2011), 'Education and Utopia: Robert Owen and Charles Fourier', *Oxford Review of Education*, 37, no. 5: 619–35.

Pring, B. (1937), *Education: Capitalist and Socialist*, London: Methuen.

Simon, B. (1965), *Education and the Labour Movement*, London: Lawrence and Wishart.

Terrill, R. (1974), *R. H. Tawney and His Times: Socialism as Fellowship*, London: Andre Deutsch.

Woodin, T. (2015), *Co-operation, Learning and Co-operative Values*, Abingdon: Routledge.

5

Education for a Global Society

Introduction

Social change can no longer be seen purely from a local or national angle. Global forces influence all aspects of life including education.

As has been shown through the Climate Emergency initiative in 2019 and the Black Lives Matter movement in 2020, many of the campaigns for social change, whilst they may have started in a particular country, are increasingly global in context and impact. The world of the third decade of the twenty-first century is a globalized world. What happens in one part of the world very often has an impact elsewhere. The 2020 Covid-19 pandemic is the most direct and devasting example of this.

Another feature of these global initiatives for social change has been their emphasis on social action, often initiated via social media. What these initiatives pose is where is the role of learning and understanding, and what forms of social action should be taken. A theme this chapter will address is: within the calls for social change, what is the contribution and role of education?

Discussions and activities on education as a vehicle for social change therefore need to include a recognition that globalization and global forces are likely to be the motors for change today. These forces may well be economic, social or cultural.

The main focus of this chapter, in recognizing the points outlined above, is to suggest why, what, and how globalization and global forces are key to addressing social change today through education. Reference will be made to understanding the significance and characteristics of the influence of globalization, through its impact on the nature, composition and economic basis of communities. Globalization has resulted in significant de-industrialization in some parts of the world but increased industrialization elsewhere. It will be noted that in a number of countries it is the right wing rather than the left wing which is today more anti-globalization.

A second theme will be specifically to look at how education is being perceived through human capital and the creation of knowledge-based economies. A third theme is the way in which the relationship between globalization and global social change has changed since the turn of the century. Consideration will here be given to the influence of social media and what Castells (1996) has called the 'network society'.

As with all of the remaining chapters in this volume, a specific section is set aside to consider research on these themes, particularly from doctoral-level dissertations. Finally, the chapter will review examples from different regions of the world that have tried directly to link learning with using global technologies in order to encourage social change. These include 'Send My Friend to School', 'Connecting Classrooms Through Global Learning' and 'Inspiral Education'. The purpose of these case studies is to provide descriptions of practical examples of putting education for a global society into practice.

Globalization and a Global Society

Globalization has a direct influence on people's lives in all regions of the world. However, its meaning and interpretation is complex. Giddens (1991) is often used as the starting point of definitions of globalization. He defines it as the 'intensification of worldwide social relations which link distinct localities in such a way that local happenings are shaped by events occurring far away and vice versa' (ibid., 64).

Other key figures who have defined the term are Harvey (1989), who refers to cultural de-territorialization and time space compression, and Held and McGrew (2000), who see it as a complex process of the transformation of economic, political and cultural social relations. This sense of connectedness at social, economic and cultural level is therefore a common theme in much of the literature around globalization (Baylis and Smith 1999: 7). Castells (1996) has developed this sense of connectedness with his work on 'the network society'.

Lissovoy (2008: 157–8) notes that globalization as a term can be seen as conflating two different meanings. The first are the economic and political initiatives undertaken by global elites as part of a new phase of capitalism. But it can also be taken to refer to a more fundamental process of 'the withering of the nation state system as the primary framework for organising social and political life and the worldwide cultural interpenetration that reorganises human society and identities on a planetary scale'. This second sense is often referred to as globality.

As well as being about connectedness and forms of interaction beyond the nation state, globalisation could also be seen in terms of a number of dimensions: economic, cultural, social, technological and political. Economically this can be seen through the movement of capital and goods around the world and the ways in which materials are produced in different parts of the world. The world-famous Swiss watch, for example, whilst being designed in Switzerland, has its components made and assembled in different countries. The global supply chain is a direct result of globalization and relies heavily on an easy exchange of goods and materials between countries.

Socially, it can be seen through the movements of people and ways in which communities have become more diverse. This diversity has resulted sometimes in divisions between cultural groups, often with those from migrant communities being used as cheap labour with minimal rights.

Culturally, it can be seen in the ways in which people and communities have become influenced by forces elsewhere in the world. This has often resulted in forms of homogeneity and Western dominance, particularly in terms of 'bland product conformity' (McDermott 2007: 120) and what has been called 'McDonaldisation' (Ritzer 2000). It has also had an impact on people's cultural lifestyles and sense of identity. As Ray (2007) notes, these influences can result in a complex individual identity influenced by a range of social and cultural forces. What is also evident is that globalization can often lead to increased individualism and a sense of insecurity and uncertainty.

Technologically, through the internet and social media, people can communicate more easily with people elsewhere in the world and have greater access to information and knowledge.

Finally, politically, it can be seen in the ways in which there has been a recognition of international collaboration, be it through global institutions such as the United Nations, regional bodies such as the European Union, groupings of leading countries in the world such as the G7 or increasing usage of international agreements to address common problems such as those of climate change.

These differing approaches therefore raise questions about the ways education is influenced by global forces. There are two themes which bring together the dimensions addressed above and which relate directly to what learning takes place and how. The first theme is what Beck (2000) calls 'globalism' which he sees as the 'ideology of the market place' with globalization being the analytical tool. This concept of globalism is closely aligned with the ideology of neoliberalism. Harvey (2005: 3) defines neoliberalism as an ideology of:

political economic practices that propose that human well-being can best be advanced by liberating individual entrepreneurial freedoms and skills within an institutional framework characterised by strong private property rights, free market and free trade.

The second theme is that globalization can provide spaces for new identities and contestation of established values and 'norms' (Stromquist and Monkmann, 2000: 21) and broadening perspectives, experiencing different cultures and ways of living (Kenway and Bullen 2008: 33–34). Burbules and Torres (2000) refer to this as 'globalisation from below' which can and has resulted in a range of global social movements. Key initiatives here include the 'Arab Spring', 'Climate Emergency' and 'Black Lives Matter'. What is also significant about these movements is the way they have used social media not only to raise awareness of issues but to mobilize millions of people around the world.

What this usage of global forces also shows is that people and communities are not passive consumers but actively involved in reusing globalization for their own purposes, identity and engagement communities.

At the same time, however, it should be noted that globalization can have negative influences on societies, communities and individual outlooks. As Lissovoy (2008: 158) has commented:

> Globalisation has so far meant . . . the decline of stable jobs and good benefits for workers, the proliferation of conditions of super-exploitation for others, the abandonment of many to no livelihood at all with the dramatic movement of firms around the globe, the destruction of traditional economies and forms of life, forced migration, cultural imperialism, and predatory consumerism, not to mention environmental degradation and perpetual war.

This, he suggests, presents major challenges for children and young people in terms of threats to security, and unstable and insecure futures. In addition, he notes the shift to globality has meant the re-organization of much of human life to a global and much more complex scale which can often result in a sense of powerlessness. This includes the 'replacement of familiar frameworks and modes of communication by alien ones; the deterritorialization of identities and the assimilation of daily practices to a new set of general and planetary social habits' (ibid.,159).

The emphasis on consumerism, for example, as a result of increased competition for the sale of products, has led to a more individualized approach to ways of living in many communities. Secondly, global influences have led in a number of countries to a retreat to forms of nationalism and xenophobia. This can be seen in the UK through Brexit and forms of populism in Europe and America.

What these trends suggest is that key to the ways in which individuals and communities respond to global forces is the role of education. One response to these changes in societies and economies has been the increased influence of the human capital approach, which perceives educational priorities in terms of skills development of the workforce. It is not the purpose of this chapter to discuss in detail the merits or otherwise of human capital theory, merely to note that in many ways it is a continuation of traditions that go right back to the nineteenth century of seeing more education as the primary vehicle for economic development. Where human capital theories have been particularly influential has been where there has been a strong emphasis on competition, emphasizing the needs of the highly skilled and individualized forms of learning. What tends to get either ignored or considered to be of less importance is the value of a broad, holistic education and the social developmental needs of the learner.

Role of Education

It is these two interpretations on the role that education can play in using global forces for social change that is the focus of this section. There is the economic interpretation which equates with using global forces to develop a more 'highly skilled workforce' and which sees competition and the use of market forces as the way in which education systems should be organized. Alternatively, there is the view that sees global forces as a means for addressing injustices and inequalities around the world and promoting a sense of being a global citizen.

The focus on addressing economic needs through education can be seen in a range of policy statements from bodies such as the OECD (2011, 2015, 2016, 2017). Here the emphasis is that educational programmes should be primarily related to the skills needs of the workforce. Whilst within the initiatives around skill there is a recognition of what could be called 'softer' or twenty-first-century skills, the agenda is geared towards learning to compete in the global marketplace (Bourn 2018b).

The alternative is to see global forces as a vehicle for promoting a sense of global social justice. As already suggested in this chapter, globalization does not necessarily lead to conformity and homogeneity. As Scheunpflug notes (2011: 30), 'globalisation does not have a single face, but a plurality of aspects, depending upon where and how one lives. The universal process of globalisation shapes national patterns in different ways'.

Instant access to knowledge and information, whilst enabling the learner to have instant access to a range of perspectives, can also lead to 'fake news' and distorted views of reality. This means that a key element of educational responses to these challenges has to be a clear strategy of what could be called 'global skills' (Bourn 2018b).

This means promoting approaches towards learning that encourage the development of critical thinking and understanding a range of worldviews. Elsewhere this is discussed in more detail and can be summarized as follows:

- An ability to see the connections between what is happening in your own community with those of people elsewhere in the world.
- Recognizing what it means to live and work in a global society and the value of having a broad global outlook on the world that respects, listens to and values perspectives other than one's own.
- An ability to understand the impact of global forces on one's and other people's lives and what this means in terms of a sense of place in the world.
- Understanding the value of using ICT and how best to use it in a way that is self-reflective and critical and questions data and information.
- Openness to a continued process of self-reflection, critical dialogue and questioning one's own assumptions about the world.
- Ability to work with others who may well have different viewpoints and perspectives to you, being prepared to change one's own opinion as a result of working with others and seeking ways of working that are co-operative and participatory in nature.
- Confidence, belief and willingness in wanting to seek a more just and sustainable world (Bourn 2018b).

Each of these themes seeks to link globalization issues with specific knowledges, values and attitudes, skills and related pedagogical needs. They move beyond generalized terms such as teamwork and co-operation and locate skills development within specific contexts. They are also skills that have a social function beyond individual attributes. This approach also means that social change becomes an element of educational initiatives and the skills emphasis has to have a direct relationship to knowledge and values.

Global forces, and particularly the use of the internet, can enable learners to share ideas and experiences with others elsewhere in the world. This connectivity has to be organized so that all learners can have equal access to resources and sharing of ideas. The education also has to be in a form where all partners can benefit and there is a sense of mutual learning. What, however, is clear from the examples shown later in this chapter is that technology can enable learners to develop a global outlook, to share experiences and feel part of a broader community committed to social justice.

Global Social Movements

A feature of debates on globalization and social change has been the role of social movements. From the movements against global corporations and international organizations at the turn of the century to more recent campaigns on climate change, social movements have played an important role. But what is significant about movements today is the way in which the use of global technologies has resulted in a move away from formal institutions to more grassroots-based groups and in some cases more informal networks. As Cohen and Rai (2000: 6) have noted, 'old social movements spoke primarily to or against the nation state, the voice of the new movements (have) reached beyond the borders of the nation'.

What is relevant for discussions in this chapter is the extent to which these movements have been simply against something and/or been a promoter of a vision and positive alternative and way forward. To some a social movement has been seen as being just a form of protest (Della Porta and Diani 1999: 14-15). Gibson goes further and suggest that social movements are ultimately 'fought against the same neoliberal order' (Gibson 2008: 255).

An alternative perspective is to see global social movements as providing the space and opportunities for voices from communities to be heard and organized so that they can make a difference (McDonald 2006: 25). This relates to themes outlined by Paulo Freire who, whilst critiquing education, said there was a need to 'announce the dream for which one fights' (Freire 2004: 18). Tarrow (2005: 56) suggests that it is 'social justice' which provides the glue to having a vision for social change.

There have been many campaigns around the world that have lobbied for global policy changes. One of those, which mobilized millions of people, was Make Poverty History in 2005. But like many other campaigns and initiatives, this example reinforces the view that such calls for policy changes emphasize more the imparting of information in order to gather support rather than encouraging a deepening of knowledge and ownership (Darnton and Kirk 2011; Hudson and van Heerde-Hudson 2012). These campaigns have also tended to be based on what Chan (2009) calls an activist based political pedagogy.

The response to these challenges suggested here is the need for clear educational strategies; and, secondly, the identification of possibilities and alternative scenarios for social change around the creation of a vision for global citizenship. Chan has summarized these responses as:

- Education as counter analysis — providing evidence to challenge dominant orthodoxies, looking particularly at difference and power.
- Education as possibilities — identifying alternative possibilities, including development approaches and global governance reform; there are alternatives to free market approach.
- Education as new subjectivities/citizenships — fostering cosmopolitan/global citizenship (ibid.).

Understanding Globalization

For education to provide a counter analysis that could inform global campaigns and initiatives, there is a need for the learning to include an understanding of the impact of globalization. As I have noted elsewhere (Bourn 2018b), initiatives on education for a future society and economy rarely mention globalization. This can be seen, for example, in the various programmes about twenty-first-century skills or sustainable development. Scheunpflug (2011: 35) suggests instead that an understanding of globalization should have factual, temporal, spatial and social dimensions. This means:

- Factual includes knowledge about globalization and literacy, mathematics and sciences.
- Temporal includes information-seeking and tolerance to ambiguity.
- Spatial includes thinking and working in networks, and thinking and working in virtual spaces.
- Social includes knowledge about diverse lifestyles, cultures and religions.

What is significant and important about this rationale for understanding globalization is that not only does the learner need to develop more knowledge about the term, they need to consider the term in relation to their own sense of place in the world and what could be their contribution to engage in this global society.

Where globalization has been the subject of educational resources, particularly for schools, there has been a tendency to focus on multi-national companies. This can be seen in a range of materials produced by NGOs such as 'The Trading Game'.

Egan (2012) has suggested that 'understanding corporate power should be central to learning' and proposed that the key to this was 'critical literacy'. This means learning about global issues needs to give greater attention to the impact of global forces and how people and communities respond to these challenges.

Alternative Perspectives

One form of educational response can be to promote different scenarios to the dominant neoliberal discourses around globalization, including not only knowledge about global forces but the development of skills to effectively engage in models for social change.

What this means is recognizing the opportunities that globalization can provide in terms of access to differing ideas, particularly through social media. Key here is critical media literacy and enabling the learner to develop skills to make a difference. Finally, and this is outlined further below through the examples, is how social media and the internet can enable learners to connect with fellow learners around the world and listen to and understand different perspectives.

As Lissovoy (2008: 166) notes:

Globalisation provokes questions about new dimensions of power as well as the challenges and possibilities for democracy; critical education must analyse and explore these questions.

This means that any form of educational programme with a global component, be it in schools, youth work, colleges or universities, or in lifelong learning, has to consider the following:

- What is meant by inequality?
- Why are some people rich and others poor?
- What impact has colonialism had?
- To what extent do powerful economic and social media forces influence what and how subjects are taught?

This is because if an educational initiative includes any form of dialogue or interaction with others elsewhere in the world or just includes understanding about people elsewhere in the world, there will be factors that influence how learning takes place. For example, there will be external factors that will influence an individual's approach towards learning about the other, including inter-cultural experience, possible stereotypical views, willingness to reflect upon and reconsider one's own opinions, and the extent to which their values base is rooted in social justice and human rights.

Research on the impact of students from North American universities visiting community projects in Brazil showed the complexities and challenges of such initiatives and the ideological factors that influenced the students' learning. Like many such initiatives, the young people came away from the experience seeking to take further action to address the poverty and inequality they faced. As Sutherland, Susa and Andreotti noted:

> Their expectations were framed in narratives of intercultural exposure, of developing an increased awareness about the world, and the development of individual qualities and mindsets to foster social change and avoid reproducing unjust structures that are often found in mainstream rationales for global citizenship education. (Sutherland, Susa and Andreotti 2020: 394)

What their research also showed was that despite the positive value of the encounters upon all involved, it did lead to a sense of powerlessness and recognizing the need to develop more meaningful relationships. What was also evident was that such experiences expose the need for deeper learning around such projects to deal with the complexities and uncertain outcomes that may emerge. As the authors noted:

> Only in learning how the kinds of knowledge that we have been socialized into are foreclosing on the possibilities of seeing the world from someone else's eyes, in acknowledging the epistemic and ontological erasures, can we break with some of the more harmful exploitative and hegemonic patterns of behaviour that more often than not dominate the North-South encounters. (ibid., 398)

Being able to have access to a range of cultures, knowledge and experiences from around the world brings with it questions of power, ideology and personal challenges. This is why education is so important. Without opportunities to reflect on one's own experiences, to learn about different worldviews and to understand specific local circumstances, so-called inter-cultural experiences can reinforce rather than challenge existing perspectives.

Research on Students as Global Citizens and the Global University

Terms such as being a 'global graduate' and a 'global university' have become popular within many universities around the world. They have become used as a way of recognizing the globalized world within which universities operate and aiming to equip all of its graduates with the knowledge and skills for a career in the economy and world of the twenty-first century. North Eastern University in the United States, for example, states that it attracts 'students and faculty who believe in experiential learning, a cornerstone of what it takes to succeed in different cultures and with people from different cultures. Our students are going out into the world, and the world is coming to us' (North Eastern University n.d.).

Coventry University in the UK promotes itself as a 'A Global University: An Innovative and Enterprising University in a Globalised World'. This interpretation of a global university includes 'making our excellent programmes available to students around the world'; their programmes aiming to be 'global in orientation'; and their students having 'the opportunity to acquire a new language or deepen competence in an existing second language alongside increased cultural proficiency and knowledge of global issues' (Coventry University n.d.).

Like many universities, Coventry also refers to international mobility experiences so that their students 'are better equipped to be global leaders and employees of the future'. Where perhaps Coventry goes one step further is that their 'courses draw on material and case studies sourced globally and encourage the examination of issues from different cultural, economic and socio-political perspectives' (ibid.).

Benhayoun, an academic based at a university in Morocco, has suggested that technology and global events of 2020 indicate that there is a need for a new approach to the concept of the 'global university':

> The new global university has to make a statement of its own through the actual diversity of its community of staff and students and by its power to network and influence academe irrespective of the time difference, geographical location and cultural background. (Benhayoun 2020: 1)

He goes on to suggest that this needs to be done by the 'new global university' becoming an 'an open access establishment influenced and enriched by the cultural and intellectual import of its community across distances and locations' (ibid.).

These perspectives pose important questions about the role and purpose of the university in the context of the global world but what is less evident from these observations is the extent to which there is a broader sense of social responsibility. There has been some valuable research, by Killick, that looks at the value of cross-cultural capability which seeks to:

demonstrate the relationships between local actions and global consequences, highlighting inequalities, helping us reflect upon major issues such as global warming, world trade, poverty, sustainable development, human migration, and promoting a response based on justice and equality not charity. (Killick 2006: 4)

Killick's completed research (2011) on Students as Global Citizens provides us, however, with some valuable evidence from UK undergraduate students on the contribution of international mobility experiences to their identity, sense of place and forms of engagement in society. His thesis suggests that to live and work in a globalized world, the students need to become 'global citizens'. This process of change is seen as both a sense of the role of the individual in the world and their abilities to act in the world.

The narratives of the students Killick identified showed a:

recognition of the socio-cultural-world as being more globally situated, reconstructed in the lifeworld as one culture among many; sometimes diminished in significance, sometimes with its norms and practices brought to consciousness for the first time, and perhaps recognised as arbitrary and amenable even to change. (Killick 2011: 228)

With regard to forms of engagement and action in society, Killick found there was a greater sense of self-confidence in the students; they felt more able to express their views, tell their stories and defend their positions. A key theme identified was the form of inter-cultural communication and to learn to behave in culturally appropriate ways (ibid., 230).

Killick's research, as he himself acknowledges, opens up the value of international mobilities in the global society as a way of enhancing a sense of being a global citizen.

He later developed his ideas to question some of the passive interpretations of global citizenship by recognizing the value of Amartya Sen's capabilities approach. Killick proposed two inter-related capabilities for a graduate:

Global perspective capabilities to recognise the ways in which his/her own personal and professional actions, and those of others, impact upon the capabilities of diverse people in diverse contexts to lead lives they have reason to value. This includes not only knowledge of the ways of the world but dispositions to apply that knowledge alongside skills and emotional intelligence.

Cross-cultural capabilities to conduct his/her personal and professional life among diverse people in diverse contexts in ways which do no harm to their capabilities to lead lives they have reason to value. (Killick 2018: 73)

The research of Chris Shiel from Bournemouth University in the UK goes further and links global perspectives to sustainable development and a sense of social change.

Shiel states that universities have a 'moral responsibility to contribute toward a better society and a duty to lead the sustainability agenda, through research but also as educators of those who will be the future decision makers'. Her approach was based on the concept of 'global perspectives' which is to 'provide a curriculum and learning experience which went beyond an 'internationalized' curriculum to address the challenges of preparing and empowering students to play an active role in a complex global context, where issues such as unsustainable development, social injustice, poverty, conflict and change, require new ways of thinking, working, and indeed being' (Shiel 2013: 39).

Her research has been significant because it brings together discourses from global education and citizenship with those from sustainable development to pose a new framework under the heading of 'global perspectives' (see Bourn, McKenzie and Shiel 2006; Bourn and Shiel 2009).

Shiel relates this framework to the themes of internationalization and employability but argues that:

> developing global citizens, who understand the need for sustainable development, not only enhances other policy agendas (notably internationalisation – which must be a broader concern) but should be seen as a critical responsibility of higher education, if universities are to contribute effectively to sustainable development in a globalised world. (ibid.,102)

To Shiel, the concept of the 'global university' has an institutional wide validity. A lot of her detailed research was in the areas of business and management education and from this identified a distinctive pedagogical approach that is clearly influenced by Freire and transformative learning theorists. Finally, and particularly related to social change, she recognizes the importance of engaging with the policy initiatives on leadership in higher education but in a form that aims to secure not only a 'sustainable university' but aims to engage in global social change.

Case Studies

Outlined below are educational initiatives that start from recognizing the importance of the influence of being part of a global society and how young people, civil society organizations, teachers and educational bodies can connect with each other around the world.

Connecting Classrooms Through Global Learning – Example of Partnerships Between Schools in the UK and Nepal

Connecting Classrooms Through Global Learning is a global programme for schools and teachers managed by the British Council in the UK. The programme focuses on professional development courses for teachers and funding and support for international partnership projects for schools in the UK and schools in Africa, Middle East and Asia. The partnership projects have to be related to the Sustainable Development Goals.

One example of practice within this programme that demonstrates being part of a global community has been the partnership initiatives between schools in Nepal with schools in the UK. Nepal is a country which provides different cultural experiences for teachers and children in the UK. For Nepalese children, the development of their English language skills is seen as a key motivator factor for the children.

A good example of the type of partnerships between schools in the two countries is one between Stevenage in England with schools in Kathmandu and Pokhara in Nepal. Teachers from the Stevenage schools, with funding from the British Council, travelled to Kathmandu and Pokhara in September 2019 where they had the opportunity to visit their partner school and meet with their fellow Nepalese teachers to discuss and agree the specifics of a planned joint educational project.

Recognizing the inequalities that exist in the world, the teachers agreed on 'gender equality through citizenship' as a collaborative project. Specifically, the project aimed to address how gender roles and expectations influence identity and rights. A feature of the project was to encourage the pupils to question their own assumptions about inequality and how to empower all women and girls to play a positive role in society and to seek a more just world. These goals were noted by the teachers and clearly gained support from pupils.

As one of the Stevenage teachers noted:

> The participating schools are all passionate about providing their students with the knowledge, skills and values that will enable them to play an active role in their community, whilst working with others to make our planet more equal, fair and sustainable. (Bourn and Pasha 2020: 36)

To the Nepalese teachers, the partnership project also provided opportunities to learn about and develop different approaches to teaching that moved beyond a traditional 'chalk and talk' approach.

For schools from both countries, the partnership helped to develop 'inclusive values', pupil motivation and engagement and school-community links (ibid.).

International partnerships like these can all too easily fall into the dangers of reproducing neo-colonial relationships. This was recognised by the teachers in both the UK and in Nepal particularly in terms of the dangers of stereotypes and exoticism. This is why global learning professional development courses are recognised as an important prerequisite of such partnerships.

Send My Friend to School

Send My Friend to School is an initiative in schools in the UK which has the support of over twenty organizations including development NGOs, teacher trade unions and educational foundations. It is linked to the Global Campaign for Education which is a global organization working to ensure quality education for all children, with members in over ninety countries. The focus of Send My Friend is to encourage schools and young people to campaign for better education around the world. It has been running since 2005 and has involved over 10,000 schools in the UK. Its focus has been to influence and lobby policy-makers, particularly Members of Parliament, to support the campaign and the actions Send My Friend has identified.

The Campaign produces educational resources to support their activities. The focus of their 2020 pack was on Climate Change. It included information about the issues, activities such as producing posters and other visual material to influence their peers and also their local Member of Parliament. The Pack also included case studies of the impact of climate change on various communities around the world and a series of issues that need to be tackled with suggested solutions.

An important part of the materials Send My Friend produces is to provide guidance for young people on how to campaign including influencing the local press and a Guide on how to approach Members of Parliament.

One of the most important materials from the organization that is relevant to the theme of education for social change is their factsheet on local to global links and how their actions can help make sure every child has an education. It shows how by influencing your local Member of Parliament, the campaign by the young people could influence government and thereby try and change national and international policies. The factsheet also shows the importance of being part of a global campaign and how this can have a direct impact on international bodies and also influence other countries around the world. The factsheet also notes the importance that by bringing these different influences together you are more likely to influence international forums such as the United Nations, the G7 and the G20 (Send My Friend 2016).

Inspiral Education

This organization, through support from entrepreneurs, has developed an international online educational resource that enables young people based in schools to learn about global issues with their peers from elsewhere in the world. It is a social learning platform that enables 11–16-year-old school students to learn about topics such as freedom of expression and human migration and to share their ideas with fellow students from other regions of the world. Its aim is to better prepare students for living and working in an uncertain world. It aims to 'improve their global competencies and sense of global citizenship by connecting students to learn and make sense of their world together'.[1]

Each topic follows a structured learning programme that will include the use of videos, background information and group and individual-based tasks. An important component is the lesson plans produced to support the activities, with critical thinking skills regarded as particularly important.

A feature of the programme is shared spaces for students to express their views but also to engage in active listening with the aim of reflecting on their experience. Dialogue and activities can also take different forms from groups within a classroom to international teams.

The evidence from the Freedom of Expression activities show that students valued the learning process with one commenting: 'I've learnt that people have different opinions and that's okay'. Another said that they had learnt 'how to be respectful and understand other people's difficulties'. The evidence from students also shows the importance to them of learning about differences and similarities. This included 'to see the other person's views and how actions or events impact your perspective, and that loads of people have different ideas'. The development of new skills was also as important to them; they now felt more able to express themselves including to 'share my opinion more often, listen to others'.

Values were also recognized by the students as things they had gained. This included respecting others, tolerance of difference, empathy and equality of all people as the most valuable thing they had learnt.

Within the Inspiral methodology, there is a clear pedagogical approach that starts from a stimulus activity, often a video, with a global overview, followed by activities, that encourages connections to personal viewpoints which are then shared and discussed with others. This enables a recognition of and consideration for different viewpoints. This is then followed by online discussions with peers from other countries with final activities to assess the level and nature of the learning that has taken place.

Conclusion

Globalization has resulted in widespread changes to economies, societies and cultures around the world. It has also posed major questions as to what and how people learn. It can lead to a focus within educational programmes on the dominance of economic agendas, the influence of market forces and a concentration on technological skills. But these global skills can also be seen from a different perspective such as equipping the learner to understand different world perspectives, how to make an active contribution to society and challenge existing assumptions about people from other cultures.

An impact of globalization, as this chapter has shown, has been the way in which higher education institutions and students have used these global forces to broaden horizons, provide opportunities for inter-cultural understanding and encourage a sense of being global citizens.

Social media has clearly had a major influence on learning and what people do with the knowledge and skills they have gained. The examples identified in this chapter,

'Send My Friend to School', 'Connecting Classrooms Through Global Learning' and 'Inspiral Education' show the positive value of learning about global issues and its impact upon seeking a more just world. What the chapter has, above all, shown is the challenges that international partnerships can create. As has been shown, there are dangers of paternalism and stereotyping, but they can also help to create a global mindset and encourage a recognition of the inequalities that exist in the world and what can be done to reduce them.

Questions for Further Consideration

- What does globalization pose in terms of challenges and opportunities for learning?
- To what extent is 'global skills' a useful term in equipping learners with playing a positive role within a global society?
- What do you see as the strengths and weaknesses of universities using the term being a 'global university'?
- To what extent does making links and connections with learners elsewhere in the world contribute to feeling being part of a global society?

Further Reading

Bourn, D. (2018), *Understanding Global Skills for 21st Century Professions*, London: Palgrave.

Chan, J. (2009), 'The Alternative Globalisation Movement, Social Justice and Education', in W. Ayers, T. Quinn and D. Stovall (eds), *Handbook of Social Justice in Education*, 554–64, New York: Routledge.

Held, D. and A. McGrew (eds) (2000), *The Global Transformation Reader*, Cambridge: Polity Press.

Lissovoy, N. (2008), *Power, Crisis and Education for Liberation*, New York: Palgrave.

Scheunpflug, A. (2011), 'Global Education and Cross-Cultural Learning: A Challenge for a Research-Based Approach to International Teacher Education', *International Journal of Development Education and Global Learning*, 3, no. 3: 29–44.

Shiel, C. (2007), 'Developing and Embedding Global Perspectives across the University', in S. Marshall (ed.), *Strategic Leadership of Change in Higher Education*, 158–73, London and New York: Routledge.

6

Pedagogy for Global Social Justice

Introduction

The focus of this chapter is social justice and, in particular, what is meant by a pedagogy for global social justice. The rationale for this focus is that all societies have elements of social injustice within them. Education can play an important contribution towards reducing inequalities through raising awareness and understanding of issues and equipping learners with the skills and opportunities so that people of all ages can make a constructive contribution to society.

To understand what social justice means within the context of education for social change, it is necessary to recognize and consider the influences of power and inequality in the world, the importance of human rights, and how people can make a difference. Building on themes identified in earlier chapters, particularly through the influence of Paulo Freire, this chapter first outlines what pedagogy means in the context of social justice. Pedagogy is conceived as meaning more than 'methods of teaching' and 'subject and curriculum knowledge' and includes reference to broader social and cultural factors. The contribution of Henry Giroux to these debates and his approach of 'critical pedagogy' is recognized. The chapter then discusses various interpretations and approaches to social justice and looks specifically at human rights and power relations. With regard to research, the chapter reviews evidence gathered particularly in the United States on what is meant by social justice education and how teachers have engaged with the term. Finally, the chapter reviews some examples of practice that have demonstrated a pedagogy of global social justice, most notably in the UNICEF UK's Rights and Respecting Schools Award programme, the Fairtrade Foundation's Fairtrade School Awards programme and the Chicago Freedom School approach from the United States.

What is Meant by Pedagogy?

The term 'pedagogy' is usually summarized as the method and practice of teaching, the way teachers deliver the content of the curriculum within a classroom.[1] But there are many ways in which teaching can be delivered related to styles of delivery, needs and backgrounds of students, resources available and the extent to which the learning is assessed. Teachers are also likely to have their own views and principles as to what and how learning should be conducted.

For some educationalists and policymakers, pedagogy is defined in these rather narrow terms related primarily to forms and approaches to how people learn. There is, however, a wider view that includes 'ideas, values and evidence' about 'children, learning, teaching, curriculum and culture' (Alexander 2004: 7–8). Alexander further refers to pedagogy as involving 'what one needs to know and the skills one needs to command, in order to make and justify the many different kinds of decisions of which teaching is constituted' (Alexander 2004: 11). In many areas in Europe, pedagogy has this broader view including theories and approaches to learning.

Within the debates on what is pedagogy, a constant theme is the extent to which it is teacher- or learner-centred. The nature of the interaction between the teacher and the learner and the environment in which it takes place are therefore central questions to pose in any discussion on pedagogy. These could be summarized as three distinct approaches:

- *Teacher-Centred Pedagogy or behaviourist,* where the teacher is the centre of the process of learning and where the emphasis tends to be on large groups of learners, question and answer format with a clear power relationship.
- *Learner-Centred Pedagogy or constructivist,* where it is assumed the learners play an active role using their own experiences and existing knowledge. The role of the teacher is as a facilitator and to create the frameworks for the process of learning.
- *Learning-Centred Pedagogy or social constructivist* in which, whilst recognising the value of both approaches mentioned above, the learning environment becomes recognised as being central to the methodology and approach. This means taking account of the resources available, the physical environment, size of the classroom (UNESCO International Institute for Educational Planning n.d.).

Whilst all of these approaches have some value, depending on educational and cultural context, there is an area that needs to be added and that is one that recognizes power and inequality in the world and sees the learning as being equally appropriate to the teacher and the learner. This fourth approach is that referred to in earlier chapters from the works of Paulo Freire and Henry Giroux. This approach is usually summarized as 'critical pedagogy' and puts social justice and seeking social change at the heart of the learning process with an emphasis on democracy, freedom and liberation.

Critical Pedagogy

The term 'critical pedagogy', as developed by Freire and later by Henry Giroux and Peter McLaren, amongst others, suggests that learning not only needs to be democratic, it needs to recognize the power dynamics that inform how knowledge is constructed and applied (Freire 2004; Schugurensky 2014; Giroux 2005; McLaren 1998; Rouse 2011; Cho 2013). As outlined in earlier chapters, the perspectives from Paulo Freire were based on challenging the dominant oppressive modes of education and posing an alternative liberating model. Central to his thinking was the relationship between teacher and student where they both become empowered through a joint learning process (Shor 1992). As Shor notes, this form of pedagogy invites 'students to think critically about subject matter, doctrines, the learning process itself, and their society' and asserts that 'teachers pose problems derived from student life, social issues, and academic subjects, in a mutually created dialogue' (ibid., 25).

The work of Henry Giroux is particularly important here as he has developed Freire's thinking into a distinctive methodological approach that has social justice at its core. He suggests an approach to critical pedagogy that puts critical thinking at its heart where learners move beyond a slavish rote learning approach to one of exploration, questioning authority and challenging dominant assumptions. What makes Giroux's work so important for the themes in this volume is that whilst he critiques the dominant oppressive nature of many of the education systems around the world, he proposes a framework for change. This means enabling the learner to develop the:

> knowledge, passion, civic capacities, and social responsibility necessary to address the problems facing the nation and the globe; this means challenging those modes of schooling and pedagogy designed largely to promote 'economic

gain' etc. and substitute training for critical thinking and analysis. (Giroux 2011: 12)

Building on the work of Freire, Giroux suggests that education cannot be neutral. But in answer to the suggestion that his view of critical pedagogy is based around 'ideological propaganda', he states:

> critical pedagogy begins with the assumption that knowledge and power should always be subject to debate, held accountable, and critically engaged. Central to the very definition of critical pedagogy is a common concern for reforming schools and developing modes of pedagogical practice in which teachers and students become critical agents actively questioning and negotiating the relationship between theory and practice, critical analysis and common sense, and learning and social change. (Giroux 2011: 172)

There is a consensus amongst many of the proponents of critical pedagogy that its focus and approach are based on a vision of justice and equality that not only critiques societies but suggests the role that education can play in their transformation (Kincheloe 2004; Lynn & Jennings 2009). Critical pedagogy aims to challenge the dominant power relations in societies through a process of reflective learning and the promotion of social justice. As McLaren (1998: 160) has noted, what unites those promoting critical pedagogy is the objective to empower the powerless and transform existing social inequalities and injustices. He considers that forms of knowledge central to critical pedagogy are emancipatory, or directive knowledge. By this, McLaren (2003: 73) means:

> Emancipatory knowledge helps us understand how social relationships are distorted and manipulated by relations of power and privilege. It also aims at creating the conditions under which irrationality, domination, and oppression can be overcome and transformed through deliberative, collective action. In short, it creates the foundation for social justice, equality, and empowerment.

Another key element of critical pedagogy, first outlined by Freire but developed further by Darder, Baltodano and Torres (2003), is dialogue and his usage of the term *conscientização*. This means a problem-posing approach to learning with a constant process of conscious reflection that leads to an understanding of the social and political dimensions of one's life. Conscientization is the process that happens in dialogue.

Cho (2013) provides perhaps the clearest indication of the relationship between critical pedagogy and social change by posing that one of its functions is to construct alternatives to or counter-hegemonic forms of knowledge.

One of the areas of criticism of critical pedagogy is its apparent lack of engagement with racism and feminism. One person who directly addresses these areas is bell hooks, whose work was discussed in Chapter 4. Critical Race Theory (CRT), however, deserves some discussion here. Ladson-Billings and Tate (1995) put race centre stage and challenged dominant ideologies around neutrality, objectivity and colour blindness. But they also see CRT as part of a broader commitment to social justice and challenging all forms of oppression. Criticisms of CRT have suggested that it plays down the significance of class (Darder and Torres, 2004). But as Gillborn and Youdell (2009) have suggested, the notion of intersectionality can be helpful because it can be used to show how cultural patterns of oppression are interrelated. They note moreover:

> Intersectionality incites us to pay attention to more than one axis of subordination and inequality, more than one category of identity, and to attend to the relationships between inequalities, between identities, and between inequalities and identities. (Ibid.183)

Parker and Stovall (2004) in discussing the relationship of CRT to critical pedagogy suggest there is a need to locate the debates within a broader and ideological power struggle and to open up a new space with social justice at its centre. This framing around social justice provides not only an important conceptual basis, but also the basis of a distinctive pedagogical approach. It is to that term that the chapter now turns.

Social Justice

As Quinn (2009: 110) has noted: 'Educating for a more just society has been a perennial goal of educators'.

From Dewey to Counts, Freire, Rawls to Sen, there have been calls for education to be more closely related to achieving a society where there is a greater degree of equality and sense of fairness and for addressing the power relations that exist around the world. But what it means beyond this has been open to many different interpretations.

Within the United States, George Counts is a particularly important figure. He took Dewey's ideas, outlined in Chapter 3, one step further and posed questions such as the title of his influential pamphlet, *Dare the School Build a New Social Order?* (1932). He wanted schools to play a central role in replacing the individualist culture that dominated schools and society with one based on social justice (Boyles, Carusi and Attick 2009).

More recently, there have been academics who have seen a connection between social justice and liberation, empowerment, anti-oppressive practices and social transformation. Novak (2000), for example, states that 'whole books and treatises have been written about social justice without ever offering a definition of it. It is allowed to float in the air as if everyone will recognize an instance of it when it appears' (ibid., 1). As Rizvi (1998: 47) has suggested, 'the immediate difficulty one confronts when examining the idea of social justice is the fact that it does not have a single essential meaning – it is embedded within discourses that are historically constituted and that are sites of conflicting and divergent political endeavours.'

Zollers, Albert and Cochran-Smith (2000) found that within their teacher education programme, whilst there was support for the goal of teaching for social justice, what this meant was open to many different interpretations. For many within education, the sense of social justice is related more to wanting to see a fairer society with a more equal distribution of resources and greater access to engaging in a more democratic society. This view of social justice is most commonly associated with Rawls and has its roots in rights, liberties and a sense of fairness, with education being a major vehicle for giving advantage to the disadvantaged (Rawls 1971; Sen 2010; Singh 2011).

To Rawls (1971, 1993) social justice is perhaps most closely linked to fairness as can be shown here:

- Each person has an equal right to a fully adequate scheme of equal basic liberties which is compatible with a similar scheme for all.
- Social and economic inequalities are to satisfy two conditions. First, they must be attached to offices, and positions open to all under conditions of fair equality of opportunity; and second, they must be to the greatest benefit of the least advantaged members of society (Rawls 1993: 291).

But what this definition does not consider is how social justice relates to the realities that exist for many people in terms of social, economic and cultural inequalities. What needs to be an integral component of any discussions on social justice are to understand and address the causes of these inequalities and see them in the context of oppression. This also means that there has to be a degree of consciousness and understanding about this oppression and a wish to change it (Tyson and Park 2008).

Sant et al. (2018) identify three different discourses on justice: economic, recognition and democratic justice, influenced by the work of Fraser (2003). Economic justice is usually seen in relation to distributive theories of justice.

This can take liberal forms of assistance to people to achieve basic needs or in Marxian form of notions of exploitation. Behind this approach to social justice, which is often called 'distributive justice', is an individualistic approach which is about rewarding freedom and having access to resources. 'Recognition justice' on the other hand relates closely to discussions of identity and lifestyle, and is often associated with addressing the needs of marginalized groups. Finally, 'democratic justice' is concerned with making connections to ways in which people can participate in society.

A slightly different approach, developed mainly by Young (1990), focuses primarily on 'Recognition Justice' in which she says there is a need to counter traditional divisions within societies, that is, between masculine and feminine roles which can lead to oppressive relationships. Similar views can be seen in Gewirtz (2006) which is located within the discourses around cultural studies and the goal of challenging cultural domination.

What is clear from a range of international policy initiatives over the past twenty years is that social justice has become part of the vocabulary of decision-makers concerned with education. Whilst many of these initiatives have tended to follow the distributive justice model, there have been attempts, whilst using a rights-based approach, to include reference to addressing questions of power and inequality in the world and how to empower the oppressed and disenfranchised. What is evident, however, as Delanty (2003) has shown, is that the usage of the term 'inclusion' does not necessarily mean changes in power relationships. As Mala Singh (2011: 492) notes:

> The challenging times in which we live could benefit greatly from a rigorous investigation of the conceptual, normative and strategic potential of the notion of social justice as currently invoked in higher education but also of the modalities being used to give expression to it and their accompanying ambiguities and rhetoricisms.

Within both school-based and higher education, whilst it is possible to find many references around the world to social justice, they tend to ignore questions of power and inequality with the focus on access and the individual. Whilst these areas are important, they tend to ignore the linkages between social justice and the influence of global forces. Rowan (2019: 16) suggests that in terms of higher education there is a need to consider relationship-centred education. This position 'recognises the power of education and its fundamentally constructed and negotiated nature . . . It is a commitment to transformation. . . . Moving from what is to what might be'.

Rowan further suggests that academics who hold positions of power have a moral obligation to reflect how we challenge, transgress, subvert, interrupt and transform those aspects of university culture relating to curriculum, pedagogy and assessment. This relates to her suggestion of the usage of the term 'responsibility educators'. Rowan states that it is the responsibility of academics to aim for destinations within which diverse learners have the greatest possible opportunity to develop kinds of positive relations that are aligned with the practice of freedom.

These debates pose the need to recognize power and inequalities. This leads to another approach to social justice and that is associational or participatory justice where engagement in society to secure a more just society is seen as of central importance. It is this approach which has the closest relationship to critical pedagogy. However, what also needs to be added to the debates around social justice, even from a critical pedagogical perspective, is the 'global' nature of inequalities in the world.

Bringing the Global into Social Justice

Within much of the discourse around social justice, there tends to be a focus on individual rights and specific local or national needs. As this volume suggests, all learning today has to be contextualized within a global context.

Whilst there are numerous references within the debates on social justice to the importance of the global, many of them still tend to follow an individual rights perspective. Brock (2009: 326), for example, whilst promoting the term 'global justice' still sees the term as relating to every person having the right to be 'adequately positioned to enjoy prospects for a decent life'. She states that it also means understanding 'what is necessary; for everyone to meet their needs, along with certain guarantees about basic freedom, fair terms of cooperation in collective endeavours, and the social and political arrangements that can underwrite these important goals' (ibid.). This perspective builds on the work of Rawls and Nussbaum's capabilities approach who sees global justice as a set of basic entitlements (Nussbaum 2006).

Catherine Odora Hoppers, on the other hand, brings in the power dimension. To her, the concept of social justice, and its usage and interpretation, often favoured the strong and the powerful. She states that social justice should be seen as the ideal condition in which all members of society have the same basic rights, security, opportunities, obligations and social benefits. She goes on: 'social justice is based on the idea of a society which gives individuals and groups fair treatment and a just share of the benefits of society' (Odora Hoppers 2009: 608).

It is the connection between power and inequality, whilst recognizing the importance of rights and responsibilities, that is particularly important when referring to global social justice. As this volume has suggested, globalization and global forces dominate all aspects of life, societies and economies around the world. The usage of the term also relates to the influence of international treaties and agreements and particularly the inequalities between countries in terms of aid and debt.

The term 'global social justice' is often associated with campaigning organizations and social movements that are seeking to reduce poverty and tackle global inequality. It has been used by a number of social movements who have been seeking to question the role of the World Trade Organization and to promote fairer and more equitable trade relationships between states. The most well-known is probably the Occupy Movement, which began in New York in 2011 in response to the power and influence of multinational corporations. The movement captured the imagination of many thousands of people, and within a few weeks of its launch, over 900 cities around the world organized similar protests. Although the movement did not last longer than a year, it did provide the inspiration for many social movements fighting for greater social justice in the Middle East and Hong Kong. The movement could be criticized for lacking clear goals, but as later chapters in this volume will show, the power of social media, which was so evident within Occupy, has transformed how people seek social change.

The influence of Occupy can be seen in the way in which global justice has now become more directly associated with calls for social change. In the United Kingdom, the international development campaigning organization formerly known as the World Development Movement now calls itself 'Global Justice Now'.[2] The organization states that it is a:

> democratic social justice organisation working as part of a global movement to challenge the powerful and create a more just and equal world. We mobilise people in the UK for change, and act in solidarity with those fighting injustice, particularly in the global south. (Global Justice Now 2020)

This movement and other similar ones around the world have clearly had an impact in relation to debates on international trade and most recently on climate change, which is discussed in more detail in later chapters. But what is often missing, particularly in organizations that came out of Occupy, has been engagement with education. As will be shown, the educational movements around social justice have had a different starting point.

Social Justice Education

Different political ideologies have promoted social justice through education. Many political figures have made reference to the role of education in reducing poverty and inequality and promoting social justice. Some on the left saw it is as the role of the state, whilst those on the right put the responsibility on the individual.

Grunsell (2007: 83–4) makes a valuable distinction between three types of social justice education:

- Education about social justice, which can involve learning about issues such as colonialism, struggles against slavery and apartheid.
- Education for social justice, which includes bringing more values-based approaches into the classroom and wider society through themes of inclusion and fairness. Role-play games around fairtrade is one of the examples of this approach.
- Education through social justice, including how learners take action for change, challenging racism, for example, and developing positive forms of activity to change attitudes and behaviour.

Ayers, Quinn and Stovall (2009: xiv–v) state that social justice education rests on three principles or pillars:

- Equity – principle of fairness and equal access to all educational experiences.
- Activism – participation and engagement to change.
- Social literacy – understanding own sense of identity in complex world.

To them, social justice education has to be relevant, rigorous and revolutionary.

Adams, Bell and Griffin (1997) define social justice education as both a process and a goal. 'The process for attaining the goal of social justice we believe should also be democratic and participatory, inclusive and affirming of human agency and human capacities for working collaboratively to create change. The goal of social justice education is full and equal participation of all groups in a society that is mutually shaped to meet their needs' (ibid., 3–4).

Whilst all of these interpretations have some value, what is sometimes missing is the need to not only learn from different voices, but also question one's own assumptions and then consider how to be most effective in seeking social change. Wade, for example, suggests that social justice education should begin with students' lived experiences, including their concerns and dreams, and then move towards multiple perspectives with an emphasis on social action (Wade

2004: 65). Similar perspectives can be seen in Bigelow et al. (1994). In their *Rethinking Our Classrooms*, they suggest that a social justice-oriented classroom should be grounded in the lives of students, including critical, multicultural, antiracist, and pro-justice, participatory and experiential activities. It also means to have an approach that is hopeful, joyful, kind, culturally sensitive and visionary (ibid., 4–5).

Where the term 'social justice education' has followed these perspectives, it is clearly seen as a break from multicultural or intercultural education. It shifts the focus from issues of cultural diversity to issues of social justice, making social change and activism central to the vision of the teaching and learning promoted. The evidence from North America is that where social justice programmes have been promoted within schools, for example, they attempt to prepare teachers to take both individual and collective action towards mitigating oppression (McDonald and Zeichner 2009: 597).

Tarozzi and Torres (2016) have, however, raised a word of caution as the term can be ambiguous. What they did find from empirical studies was that social justice could be promoted as a distinct educational approach if it included:

> social change as a purpose and community as priority area of intervention; critical thinking as being aware of injustices and social inequalities, school both as a site of the reproduction of injustice and as a place of emancipation. (ibid., 126)

However, they also noted that the notion of distributive justice has been criticized from both the right and the left. From the right, there is the view that justice should be related to individual and free movements related to the market. From the left, there is criticism that this approach is founded on an ethical neutrality of justice and still focused on individualism.

'Social justice in American education' has often been related to inequalities between black-and-white communities, and the usage of this term has become popular again as a result of the Black Lives Matter initiative. However, the tensions between an approach that focuses on power relations and one that emphasizes distributive justice remain. When social justice education has been promoted, there has been a tendency to conflate the two forms of justice, social and distributive, emphasizing the allocation of property at the expense of less quantifiable qualities that society entails, such as virtues, actions, and ideas, each of which comprises in part the very 'good' social justice that promoters of the term seek to attain. This is not to say distributive notions of justice should be removed or replaced (Boyles, Carusi and Attick 2009: 38). What is missing from this approach is the emancipatory approach which seeks to free people from oppression.

That is why it is suggested here that a more effective approach is one that is rooted in critical pedagogical perspectives which relates social justice to addressing the inequalities that exist, including in the educational process itself. This emancipatory approach aims to relate social justice to the role that education can play in the social and political transformation of poor communities. Torres calls this 'transformative social justice education', and Tarozzi and Torres define it as:

> Social and pedagogical practice . . . when people reach a deeper, richer, more textured and nuanced understanding of themselves and their world. (Tarozzi and Torres 2016: 129)

This approach is heavily influenced by the ideas of Freire, and they make reference to transformative social justice as calling for conscientization and people to develop social and individual awareness.

Contribution of Human Rights Education

As this chapter has indicated, discussions of social justice cannot be divorced from talking about human rights. Whilst there may be differing views as the extent to which educational initiatives should be framed with a rights-based approach, what is clearly evident from numerous studies (Osler and Starkey 2010; Banks 2008) is that learning about international declarations on human rights can be an important stepping stone to developing a social justice-based approach to learning. Through a human rights lens, themes such as inequalities, denial of free speech and inclusivity can be taught. There has been growth particularly in the popularity of learning about specific children's rights, including the UN Declaration of the Rights of the Child. This has been a specific focus for the educational work of UNICEF, and this is discussed in more detail later in this chapter.

One of the leading promoters of human rights education has been Audrey Osler and she has made an important distinction between education about human rights, education through human rights and education for human rights (Osler 2016). To her, education about rights is a knowledge-based approach, learning particularly about specific legislation or agreements either national or international. Education through rights is more of an experiential or skills-based approach and can often be seen within various initiatives around citizenship education. Education for human rights is more likely to have a more activist approach making a linkage between learning about specific rights and calling on governments or international bodies to fully implement agreements such as the Convention on the Rights of the Child (ibid.). It is this education for human rights that brings in themes of solidarity with peoples elsewhere in the world and the protection of democratic rights.

This approach, Osler suggests, can ensure that human rights education has a transformative goal, and it is here, she suggests, there is a clear relationship to social justice. It moreover, Osler poses, 'implies addressing oppression at the microlevel of interpersonal relationships, including student-student and student-teacher relationships' (ibid., 30).

Osler suggests that one of the key aims of education for social justice is to encourage learner participation and 'critical engagement with knowledge, ideas and other learners'. This is to include, she suggests, three elements:

- Information about and experience of democracy and human rights in theory and practice.
- Opportunities to explore and reflect on various identities and cultural attributes, create personal narratives and develop processes of self-learning.
- Co-operative practice, teamwork and the development of collective narratives and study of cognitive models that enable learners as a group to make sense of the world (ibid., 53).

Whilst supporting the value of human rights education in schools, Osler notes that it could be seen as encouraging conformity and obedience, part of the 'modern civilising mission of schools' (ibid., 76), and using rights as a way of managing behaviour in the classroom. She also notes that there is a risk human rights education might ignore power relations, and it is by encouraging rights to be linked to real-world situations, where connections can be made to local and global issues, that it can be most transformative.

Therefore, whilst human rights clearly have an important contribution within all forms of education, the connection to social justice and addressing power relations and inequalities in the world needs to be recognized. Also, as Osler suggests, human rights education needs to be based on a pedagogical approach that encourages participatory forms of learning, recognizes different cultural perspectives and includes self-reflection and critical thinking.

This, for example, can be seen in Bettez (2008: 279), in her discussion of university teaching. She outlines seven skills, practices and dispositions of an activist social justice education approach. These include '(1) promoting a mind/body connection, (2) conducting artful facilitation that promotes critical thinking, (3) engaging in explicit discussions of power, privilege, and oppression,

(4) maintaining compassion for students, (5) believing that change toward social justice is possible, (6) exercising self-care, and (7) building critical communities'.

These examples demonstrate the close linkage between human rights and social justice and, above all, the need for a distinctive pedagogical approach.

Pedagogy for Global Social Justice

Elsewhere I have defined a pedagogy for global social justice along the following lines:

> a pedagogy of making connections between the individual and personal, from the local to the global, and which by its very nature, is transformative. It needs to be seen as an approach to learning that challenges dominant orthodoxies on education and perceptions about the world and enables the learner to look at issues and the world from a different place. (Bourn 2008: 18)

Central to this approach is a *problem-posing education* that includes *critical dialogue* and *questioning* and includes a mutual learning process for both teacher and learner (Freire 2004; McLaren and Leonard 1993). This means the teacher poses thought-provoking questions and encouraging a sense of constant review and examining their own assumptions. This is where critical dialogue becomes important as it enables this process of reflection from which a more informed action is likely to emerge.

This pedagogical approach also means that the learner investigates global issues, looks at their relationship to their experiences of the wider world and considers their own personal values base before engaging in forms of social action to encourage a more just world.

Within a pedagogy of global social justice, there needs to be a recognition of power, inequalities and oppression in the world and its implications for cultures and communities. There needs also to be a process of what Freire calls *conscientização*, or critical consciousness (Freire 2004), within which the learner develops a deeper understanding of what is meant by social justice and their own identity within the world. Finally, there is the active component of supporting and promoting social justice through relevant forms of social action.

Tan (2009) refers to this approach under the five Es of emancipatory education:

- Engage – building trust, respect and buy-in with students, families and communities.

- Educate – developing academic and critical competencies.
- Experience – from exposure to lived experience.
- Empowerment of self – knowing that there is hope.
- Enact – what are you going to do about it?

Another perspective is that of Shultz (2011a), who suggests that it is important to distinguish between the path to social justice and the path of social justice with the latter holding the possibility of achieving decolonization, the deep democratic project that is needed to address the multitude of global and local issues and to position dignity as a foundation of human existence. Shultz concluded that it is important to understand and engage with the processes of social justice rather than justice as merely an outcome or product.

A good example of bringing this range of ideas and beliefs together for educational practice is a blog comment by Tabitha Dell'Angelo (2014) from the College of New Jersey. She suggests that within the classroom it is necessary to:

> Teach your students about making positive change in the world by connecting with them, discussing real-world problems and multiple perspectives.

Key to promoting social justice in the classroom, she suggests, 'is recognizing and acting upon the power that we have for making positive change'. This means creating 'how they can be both actors and leaders in creating change'. This means, she suggests, making what is taught is 'relevant to what is going on in the world'. As suggested earlier in this chapter, this approach in the classroom also means ensuring that the voices of the learner can be heard.

A pedagogy for global social justice should therefore develop an understanding of different worldviews and perspectives on global issues, encourage a critical reflection of teachers' and pupils own perceptions and promote an emphasis on contextualising learning that places global issues and themes within historical, cultural and social traditions. Above all, this pedagogical approach should frame the learning within a vision of a more just world.

It is from this pedagogical approach that action for social change should be encouraged and supported.

However, with many debates around 'social justice education', a key challenge in answer to critics of the term, is the evidence that substantiates its value and contribution to learning in general. It is to evidence from research in this area that this chapter now turns.

Research on Social Justice Education

Three major doctoral studies from researchers in the United States on social justice education (Atkinson 2012; Robertson 2008; Rouse 2011) provide valuable evidence on the contribution of social justice perspectives to education covering different sectors of learning.

Robertson's study researched the work of one elementary public school teacher to implement a social justice curriculum unit in her fourth-grade social studies classroom. It examined the role of the teacher in terms of 'establishing a socially-just climate, creating a child-centered curriculum that allowed for voice and choice, and recognising that education is value-laden' (Robertson 2008: viii). The thesis also addressed how to implement a social justice curriculum unit in a fourth-grade school classroom.

Her research identified this definition of social justice education by a teacher which is seen to be particularly relevant:

> Social justice is the idea that working towards the fair treatment for everyone and every living thing is the right thing to do. (Quoted in Robertson 2008: 110)

Her research identified the central role of the teacher both in terms of their own expertise but also their personal philosophy and outlook on the world. A feature of Robertson's research was also the challenges the teacher had to deal with and the extent to which they could use or work around the existing curriculum. A problem the teacher in Robertson's research also identified was the lack of support within the school to teach social justice education. The findings of this research also suggested that the structure and substance of social studies, often the most popular subject to teach these themes at the elementary public school level, may not provide an adequate framework in which to promote social justice education.

Rouse's (2011) study looks at social justice as a change agent within higher education. Whilst aspects of her research are discussed further in Chapter 12 on the role of academics, there are themes that emerged from her study that are relevant to issues on developing a pedagogy for global social justice. She looked at how academic advisors could develop the 'social, cultural, and political habits of mind, understanding, knowledge and skills necessary to enact social justice leadership in academic systems and higher education'. This research posits that a contemporary challenge to the role of academics is to meet the diverse sociocultural and sociopolitical needs of today's learners. Central to her research was a social justice leadership development model. This model had three developmental phases:

critical awareness, transformation, and action, with the critical awareness phase
subdivided into three developmental stages – self-awareness, understanding
of critical constructs and multicultural awareness – to represent the broad
knowledge, skills, and awareness systems academic advisors should be guided
through. (Rouse 2011: 151)

Finally, Atkinson's (2012) research took a participatory research approach to
review youth activism within a community development and movement-building
programme, in this case the Chicago Freedom School movement, which is discussed
later in this chapter. Influenced by a range of theoretical approaches from youth
development and transformative social work, Atkinson brings into a liberatory
educational programme the importance of how anti-oppressive practices can help
young people with their social development. A key finding from her research was
the importance of young people having the space, support and opportunities to
explore their 'histories, cultural norms and personal stories' (ibid., 263).

These doctoral studies build on other relevant research on social justice
education. For example, an influential project in Massachusetts was the Social
Justice Education in Schools Project (SJES). Reilly Carlisle, Jackson and George
(2006), in analysing the impact of social justice, developed five core Principles of
Social Justice Education in Schools. These principles are as follows:

1) Inclusion and Equity: The school promotes inclusion and equity within
   the school setting and larger community by addressing all forms of social
   oppression.
2) High Expectations: The school provides a diverse and challenging learning
   environment that supports student development, holds all students to
   high expectations, and empowers students of all social identities.
3) Reciprocal Community Relationships: The school recognizes its role as
   both a resource to and beneficiary of the community.
4) System-wide Approach: The mission, resource, allocation structures,
   policies and procedures, and physical environment, exemplify its
   commitment to creating and sustaining a socially just environment.
5) District Social Justice Education and Intervention: The school's faculty,
   staff, and administration are committed to 'liberatory education', advocate
   for social justice, and directly confront manifestations of social oppression
   (Reilly Carlisle, Jackson and George 2006: 57).

Wade's (2007) study reviewed the efforts of elementary school teachers to
implement social justice education practices including relevant community
service learning. Their research mirrored other studies referred to in this chapter

of the challenges teachers faced in introducing social justice-type practices within the curriculum including obstacles within the school, pressures of testing and examinations and lukewarm support from colleagues.

Underpinning much of this evidence are the challenges for global social justice perspectives within education institutions. But as it also states, where and when it is implemented, there are considerable positive impacts upon both the educator and the learner. What the research examples also identify are the need for a clear pedagogical approach along the lines of the themes outlined earlier in this chapter.

Case Studies: Examples of Practice

Award Programmes for Schools and Promotion of Social Justice

Over the past decade in the United Kingdom, a number of organizations have developed award programmes for schools (Hunt 2012; Bourn and Hunt 2011; Gadsby and Bullivant 2010). These award programmes take varying forms but central to most of them is a structured process of learning and a way in which schools can regularly review their own level of engagement in global issues. They have become popular also because they can be a way of a school demonstrating to parents and the wider community external verifications of the quality of the teaching and learning that is taking place.

Amongst the award programmes are the Rights Respecting Schools Award (RRSA) run by UNICEF UK and the Fairtrade School Awards Programme run by the Fairtrade Foundation. Their relevance for the themes addressed in this chapter is the inclusion of social justice topics in a form that encourages elements of social action.

UNICEF and the Rights Respecting Schools Award

The Award aims to improve the lives of children in the United Kingdom by taking a whole school approach to putting children's rights at the heart of school policy and practice.

Their 2018 survey results showed that child rights education plays a key role in developing children and young people as active, engaged local and global citizens. Over 1.7 million children in the United Kingdom go to a Rights Respecting School and over 5,000 schools in England, Northern Ireland, Scotland and Wales are working through the Award.

Rights have been described as a 'heartbeat' in school life, like a 'golden thread' or 'stick of rock' that underpins and informs their practice. In a Rights Respecting School, a child rights-based approach underpins school culture, ethos and relationships as well as the more tangible changes to practice, policy and environment (UNICEF UK 2018a).

As well as becoming aware of their own rights as children, pupils in Rights Respecting Schools learn to consider the rights of other children in the United Kingdom and globally. To UNICEF, this knowledge of child rights can help 'children develop an understanding of, and compassion for social justice issues and understand how actions can promote and protect the rights of others' (UNICEF UK 2018b).

This approach to learning about children's rights is also seen as a way of connecting local to global issues. It can also, as a result, lead to the pupils being not only better informed about relevant issues but also how to participate in processes to secure change, be it within the school or wider society.

There are three levels to the Rights Respecting Schools Award:

- Bronze: Rights Committed
- Silver: Rights Aware
- Gold: Rights Respecting.

Its transformative and rigorous approach means the journey to the highest stage can take up to four years. There are four key areas of impact for children at a Rights Respecting School: well-being, participation, relationships and self-esteem.

The evidence from the impact of the Award on schools can be seen in the way that empowers pupils:

> Our views are taken very seriously. Our opinion matters because we are the pupils, we know what it is like in the school and their (adults) perspective is different from ours. (Primary pupil from a Rights Respecting School; UNICEF UK n.d.)

As one headteacher has commented:

> I am incredibly proud of the empowerment that [Rights Respecting Schools] has given to the pupils. Pupils have gone home, created their own campaigns in their areas e.g. pollution/recycling plastic linked to rights. The pupils have really taken ownership of their learning and understanding of their role on a local and global scale.

Another commented:

> During our campaigning for Outright[3] [one child] passionately took on the
> rights of others and wanted to take the lead as a prime minister to change the
> world for the better. He actively researched and extended his own learning at
> home. This demonstrated that he was a passionate world citizen. He took it upon
> himself to learn the articles at home and was then able to teach others in his class
> how they link to each other and the different lessons he was learning. (UNICEF
> UK 2018a: 2)

This process of empowerment and personal development of the child is seen by
UNICEF as framed within a moral framework of equality and respect.

Whilst other evidence (Robinson 2017; Dunhill 2018) supported the value
of this rights approach as a good basis, they also noted that the quality of the
teaching was varied, as was how teachers and school leaders interpreted human
rights education responsibilities (Robinson 2017: 134–5). A study by Tibbitts
and Kirchschlaeger (2010) identified that teachers were not familiar with human
rights education content and lacked professional development. However, a
research study by Dunhill (2018) confirmed that rights education programmes
make a positive contribution to the lives of primary age children.

More recent evidence, however, as suggested from UNICEF's own studies,
shows that their programme is not only very popular, but it has had a major
impact on empowering children and young people to take action for social
change based on a social justice approach. What has also helped is that their
Award programme is framed around a well-developed training programme for
teachers as well as a well-organized support service for teachers linked to to the
school's progression through the award process. This evidence and commitment
to professional development by UNICEF has shown that the Award programme
has made significant progress in addressing shortcomings identified by earlier
research by Robinson, Tibbits and Kirchschlaeger.

Fairtrade School Awards Programme

Fairtrade is a popular topic in many schools in Europe and the connection with social
justice themes can be seen through the emphasis on fairness and direct references to
learning about how to question unequal global trade practices and relations.

An example of promoting learning about fair trade within schools is the work
of the UK NGO The Fairtrade Foundation and their Awards programme. The
concept of fair trade has been around for over thirty years and is based on the

principle that companies and corporations in the richer countries pay a fair price to producers in poorer countries for their work.

Fair trade has become a popular theme in many schools in the United Kingdom and elsewhere in Europe (Doherty and Taplin 2008; Bourn and Hunt 2011). However, there has been a concern that fair trade activities can be reduced to encouraging learning about simple messages. This can be seen in research by Asbrand (2004), who in Germany showed the dangers of these simple solutions and the resultant lack of critical engagement with the topics. She suggested:

> The consumption of fairly traded chocolate makes sense and there is no doubt about the aim to seek greater justice in world-trade. But the issue is too complex to assume that one can solve the problems of small-scale cacao-farmers in West Africa by buying or selling fairly traded chocolate. (ibid.)

Instead of seeing fair trade as the 'politically correct' thing to do, Asbrand suggested that fair trade should be seen as an opportunity 'for self-organised learning' and to enable learners to deal with the complex issues that underpin this area such as global trade policies (ibid., 17). What Asbrand is suggesting is that fair trade should be seen as a pedagogical opportunity rather than as a campaign. It can open up the learners' thinking to see the linkages between skills development such as working co-operatively and teamwork with increased knowledge about trade relations.

These concerns about fair trade being taught in a rather uncritical way has also been noted by Gallwey (2009: 63–4) in her research in Ireland. She suggested using the term 'critical fairtrade education' as a goal as this can lead to an approach to learning looking at fair trade more critically and from a range of perspectives.

This desire for a more critical approach does not mean that fair trade is an inappropriate topic. What is suggested here is that encouraging learners to engage in campaigns around the area can all too easily ignore questions of power and inequality. It can also lead to reducing complex issues to good and evil with the answer being fair trade to combat global poverty.

This means ensuring that learning about fair trade is framed around social justice.

In the United Kingdom, this can be seen in the work of The Fairtrade Foundation, which, in addition to campaigning on the area, runs a programme for schools that includes producing resources, running training courses and organizing an Award programme.

Key to the educational work around the Award is promoting a sense of fairness and the desire to secure a more just world. One of the most popular ways this is done is through some form of role-play-type activity where pupils were split into three groups: farmers, chocolate factory owners and shopkeepers. They came to the conclusion that the shopkeepers had all of the chocolate, which they would be able to sell, and the factory owners had the most money, whilst the farmers, who did all of the work, had nothing much to show for it. They all agreed that this was not fair. Fair trade, by its very nature, poses questions around power and the nature of trade practices around the world.

One secondary school noted that its more senior pupils had, through geography, examined causes of world poverty, indicators of development, globalization, the impact of transnational corporations, issues of ethical fashion, and trade and fair trade. Another school noted that the pupils already had a knowledge of fair trade through geography and so the follow-up activities took the learning to greater depth by looking at trading inequalities in the world, especially in the developing world and the effect of unfair commodity prices on people's livelihoods (Bourn 2018a).

Many of the organizations involved in promoting fair trade in schools in the United Kingdom reflect a broader global social justice pedagogy to learning that is also grounded in participatory and learner-centred approaches.

What is evident, however, from the resources produced by the Fairtrade Foundation at least, is the intention to see fair trade products as one outcome from the learning about how bananas, cocoa or tea are grown and harvested and made available to communities all over the world. This means that the learning goes beyond what is fair trade and also brings in stories and experiences from communities around the world.

Where perhaps this Award programme is less effective than UNICEF's is that there is no direct linkage to any professional development programmes for teachers. The Fairtrade Foundation does not have the resources to provide training support to schools. However, a range of NGOs throughout the United Kingdom such as CAFOD and the local network of Development Education Centres do provide courses for teachers on fair trade themes.

Clearly there are potential dangers with teaching fair trade. The subject can be reduced to the encouragement of an emotive response from pupils to unfair trade practices. It can also be promoted as the answer to global poverty. But perhaps the biggest danger is for the subject to be taught in an uncritical manner, which reduces a pupil's engagement to some form of social action without understanding the causes of inequality in the world and why unfair trade practices exist.

Chicago Freedom School

The final example of a pedagogy for social justice in action is the Chicago Freedom School, which is a youth programme based around leadership development and anti-oppressive practice. Its programme and training aim to engage young people in developing their understanding of social problems. Social justice is central to all their work with all of their activities rooted in anti-oppressive practices.

The Chicago Freedom School (CFS) builds on a strong tradition of liberatory education using popular education methods. Freedom schools were first established by the Student Nonviolent Coordinating Committee (SNCC) during Freedom Summer in Mississippi in 1964 which sought to counter systemic under-education of Black students.

Today the CFS takes an:

> innovative approach to civic engagement, leadership development and movement building. Our programmes, resources and training invite young people and adult allies to study the work of past movements, deepen their understanding to current social problems, build new coalitions and strategies for change. (Chicago Freedom School, n.d.)

CFS has three main youth programmes:

- Project HealUs which activates and prepares 'young people of colour to explore, engage, and expand the work of the reproductive justice movement and address misogyny in their own communities'. It does this through a ten-week curriculum programme of political education and skills development.[4]
- Freedom Fellowship – helps young people of colour to develop leadership skills in order to become 'community change makers'. Fellows explore the history of social movements and current issues such as racism, access to healthy food, school to prison pipeline, sexism and climate change.[5]
- Finally, in order to continue their youth leadership skills, the CFS encourages young people to participate in the governance structure of the organization through its Youth Leadership Board.

Atkinson's research, referred to earlier in this chapter, analysed the Freedom Fellowship programme and found that it offered young people an indispensable space for developing the skills, knowledge, attitudes and relationships to undertake social justice 'activism' (Atkinson 2012: 72). Her research looked at how young people developed as activists and her findings indicated that:

young people involved in the Freedom Fellowship do, in fact, develop an activist identity as evidenced by their commitment to anti-oppressive attitudes and behaviours, dedication to community and a culture of resistance and engagement in personal and social action to end oppression. They do, in fact, perceive shifts in themselves, in terms of their leadership skills, relationships, sense of agency, attitudes and behaviours, wellness practices and self- reflexivity. They do perceive their personal power to make change as deeply connected to collective power and rooted in their social justice education. (ibid.)

In 2020, CFS gained even greater relevance and importance during the campaigns around the Black Lives Matter movement and unrest on the streets as a result of police brutality (Esposito 2020; Laurence 2020).

There are other Freedom Schools in the United States including one in Tucson, Arizona, which bears the name Paulo Freire Freedom School. This school states that its mission is to build 'a joyful and just community dedicated to environmental sustainability and social justice that embraces creative, collaborative and compassionate teaching and learning'.[6] Another is the Tyree Scott Freedom School which runs an educational programme in Seattle, Washington, with a curriculum on social justice issues and anti-racist community organizing in Seattle.[7]

This example shows that despite the pressures and challenges on educational bodies, there are social movements committed to promoting education for social change through an emphasis on social justice. Whilst they operate on the margins of the education system, their relevance and importance can be seen by their continuing success, certainly in Chicago, of engaging large numbers of young people of colour who feel marginalized from society but who also wish to change things and make their community and wider world more inclusive, egalitarian and, above all, having social justice as its core aim.

Conclusion

Crystal Belle, the director of teacher education at Rutgers University-Newark, said, in a blog in 2019 that we cannot talk about schools without addressing race, class, gender, ability, sexuality and politics.

She went on to state:

A social justice education is centered in democracy and the freedom to exercise one's full humanity. Conceptions of equity and democracy have always been practically and theoretically connected to the field of education, which is often perceived as the greatest human equalizer. Although there is some truth to this, it is important to understand that the notion of meritocracy is flawed, especially when you come from economically marginalized communities. If you work hard and get straight As in school, it does not automatically mean that you will attain social mobility. This is the very nature of capitalism: Somebody wins, and many people lose. This is particularly true if you are from a poor or working-class community. (Belle 2019: 1)

To her a social justice pedagogy has to have the following approaches:

- Acknowledge who is in the room, including where they come from and their respective cultures and communities.
- Start with the knowledge your students have and build on their experiences.
- Create unit plans and curricular maps for the entire year which means having a vision of the goals of the learning.
- Be honest about who you are and your biases which means recognising one's own prejudices and to work through them.
- Encourage students to question everything, including your teaching (ibid.).

This excellent summary of the goals of social justice education brings together many of the themes identified in this chapter. Social justice has to be more than individual liberties and has to include a recognition and understanding of power and inequality in the world. This is where and why education is so important to any campaigns for greater social justice. Critical pedagogy, as outlined by Giroux and others, provides an important framework for addressing these issues of inequality in the world.

Social justice has also to be seen through the prism of globalization because it is at a global level that social, economic and cultural forces often start and have a direct impact upon local communities. Human rights is also an important element and often a stimulus for initiatives around social justice education but, as noted in this chapter, it is where there is a clear linkage to understanding power and inequality in the world that it can have a direct relationship to calls for social change. As initiatives such as Black Lives Matter demonstrate, what happens in one part of the world can mobilize and engage people thousands of miles away.

The examples shown in this chapter from UNICEF and the Fairtrade Foundation in the United Kingdom indicate that social justice can be part of structured educational programmes. There are dangers of fair trade being reduced to simplistic messages and not addressing the complexities of global trade policies. But the Foundation's educational work is mindful of these challenges. What their work requires more of, and what UNICEF UK's work does so well, is providing professional development programmes to enable the teacher and educator to have the confidence to implement the ideas.

What the Chicago Freedom School movement shows is that young people themselves wish to be part of this process for social change. They are often the most discriminated against in communities but can, as this example shows, have the enthusiasm to change things for themselves and their wider communities.

Questions for Further Consideration

- What are the most useful definitions of social justice to consider when addressing education for global social change?
- What are the most relevant pedagogical approaches to address social justice themes within formal and higher education?
- To what extent should a social justice education have human rights as central to its approach?
- What are the most useful terms to engage learners in discussions around social justice, be they in schools, colleges or universities?
- What lessons can be gleaned from the three examples (UNICEF, Fairtrade Foundation and Chicago Freedom School) given in this chapter about promoting a pedagogy for global social justice?

Further Reading

Adams, M., L. A. Bell and P. Griffin (1997), *Teaching for Diversity and Social Justice*, New York: Routledge.

Ayers, W., T. Quinn and D. Stovall (eds) (2009), *Handbook of Social Justice in Education*, New York: Routledge.

Cho, S. (2013), *Critical Pedagogy and Social Change*, New York: Routledge.

Giroux, H. (2005), *Border Crossing*, 2nd edn, New York: Routledge.

Osler, A. (2016), *Human Rights and Schooling – An Ethical Framework for Teaching for Social Justice*, New York: Teachers College Press.

Shultz, L. (2011), 'Decolonising Social Justice Education', in A. A. Abdi (ed.), *Decolonizing Philosophies of Education*, 29–42, Rotterdam: Sense Publishing.

Young, I. M. (1990), *Justice and the Politics of Difference*, Princeton, NJ: Princeton University Press.

Education for Transformation, Sustainable Future and Being Global Citizens

Introduction

As outlined in earlier chapters, discussions today on education for social change very often bring in the themes of sustainable futures and global citizenship. These areas will be explored further in this chapter through the lens of transformative learning. This approach, as will be suggested, provides a valuable way of connecting global citizenship and sustainable development to processes of change. It could be argued that social change in itself is transformative but what this means has often been a subject of some debate. Reference will be made in this chapter particularly to the ideas of Jack Mezirow and his associates. Transformative learning will then be discussed in relation to discourses and practices around the themes of global citizenship and sustainable future. Within and around these discourses, the research of Philip Bamber, Eleanor Brown and Romina De Angelis, based mainly on doctoral studies, will be specifically discussed. Finally, the chapter will review some examples as to where and how transformative learning, global citizenship and sustainability can be seen in relation to education for social change.

What is Meant by Transformative Learning?

Throughout this volume, the term 'transformation' is mentioned as being a key feature of any approach to education for social change. The term has traditionally within education been seen as an approach to learning that is based on the ideas of Jack Mezirow and a number of his associates. Although the term was developed to be applied mainly within adult education, it has been taken on by others to frame a broader approach to learning. Like many other educational theorists referred to in this volume, Mezirow (2000: 7) notes 'The who, what, where, why and how of learning may be only understood as situated in a specific cultural' context. The key element of transformative learning to Mezirow is that it means:

> the process by which we transform our taken for granted frames of reference (meaning, perspectives, habits of mind, mind-sets) to make them more inclusive, discriminating, open, emotionally capable of change, and reflective so that they may generate beliefs and opinions that will prove more true or justified to guide action.

From this engagement, Mezirow (ibid., 7–8) suggests:

> transformative learning involves participation in constructive discourse to use the experience of others to assess reasons justifying these assumptions, and making an action decision based on the resulting insight.

This approach to transformative learning implies that there are both individual and social consequences, which 'encourages a reconstruction of narratives and one's frames of reference, to be critically reflective and challenge one's own assumptions' (ibid., 19–20). This is where, Mezirow suggests, the learning takes place. It can take a number of forms including building on existing bodies of knowledge, introducing new approaches and changing one's own views as a result of reflecting on different ideas or what he calls deeper learning that requires not only challenging one's own assumptions but changing viewpoints and perspectives (Mezirow 2000: 19).

Some of the commentaries on Mezirow's ideas for transformative learning suggest that he does not give sufficient consideration to the social action side and puts too much emphasis on individual change (Collard and Law 1989; Brookfield 2000). Mezirow, however, would argue that individual change has to come first, and only then could you influence others and work with them to secure wider societal change. Illeris, on the other hand, whilst influenced by the ideas of Mezirow, redefines transformative learning in relation to the interaction of the individual and society through their sense of identity:

> The concept of transformative learning comprises all learning that implies change in the identity of the learner. (Illeris 2014: 40)

Mezirow's later work (2009), particularly, also recognized the influence of experience and emotions which can bring in challenging debates. This is why his recognition of the importance of critical reflection and thinking as being central to transformative learning is so important. This critical thinking, Mezirow suggests, has three aspects:

- 'content', which refers to the object of perception, thought, emotions and actions.
- 'process', referred to the mode in which reasoning operates.
- 'premise', related to understanding the causes of thinking. In this way, critical thinking enables learners to consider thoroughly the beliefs and assumptions that constitute the way they understand reality for their transformation to take place (Mezirow 2009: 7, 8).

An area of criticism of Mezirow's work was his lack of consideration of the more spiritual side, and it is here one could see some differences with the views of O'Sullivan, another proponent of transformative learning, who emphasized the linkages to environment and alternative ways of seeking the world (O'Sullivan, Morrell and O'Connor 2002).

O'Sullivan (1999) offers an alternative theory of transformative learning with an emphasis on cosmology 'that is designed to initiate a deep planetary consciousness' (ibid., 207). O'Sullivan's idea of transformative learning involves addressing 'the planet as a global marketplace' (ibid.) and the injustices and inequalities that exist throughout the world (ibid., 162).

Mezirow, whilst recognizing these social inequalities, puts more emphasis on ways of thinking or 'habits of mind'. He characterizes several distinct yet interrelated habits of mind. These habits of mind might include one's beliefs, sense of identity and what is perceived as counting as knowledge. Reframing for Mezirow means reflecting on one's own assumptions, which is seen as subjective reframing. Objective reframing, on the other hand, is seen as reflecting on other peoples' assumptions. From these reflections, there is a final piece of transformative learning, based on reflective action which could result in a change of behaviour (Mezirow 2012; Robinson and Levac 2018: 113–14).

Mezirow's work is important for the themes addressed in this volume because he sees transformation as based on a process of learning. What Mezirow's work provides is a theoretical basis for action that brings together changes of thinking and experiences all based on a process of critical self-reflection.

Taylor (2009), a collaborator with Mezirow, summarizes these themes as six core elements of transformative learning:

- Individual experience
- Critical reflection
- Dialogue
- Holistic orientation
- Awareness of context
- Authentic relationships.

These elements are interconnected and form part of a learner-centred approach.

There is some debate as to whether this transformation is sudden, one big change, or, as Cranton (2006) suggests, of a more incremental and less dramatic form. Even Mezirow (2012) recognizes that the process and outcome of transformation is unlikely to be linear or straightforward. As he notes, 'critical reflection, discourse, and reflective action always exist in the real world in complex institutional, interpersonal, and historical settings, and these inevitably influence the possibilities for transformative learning and shape its nature' (ibid., 88).

Transformative Learning and Social Action

As the discussions on Mezirow and O'Sullivan suggest, there is a major debate around the role of individual as an actor for change within the discourse on transformative learning.

This debate is very relevant to broader discussions within global learning, global citizenship and sustainability education in terms of the role and importance of deeper learning as part of a process of transformation and change.

As this volume has already indicated, there are dangers within any programme that promotes social action of minimizing the role of learning. Bryan (2012), for example, has challenged what can often be seen in civil society organizations of 'obedient activism', with an emphasis on 'signing a poster or designing a poster to raise awareness of the "problem" ... thereby minimizing the likelihood that young people will think for themselves about what they see as the best course of action and foreclosing a range of other possible responses' (ibid., 273). Bryan goes further and suggests that this form of activism is based on achieving a specific goal rather than an 'ongoing commitment to social justice' (ibid.).

This implies that a key question of these forms of social activism is to what extent are they transformative. The learner may have changed some consumption patterns but their impact on societal change could be marginal. This reflects comments made in the previous chapter with regard to some of the criticisms of fair trade.

One of the pieces of research that addresses these questions through the practices of development education organizations in England and Spain has been Eleanor Brown's (2013) research on the subject. A feature of her research was to review the impact of courses run by and for NGOs. She found that 'where experiences were emotional the transformation was deeper. This was closely related to openness to participants' life experiences, recognising that transformation would be different for everyone' (ibid., 276).

She also identified the importance of the context in which the learning took place, the backgrounds and other experiences of the learner. She found also a clear process of learning with awareness coming first 'with new ideas or information offering an opportunity for critical reflection'. Key to this process of learning, Brown identified, were the importance of participative methodologies which in some cases led to a 'change in attitude, with new opinions or meaning schemes created. These attitudes could then be employed in new ways of behaving' (ibid.). Brown further identified that any changes in behaviour often came as a result of further critical reflection.

In terms of social change, Brown noticed that whilst many people took individual actions, it was where there were elements of 'multiplier effects', of learners passing their views and ideas to others and also through making connections to the aims of broader networks and social movements. What Brown's research above all identified was that where NGOs provided spaces for learners to creatively develop their ideas, then there were more opportunities for transformative learning (ibid., 280).

Sustainability and Sustainable Futures and Transformation

An increasingly influential and popular feature of international education policies and practices has been the recognition of the need to address themes around sustainable development. Whilst some of these date back to the implementation of the recommendations of the Rio Summit and the use of Agenda 21, it has been since the UN Decade on Education for Sustainable Development (ESD) from 2005 to 2014, and its references in the Sustainable Development Goals (SDGs) and policies from UNESCO, that ESD has begun to have visibility in many national educational programmes.

Conclusion will look at these policies in more detail but here the focus is on how the literature around sustainability, including theoretical approaches, demonstrate a relationship to transformation and social change.

Whilst merely posing an approach to education that is about sustainable change could be said to be transformative, much of the influence on this approach to learning has come from environmentalists where there has been a tension between proponents of preserving the natural environment and those seeking a more radical approach.

One of the most influential academics who has addressed some of these tensions has been Stephen Sterling. Influenced by Gregory Bateson's (1987) three orders of learning, he suggests (Sterling 2003; 2010) there are three levels of sustainability pedagogies: transmissive, transactional and transformative. As learners move from one to the next, they experience a shift towards a deeper form of engagement. In transmissive learning strategies, there is a focus on information transfer. Strategies are related to learning about things rather than challenging the assumptions of the learner. In transactional strategies, the learning includes an understanding and inclusion of cultural forces and recognizes social context. However, in transformative learning strategies, learners focus on critically questioning their assumptions, beliefs and values. It emphasizes encouraging learners to question and change their ways of seeing and thinking about the world, in order to further develop their understanding of it (Mezirow, 2000). Put more simply, the first level of learning could be seen as education about sustainability which has a role but does not challenge dominant assumptions. The second level is 'education *for* sustainability' and includes consideration of broader issues and forms of action. Finally, the 'third' level of learning, which Sterling calls 'sustainable education', is about systematic change, which means that where there is a constant process of change and nothing is certain. This level could also be called 'learning *as* change'. Central to this approach is the transformation within the learner and the opportunities for broader societal change.

Alun Morgan (2007) in his research developed a further level by including a more eco and spiritual dimension which not only brings more directly some of the ideas from O'Sullivan but also a more holistic concept of wisdom where thinking is seen as being more reflective and relational or dialectical. This means a more multi-perspectival and transdisciplinary view on the nature of reality, where some perspectives are more suitable than others to satisfy sustainability purposes (Morgan 2007; De Angelis 2020).

There are obvious similarities in Morgan's approach to that of Sterling and 'multiple loop learning with single loop related to acquiring skills about sustainability, double loop to consider critiquing existing viewpoints. Triple-loop learning goes a stage further in changing existing views and ideas and development of a 'whole new worldview' (Bourn and Morgan 2010: 279). Finally, the fourth level brings in more the spiritual and consciousness dimension. Whilst Morgan recognizes that all levels of learning are needed for sustainability education, the emphasis is clearly on a process rather than a set of outcomes to be achieved by learners. The focus on the ever-evolving nature of this type of learning represents a key feature in this approach, for measuring it in terms of accomplishing a specific goal would represent a limitation rather than an advantage (Bourn 2015).

Similar approaches can be seen in the work of Van Poeck et al. (2019), who refer to three views in relation to change towards sustainability issues. The first is an acceptance of working within the existing economic system and that market forces and technology can address the major issues of the day. The second view aims to reform the present system, criticizing existing practices but not seeking systematic change. Finally, the third view recognizes and addresses the dominant neoliberal forces and recommends that only transformative action will secure real change.

Another approach, but covering the same themes, are Vare and Scott (2007), who suggest that there are two types of 'learning for a change':

- Approaches that assume the problems are essentially environmental and can be understood through science and resolved by appropriate environmental and/or social actions
- Approaches that assume fundamental problems are social and political and that these problems produce environmental symptoms. Such fundamental problems can be understood by means of anything from socio-scientific analysis to an appeal to indigenous knowledge (ibid., 192).

There are also other studies that emphasize the importance of transformative learning (Moore 2005; Bell 2016; Sarabhai 2013; Wahr, Underwood, Adams and Prideaux 2013). As stated in these studies, the aims of ESD and transformative education overlap. As transformative learning facilitates action and social change, it can help ESD to reach its aims for a change to educate responsible global citizens. It was emphasized by UNESCO (2016b: 288) that embedding is thought to provide double-purpose learning. In this type of learning, students will have both the required subject knowledge and skills, and will learn how to contribute to a sustainable transformation of society by living together with a deep respect for the environment and dignity for all humans.

Elements of some of these ideas can be seen in ESD as 'action-oriented learning' (Leicht, Heiss and Byun 2018). In this approach, learners should be active in their learning and reflect their own experiences to construct their own knowledge. Their experiences may be gathered from engaging in or implementing a project. To provide this, educators should create learning environments that promote learners' experiences and make them active in their learning process.

Another model is called the Head, Heart and Hands model. As Singleton (2015) has stated, this model is developed by Orr (1992) and expanded by Sipos, Battisti and Grimm (2008) to reflect the multidimensional process of transformative learning. The model suggests adding the cognitive (head), psychomotor (hands) and the affective domain (heart) to learning. 'Head' indicates the cognitive domain by understanding sustainability, 'hands' indicates psychomotor domain by developing practical skills and 'heart' indicates the affective skills by developing values and attitudes for a behavioural change as a basic aim of transformative learning.

What all of these models and approaches suggest is that sustainability education can be seen in terms of transformation, but that this can take many forms with processes of learning and distinct pedagogical approaches being seen as key.

Global Citizenship and Transformative Learning

Like education for sustainability, global citizenship has a multitude of voices and perspectives but within them a common theme of seeking social change can be identified. In many respects, 'global citizenship' has become used as the new buzzword by bodies such as UNESCO, leading universities around the world and an abundance of NGOs. The term has become popular because it can reflect both the globalized and interconnected world we now live in but also the complex forms of identity that many people now have. The development of a major educational programme on this theme by UNESCO, which is discussed more in Chapter 12, has also been helped by the explicit mention of the term within Goal 4.7 of the Sustainable Development Goals.

Within the plethora of literature around the term 'global citizenship', there have been a number of attempts to categorize clear themes. Some of these categorizations reflect similar themes to those of ESD, most notably Andreotti's distinction between 'soft' and 'critical' global citizenship with the former focusing around a sense of common humanity and a more cosmopolitan outlook and the latter emphasizing inequalities and injustices and seeking social change (Andreotti, 2006). Oxley and Morris (2013), in their categorizations of global citizenship, distinguish between cosmopolitan (political, moral, economic, cultural) and more advocacy-based (social, critical, environmental and spiritual) approaches.

Goren and Yemini (2017) take a slightly different approach and identified the following educational themes from their literature review: globalization and culture, language learning, and education for environmental sustainability. Finally, Pashby, da Costa, Stein and Andreotti (2020), using a social cartography approach, identified neoliberal, liberal and critical approaches but also added the linkages between them through neoconservatism and post-criticality. Other variations on these categorizations can be seen in Shultz (2007), who makes a distinction between radical and transformative. Gaudelli (2016) brings in Marxist and world justice categories, and others such as Schattle (2008) and Camicia and Franklin (2011) bring in themes of environment and democracy.

What is also relevant in discussions on global citizenship and transformative learning is the role and influence NGOs and civil society organizations have played. The most notable of these has been Oxfam, whose conception and usage of the term, whilst building on the practices of development and global education, sought to make a more explicit connection to citizenship and social action. This could be summarized in their slogan of learn, think and act.

In relation to the themes of this chapter, global citizenship has been most closely related to transformative learning with regards to personal experience, especially studying abroad and being exposed to different cultures and ways of seeing the world, and forms of social action. It also needs to be noted that these perspectives of global citizenship can also be seen as applicable to a Western elite who have the resources for international travel and to be socially and economically mobile.

Global Citizenship for Transformative Social Action

One area where 'global citizenship' has been used as a term has been in relation to engaging in social action for social change. This can, for example, be seen in the usage of the term in campaigns around the climate emergency. It has also been more widely used as part of broader 'global citizens' movements' for change. This means some form of conscious recognition of being 'global citizens' and those who wish to see a more just and sustainable world.

What is particularly significant about a number of these initiatives is the interrelationship between personal transformation and that of seeking systematic and structural changes.

This sense of seeing global citizenship as some form of conscious movement for transformation and change has been one of the reasons why it has become popular within progressive educational circles. It is this transformative dimension of global citizenship education – which seeks not only institutional changes but also personal and cultural mindsets that cut across national boundaries – that has helped to gain it support amongst a range of global educationalists such as Andreotti (2006), Dill (2013), Gaudelli (2016), Torres (2017) and Shultz (2007, 2010, 2011b).

Research on Global Citizenship, International Experience and Transformative Learning

The role of international experience has been seen in many studies and projects as a form of transformative global citizenship. Engaging in some form of international volunteering or study visit has been seen as a way of not only exposing people to new cultural experiences, but to transform their world views and their sense of place and identity.

There are numerous studies that have looked at the value of such experiences (Anderson, Lawton, Rexeisen, and Hubbard,2006; Dalby 2017; Bentall, Blum and Bourn 2010; Findlay, King, Stam, and Ruiz-Gelices, E. 2006; Llanes, and Muñoz, 2009; Paige, Fry, Stallman, Josić, and Jon 2009 Zemach-Bersin 2012). These studies have reviewed the value of both short-term and long-term study abroad experiences. They demonstrate a range of perspectives as to the relative value of such initiatives including areas such as cognitive, intrapersonal and interpersonal areas. Braskamp et al. (2009) have suggested that this includes increased awareness, knowledge development, challenges notions of identity, personal attitudes and emotions and behavioural patterns and sense of social responsibility.

Whilst some of these themes were discussed in Chapter 6 with regard to international mobility by university students in reference to the research of Killick, it is an area that has seen important research in relation to transformative learning.

Perhaps the most relevant for the themes discussed in this chapter is the research and follow-up publications by Phil Bamber (2016). The relationship between global citizenship and transformative learning through a form of international service learning was the focus of Bamber's research.

Bamber developed Mezirow's ideas on transformative learning by adding an 'ethical ecological' approach which means 'elevating the importance of the context within which the learning self is embedded'. Context, Bamber (p. 182) suggests, is:

understood here not simply as the physical environment in which learning takes place. It is concerned with the totality of relationships nurtured by the learning self with knowledge, ideas, places, individuals and communities, locally and globally.

He also added to his framework the development of the authentic self: 'an ongoing process of becoming oneself, becoming persons-in-relation and becoming other-wise' (ibid., 7).

Based on his doctoral research, Bamber investigated the activities and experiences of a group of higher education tutors and students as they undertook a curriculum development project titled 'International Experience for Engaged Global Citizens in Education'. The initial phase of the project sought to develop an understanding of the value of international experience in relation to notions of global citizenship, as experienced by undergraduates. This led to the development of a 'framework for engaged global citizens in education' and the subsequent development of interventions to internationalize the curriculum for all students at home.

His research is based on a project that brought together eight academics from a range of disciplines and cultural backgrounds based at a university in the United Kingdom. They were joined by eleven undergraduate students to form a 'conceptual steering group' (CSG) for the project. Bamber's research identified that values and attitudes such as openness (to difference, others, diversity), self-respect, an ease with uncertainty, and a commitment to social change must lie at the heart of their framework for engaged global citizenship, and that these values came through lived experiences.

His research also found that the transformational aspects came through ongoing dialogue and conversations between the staff and the students. A process of doing and undoing, learning and unlearning, was, in fact, the very process of learning that the framework sought to capture (Bamber 2016).

Other studies such as young people engaging in projects in Latin America (Dalby 2017) show that whilst such experiences can be of personal transformative value, the extent to which they have a direct impact on the local communities is perhaps more open to question.

Whilst these might appear to be laudable aims, research in the United Kingdom by Bentall, Blum and Bourn (2010) suggests that whilst some form of international experience might have a personal transformative experience, it did not necessarily lead to the students and learners becoming 'agents for change' in the way the organization had envisaged. For example, some people who had been volunteers found the international experience had questioned their perceptions about development and aid.

Global Citizenship for a Western Elite

Whilst there are numerous studies that relate to a sense of being a global citizen within transformative learning, there is considerable evidence that this has only been seen to be appropriate to people who are economically and socially mobile and have the resources and background that can enable them to take part in such experiences. Larkin (2018: 563) notes:

> Narratives of global citizenship promote an image of an idealised individual whose personal/social responsibilities extend well beyond the local and expand the boundaries of an individual's identity to include the values of an imagined global community.

Dalby (2017), in his research with young people from North America spending time in Latin America, developed the concept 'pedagogy of the privileged' outlined by Curry-Stevens (2007). Despite the perceived transformative pedagogy used in the project he was researching, he identified several cases that appeared to 'facilitate processes in which students reinforced their pre-existing, problematic understandings of social inequality'. Dalby recommended that this field of global learning and citizenship needed to give more consideration to power relations.

Jooste and Heleta (2017) question the use of the term 'global citizenship' in higher education when the majority of students in the Global South live in an unjust world. My own research (Bourn 2009) with students at UCL over a decade ago found that students who had limited or no international experience were uncomfortable with identifying themselves with the term. It was only those students who were economically and socially mobile and who had hybrid identities who were most comfortable with the term.

Research on Curriculum Initiatives and Education for Transformation

A theme of this chapter alongside others in this volume is the interrelationship of pedagogy and learning to social change. One example of research that looks at the potential value of the usage of the term 'transformative learning' in relation to specific curriculum-based initiatives has been the doctoral research by De Angelis (2020) on environmental education in Jamaica.

De Angelis found elements of transformative learning within the curriculum of a primary school in the Integrated Studies and Social Studies subjects, and 'uncovered elements that represent a potential towards a more "transformative" turn in the teaching/learning approach'. She said that if 'a transformative pedagogy is intended as a way of teaching and learning where students develop critical thinking abilities through co-constructive and reflective activities that enable them to envision new meanings for the environment and sustainable behaviours', then this could be seen in a number of activities (ibid., 94). For example, she found that the:

> writing of the poem can allow students to relate their surrounding reality and critically reflect upon it (e.g., the bamboo constituting a tourist attraction). Thus, students can better realise the interconnections between humankind and nature and the latter's intrinsic value (e.g., the bamboo is valued for its beauty and should not be polluted). The student who composed this poem also reflected on problematic actions from other students and community members (e.g., students throwing 'bag juices' and a man cutting the bamboo). (ibid. 223)

Another area she found that could facilitate a transformative approach was related to outdoor experiential activities. This included bringing in plants from home to their school which enabled them to apply their local knowledge to curriculum content and could transform their perceptions about plant life and protecting the environment (ibid., 224).

These examples from research demonstrate that the concept of transformative learning is relevant to discussions on both sustainable development and global citizenship and social change more widely. What they pose however is that this process of transformation is often related to forms of personal experience or exposure to different modes of learning.

Case Studies and Examples of Practice

If transformative learning is about 'habits of mind' that comes as much from experience as from more formal forms of education, it is not surprising that studying abroad, as this chapter has noted, is an obvious example. As already noted earlier in this chapter, studying abroad has been promoted as a way young people can develop concepts relevant to being a global citizen including intercultural understanding, inter-personal skills and language learning (Hammond and Keating 2018; Bourn 2018b).

Three examples are reviewed here that demonstrate these themes, one from University College London (UCL), one from Southern Africa and the third from a very influential publication which has had an impact on educational practices in Ireland and elsewhere in the world. These examples have been chosen because the aims of the first two clearly link international experience to transformative learning. The third example focuses more on a very influential publication that connects transformation learning directly to global social justice educational practices.

The first is research undertaken with undergraduate students on UCL's Arts and Sciences (BASc) programme. Between 2014 and 2018, undergraduate students had the opportunity to spend a year abroad in which they participated in courses at their host institution, developed language skills and completed a study abroad dissertation on the themes of globalization and global citizenship.

The aims of the research with these students from UCL were to:

- Identify the impact of the study abroad experience on BASc students' world outlook and their views about being global citizens.
- Investigate the extent to which the study abroad programme enables students to develop new knowledge and skills.
- Consider the extent to which the study abroad experience has influenced students' plans for their future careers.[1]

The evidence from the interviews with the students reflected many of the themes relevant to transformative learning, often initially very personal:

I wanted to reinvent myself, I wanted to achieve academically.

Whilst many hoped that studying abroad would help them to build particular knowledge and skills, others hoped for an even more transformative experience:

I came to McGill thinking I'm going to reinvent myself as a person.

But this student found that 'radical change of personality doesn't come easy'.

When asked to reflect on their experiences, the students found they had learnt to look at issues more critically. What the evidence also showed was that a study abroad experience can lead to thinking more deeply about the world and their place in it, and that the usage of the term 'global citizenship' had some relevance to them:

Studying abroad was the first time I felt like I could call myself a global citizen. Before this, I had some awareness and interest in international issues, but had never left Europe and only travelled for brief periods of time. On returning, I found I had a reverse culture shock, and could relate better to international students studying in the UK.

The evidence also suggests that a number of different kinds of learning take place during study abroad, including learning about particular topics/issues, experiences of particular places and/or exposure to new ideas. Whilst these experiences can be highly significant for individuals, it is important to recognize that transformative learning may not happen without support. Students in this research clearly recognized the value of their study abroad learning and experiences, but also the need for more ways to reflect on this with programme organizers and with peers, particularly if they are to be able to take their learning forward.

EDU Africa[2]

Another example of this more personal transformative experience is the EDU Africa-facilitated programmes, with the goal:

> for all students to experience holistic transformation during their study abroad time in Africa, and that they will become global agents of that change. We aim to encourage student growth in our five transformation learning goal areas: Intercultural Competence, Global Citizenship, Personal Growth, Intellectual Growth, and Professional Development. (EDU-Africa, n.d.)

Born out of a deep passion for the continent, EDU Africa was launched out of Harare, Zimbabwe, during 2003 – a couple of years after the founding members first began exploring the concept of offering travel experiences in Southern and East Africa that benefitted the community and environment. EDU Africa provides educational programmes and service learning experiences for young people, often university students.

Barry Rawlings, managing director and Southern Africa (Central) director, explains why the offering is so unique:

> We understand education. We aren't a tour operator putting an educational spin on what we do, we are genuine educationalists and appreciate outcomes, curriculum and pedagogy.

What is interesting about the approach of this organization is their recognition of the problematic nature of the term 'global citizen', which can and has been used to promote one world view. Like Bamber, they recognize the complexity of the issues and the need to understand the context within which the learning experience takes place.

EDU Africa, like other organizations such as Voluntary Service Overseas in the United Kingdom, see international experience as not only developing the knowledge, skills and value base of the learner but also hoping that they would become 'change agents'.

Transformation for EDU Africa 'is a deepening of perspective that can result from venturing outside of one's comfort zone' (Edu-Africa, n.d.). The organization further notes:

> Our Transformative Learning Journeys might be short-term, but we do believe that the transformation process is not. After participating in our programs, our sincere hope is that students will continue to transform and, ultimately, become global agents of the change they experience. (ibid.)

Training for Transformation

One of the most influential training volumes around the theme of transformation has been the series of volumes produced by Hope and Timmel (1989) on Training for Transformation. Initially three volumes, but later supplemented by a fourth, they provide a Freirean, combined with a Christian philosophical, outlook, for the training of community workers. The volumes emphasize participatory methods alongside organizational development, and leadership skills within the context of how to develop self-learning communities. Central to their approach is the DELTA training programme which builds on Freire's work on critical awareness, role of human relations within a training context, organizational development, social analysis and the Christian concept of transformation. Reflecting themes discussed elsewhere in this volume, Hope and Timmel make reference to liberation, socialism and democracy.

Training for Transformation has as its basic philosophy the belief that we should all participate in making this world a more just place to live in. A feature of each volume are examples of activities for training courses that are problem posing with themes such as building a co-operative, storytelling and use of role play.

This approach to learning has been influential in many countries around the world. One organization that has been developed around the philosophy and approach of the volumes is Partners Training for Transformation based in Ireland which sees itself as 'working for social justice through grassroots community education'.

Influenced by development traditions from a Global Southern perspective, the organization runs a range of training courses for adult educators. Relevant to themes outlined in this chapter is their methodological approach which is based on the following:

The bag: Partners recognizes that participants entering the learning group come as if with a bag already full of their experience, theory and values.

The three circles: personal, interpersonal and the wider society which are seen as three overlapping circles.

Partners see a group of participants as a *temporary learning community*. By working together, they develop a sense of a community and learn how to build communities in the wider world.

The iceberg represents the recognition of the visible and hidden dimensions of social justice work. The skills of the community activist, for example, may be visible (organizing, listening, analysing, facilitating etc.). But these are held in the water by the theories and understandings the person has; and their level of knowledge about why they are doing what they are doing. This in turn is weighted by the core attitudes and values, constructs, experience and instincts of the worker.

Make the road by walking which means 'uncovering' rather than 'covering' content. The learning process is a process that cannot be predicted. Partners' commitment is to follow the energy, interests and needs of participants, rather than rigidly following prescribed curricula. (Partners Training for Transformation, n.d.)

This example, bringing together the richness of a training manual with practice, provides an approach to transformative learning as education for social change. It reflects themes explored elsewhere in this volume influenced by the ideas of Freire and Giroux concerning critical pedagogy and social justice.

Conclusion

This chapter has reviewed what is meant by 'transformative learning' and how the term is applied in relation to sustainable development and global citizenship. 'Transformative learning' is a complex term, and, as the range of perspectives have shown, there are many different interpretations as to how it relates to processes of learning. But what is evident is that the term, if seen as a distinctive pedagogical approach, can be a valuable way of addressing the relationship between learning, experience and social action. As noted in this chapter, it is when the process of learning becomes either ignored or marginalized that transformation becomes reduced to merely behavioural change.

The research discussed in this chapter shows that the concept of transformative learning has value whether it is with regard to the practices of NGOs, the influence of studying abroad or engaging in local environmental projects. Finally, as the example from Training for Transformation shows, this approach to learning not only has similarities with perspectives from Freire but can be an effective tool for influencing both individual and collective forms of social action.

Questions for Further Consideration

- In what ways can 'transformative learning' as a term be a valuable approach to a pedagogy of social change?
- What are the most appropriate methodologies and approaches within the discourses around education for sustainable development that are relevant to transformative learning and social change?
- What are the strengths and weaknesses of international experience to developing a sense of being a transformative global citizen?

Further Reading

Bamber, P. (2016), *Transformative Education Through International Service Learning*, Abingdon: Routledge.

Bourn, D. and A. Morgan (2010), 'Development Education, Sustainable Development, Global Citizenship and Higher Education: Towards a Transformative Approach to Learning', in E. Unterhalter and V. Carpentier (eds), *Global Inequalities and Higher Education: Whose Interest Are We Serving?*, 268–86, Basingstoke: Palgrave Macmillan.

Curry-Stevens, A. (2007), 'New Forms of Transformative Education "Pedagogy for the Privileged"', *Journal of Transformative Education*, 5, no. 1: 33–58.

Hope, A. and S. Timmel (1989), *Training for Transformation*, vols. 1–3, Gweru, Zimbabwe: Mambo Press.

Mezirow, J. (2009), 'Transformative Learning Theory', in J. Mezirow and E. W. Taylor (eds), *Transformative Learning in Practice: Insights from Community, Workplace, and Higher Education*, 18–32, San Francisco: Jossey-Bass.

Sterling, S. (2010), 'Transformative Learning And Sustainability: Sketching the Conceptual Ground', *Learning and Teaching in Higher Education*, 5: 17–33.

8

Teachers as Agents of Social Change[1]

Introduction

Numerous policy initiatives and pronouncements from leading educationalists from different regions of the world often make reference to the role of teachers as agents for change. For example, in an interview on the role of teaching, Professor Arnetha Ball from Stanford University suggests that teachers should see themselves as the agents rather than the objects of change.[2] Michael Fullan, for example, has in numerous articles referred to the role of teachers as change agents. The Brazilian educationalist Paulo Freire (2005) saw teachers as central to challenging dominant orthodoxies in education. Bodies such as UNESCO in a range of policy documents have made reference to the broader social change role of teachers.

This chapter will review the literature and initiatives from around the world that have posed the role of teachers as agents of social change, including a discussion of the ideas of educationalists such as Michael Fullan, and the relevance of the term 'agency' for these debates. Discourses in and around global learning make reference to the important role of teachers, and this chapter will review the ways in which initiatives in teacher education consider them as key agents for change. Reference will then be made to the distinctions between the differing roles teachers can play as agents of change, in the school and within society. Research will be reviewed from a range of doctoral studies in the United States that bring in the theme of a pedagogy of social justice as central components of a programme for teachers as agents of social change. These studies have been chosen because they provide excellent examples of practice around teachers as agents of change. Evidence will also be shown from the United Kingdom on the potential transformative role of international partnerships and ways in which strategies that encourage movement from a charitable mentality to ones of social justice can be effective. The role that teachers play within initiatives around peace education and global learning will be discussed through examples from Europe, the United Kingdom and Rwanda. The chapter will conclude by suggesting that what this evidence and ideas suggest is that teachers have a role beyond being the mere transmitters of knowledge.

Teachers as More Than the Transmitters and the Purveyors of Knowledge

Within many societies around the world, teachers have often been seen as the experts on knowledge and the role of the learner is merely to listen to, absorb and reproduce through essays and examinations what they have been told. That is why in many languages and cultures the term 'teacher' is often combined with that of professor.

What this approach does is perceive that there is one body of knowledge and that all expertise lies with the teacher. What is missing from this approach is the role of the learner and their own experiences and perspectives.[3] As the Brazilian educationalist Paulo Freire has suggested, teachers should instead be seen as cultural workers (Freire 2005) who provide learners with the knowledge, skills and values base to consider, interpret and come to their own conclusions.

Despite the roles that teachers are often expected to play in many societies, there is also the view that teachers are looked upon as the individuals who can help to bring about positive changes in the lives of people. For example, in many countries in the Global South, teachers are seen as key players in securing change within communities (Freire 2005; Tikly and Barret 2013). UNESCO, for example, says:

> Teachers are one of the most influential and powerful forces for equity, access and quality in education and key to sustainable global development. (UNESCO n.d.)

Teachers are often seen as natural leaders who can give advice on various affairs in the community (International Labour Organization n.d.) with their role being seen as 'both significant and valuable'. They are perceived in many societies to have 'far-reaching influence on the society he lives in, and no other personality can have an influence more profound than that of a teacher' (Raina 2007).

In Namibia, for example, in the ruling political party:

Teachers (are seen) . . . as agents of change in any society. Their roles do not stop in the classroom, as educators and architects of a well-educated nation but are community activists too. Hence, they are expected to promote social change in schools and in communities in which they serve on several issues. (Nambinga n.d.)

In many societies, teachers are seen as role models who can provide inspiration to their students. As Hana-Meksem notes:

Teachers have this great opportunity to raise awareness on the world because anything they do or say is meticulously decrypted by children. Teachers are constantly watched and viewed as motivators, guides, heroes, surrogate parents, mentors, and leaders who thrive to make the world a better place. They have the power to influence children at an early age on issues. (Hana-Meksem 2014)

Teachers own professional practice, and both what and how they teach can be transformative to many students. It is the relationship of this professional practice to their own personal visions and outlooks that is a major theme of this chapter.

What has also been happening over the past couple of decades is that with the growth of the internet and social media, the role of teachers has had to change. For many young people around the world, access to information from a wide variety of sources is now possible. This means the teacher is no longer the source of all knowledge (Szucs 2009).

Instead, as this chapter will suggest, teachers should perceive their role in much broader terms that include a relationship to the needs of society. Societies around the world are still full of inequalities, and education can contribute to securing a more just society. This means encouraging teachers to see themselves as agents of change, as 'soldiers for social justice' (Grant 2009: 654). As will be shown later in this chapter, this is not easy and can present many challenges. But before this chapter reviews these challenges, it is important first of all to review some of the academic debates around the role of teachers.

Perspectives on Teachers as Agents of Change

Michael Fullan is perhaps one of the most well-known academics who has talked about teachers as agents of change. Fullan states that teachers must combine the mantle of moral purpose with the skills of change agentry. 'Scratch a good teacher and you will find a moral purpose' (Fullan 1993), he suggests, in combination with the 'skills of change agentry' (ibid., 2). Including change within the moral purpose, he suggests, enables the teacher to develop strategies to accomplish their moral goals. Moral purpose and change agentry, at first glance, can be natural allies (Fullan 1993). Having a moral purpose implies change, but teachers also need the skills to engage in change. However, as Fullan and others (Farber 1991) have noted, all too often teachers become quickly disheartened. Fullan (1993) suggests that what is needed is to encourage teachers to develop a personal vision as part of their professional development and in collaboration with others. This theme of agency will be discussed later in the chapter.

Perceptions about the Role of Teachers

Teaching has always been seen as more than just another profession or job. Hansen refers to it as a 'moral practice' (Hansen 2011: 4). Taking these elements forward within the discourses on education for social change, there is evidence that many teachers see part of their role is to be 'vision creators', to give inspiration and a sense of a positive outlook on the world to their learners, to encourage them to not only learn, but to participate in society (Jones 2009). Teachers also need to have the skills to engage others within their educational institution, to secure support for their vision. They also need to be able to reflect on their own needs, to identify areas of personal professional development that can help them to be better teachers.

What, however, needs to be noted as words of caution, is that whilst many teachers may initially support this vision, the reality of their experience as a teacher and the societal and ideological influences on their daily practice can often work against this. Since the 1980s, it could be argued that the role of policymakers has been to control and tame teachers rather than to empower them. Therefore, any discussion on teachers as agents of change needs to be predicated by an understanding of the limitations many teachers face in their desire to be agents of change.

Fullan suggests that there is a need for teachers and prospective teachers to ask themselves: 'What difference am I trying to make personally?' But as he suggests, personal purpose will be constantly changing. He suggests that constant questioning and having an inquiring approach are key (Fullan 1993). Fullan further suggests that mastery is important:

People *behave* their way into new visions and ideas, not just think their way into them. *Mastery* is obviously necessary for effectiveness, but it is also a means for achieving deeper understanding. New mind-sets arise from mastery as much as the reverse. This means the development of expertise related to ongoing professional development. (ibid.)

Finally, Fullan suggests that learning has to be a collaborative effort:

The ability to *collaborate* on both a small- and large-scale is becoming one of the core requisites of postmodern society. (ibid.)

These elements suggest that teaching for social change involves recognizing the value of working with others, understanding the subject matter, being able to articulate the key issues and constantly reflecting on one's own practice. Linked to this process of change, Fullan and others have argued that teacher agency is an important component to consider (Fullan 1993; Biesta, Priestley and Robinson 2015). This means that regardless of ideological and political constraints, what can the teacher do to change practices within an educational environment? What impact can they have on the learner?

Teacher Agency

Before reviewing some of the key literature on teachers as agents of change, it is necessary to make a distinction between this term of 'agency' and that of 'change agents'. The latter could be seen as the role of the individual in their professional capacity within the classroom and the school. The former could be seen more as the role of the teacher in securing, possibly with others, something new or different either with the school or wider society (van der Heijden et al. 2015). This chapter is primarily concerned with the former, of agents of change rather than change agents.

In reviewing the role of teacher agency as a contribution to social justice, Pantic (2015) notes:

The way teachers act in a particular environment is likely to result from complex interdependent relations of their personal and professional beliefs and dispositions, degrees of autonomy and power, and interactions within other actors within the social contexts in which they work. (Pantic 2015: 760)

Pantic develops a framework for teacher agency for social justice based on the following:

- Purpose – teachers' perceptions of their role and understanding of social justice.
- Competence – teachers' engagement in practices towards social justice and understanding of broader social forces that influence schooling.
- Autonomy – teachers' own beliefs that they can make a difference, their level of confidence and sense of belief they can make a difference.
- Reflexivity – teachers' capacity to be open to critical self-reflection and ability to articulate their own professional practices and approaches (ibid., 766).

Biesta, Priestley and Robinson (2015) raise similar themes in their recognition of the importance of teachers' beliefs in understanding agency, 'where do their beliefs come from, how do they motivate action and how do beliefs influence what is actually done?' (ibid., 627–8). This means that any consideration of teachers as agents of social change has to include their own views on the world and what they do with their perspectives. But as their research shows, despite these good intentions, many teachers struggle to locate their practices within the overall purposes of education (ibid., 636).

These interpretations of teachers as agents of change are particularly relevant when considering their role in relation to areas such as global learning. Their views on the world and their beliefs in wanting to secure change and commitment to social justice are integral to discussions on the role of teachers in delivering global learning approaches within the classroom and the school more widely.

Teachers and Global Learning

Global learning is an underlying focus of many of the chapters in this volume, and is an appropriate example to review when considering the roles of teachers because much of the literature in this area has assumptions that learning is closely linked to personal and social change (see Bourn 2015; Kirkwood-Tucker, Morris and Lieberman 2011; McCloskey 2014).

Global learning projects, for example, have tended to have a strong social change component with the educators, usually teachers, as the vehicles through which this learning and engagement takes place (Krause 2010: 13). However, underpinning some of these initiatives are approaches that can be related to learning towards predetermined goals (see Weber 2012; Asbrand and Scheunpflug 2006).

There has been a tendency to see the role of the teacher as the promoter of, and transmitter of, specific perspectives and approaches towards learning

(Hicks and Holden 2007; McCloskey 2014). This can take the form of goals the teacher has to work towards in their own professional development. This can include increasing their knowledge base, developing a strong ethical and values commitment to social justice and encouraging and supporting participatory approaches towards learning.

A range of studies has suggested that practitioners within the field of global education should nurture an approach to learning that encourages more than awareness of global issues and includes elements of promoting social action for change (Fisher 2001; O'Connor and Zeichner 2011; Steiner 1993; Merryfield 2009).

However, this approach makes a number of assumptions that teachers have the skills, confidence and capacity to encourage change as outlined earlier in this chapter. The first is the belief that the teachers can be socially responsible. Secondly, the teacher needs to have a social justice values base. For many non-governmental organizations (NGOs) involved in supporting global learning practices within schools, there is a further assumption that many teachers may not have these skills and approaches and that what is needed are professional development opportunities, the production of resources and ongoing support[4].

Whilst there are dangers with these assumptions from teachers, the evidence from numerous studies in the field suggests that whilst many teachers may be sympathetic to promoting this more active and agent of change role within global learning, they often lack the confidence and experience to deliver it (Bentall 2020; Hunt 2012; Hicks and Holden 2007).

Professional Development

The ongoing professional development of teachers is therefore suggested here as being central to the development of teachers as agents of social change. This, however, first needs some clarification as to what is meant by ongoing professional development, or, as it is often called, CPD.

Day's (1999: 4) definition is seen as particularly helpful here:

Professional development consists of all natural learning experiences and those conscious and planned activities which are intended to be of direct benefit to the individual, group or school and which contribute, through these, to the quality of education in the classroom. It is the process by which, alone and with others, teachers review, renew and extend their commitment as change agents to the moral purposes of teaching; and by which they acquire and develop critically the knowledge, skills and emotional intelligence essential to good professional thinking, planning and practice with children, young people and colleagues through each phase of their teaching lives.

What is important about this definition, as Bentall (2020) suggests, is that it rejects the deficit and technician approach, professional development being what teachers lack and what they need to have to be efficient and effective. Professional development needs instead to be about challenging teachers' own beliefs and perceptions, to encourage them to think critically and to look at issues from different perspectives. Professional development also needs to encourage teachers to ensure they have relevant knowledge to teach their own subject area. Echoing points made earlier in this chapter, Bentall suggests that professional development needs to be located within a culture of a learning community and that teachers' own learning should be seen as a collaborative and not an individual exercise.

Transformative Pedagogy

As discussed in earlier chapters, the concept of transformative learning is relevant to discussions on education for social change. For teachers, this means how they see themselves but also in terms of their pedagogical role. One author who has summarized these themes well has been Miriam Steiner (1993) in her work on the *Global Teacher*. She summarized the approach the Global Teacher should have as follows:

- A methodology that valued personal experience of both the teacher and the learner, with a range of pedagogical approaches.
- Recognising that teaching principles that come from a social justice and democratic perspective means putting them into practice within the classroom.
- Choosing diverse ways of presenting information and planning a range of approaches (ibid., 25–6).

This means that the role of the teacher as agent for social change cannot be divorced from what and how they teach in the classroom and their wider role within the school. This includes within a classroom context, exposing the learner to a range of viewpoints and prompting them to question what could well be dominant assumptions about a particular place, people or culture (Wright 2011).

Change within the School

Within a school context, for the teacher to be a promoter of social change and to have any impact, some form of designated role would be of considerable benefit. This was the case with the Global Learning Programme in England (see later in this chapter), where each school had a designated lead person. Earlier evidence from research by Cox (2011) suggested some form of distributed leadership would facilitate this role having some form of impact. Referring to the work of Durrant and Holden (2006: 169), Cox noted the importance of ways of working within the school that would encourage shared leadership and enhanced status and recognition for these champions (Cox 2011: 6). Further evidence suggests that this role within the school is further helped if there is a whole school approach. This means learning, say about global issues, is not just left to one or two teachers but is seen as relevant across all subjects and is part of whole school activities and included in the ethos as to how the school is run (Hunt and King 2015: 12).

The evidence from schools is that where such a 'whole school approach' is taken and there is an identified teacher to lead on this area which has the support of senior leaders, then it is more likely to have an impact upon the learners (Hunt 2012: 51).

Teachers as Global Citizens

There needs also to be consideration of the vision and outlook of the teachers themselves, how they see their role as agents of change. Many teachers may well be active in a range of social issues but there have been debates as to how 'political' teachers can be. There is considerable evidence to show that teachers are often reluctant to engage in what could be termed 'controversial' or political issues (Holden 2007).

This poses the extent to which teachers see themselves as agents of change, as social activists. In North America, for example, Verma (2010) has discussed this in relation to gender and race discrimination. Giroux (2011) suggests that teachers can play a role as 'public intellectuals', engaging in the debates regarding more equitable and democratic societies.

This wider social concern for change may manifest itself in other ways such as teaching overseas and directly engaging in projects that can help to reduce global poverty. There is evidence, for example, that volunteering experiences can help to radicalize a teacher's view of the world, get them to question their own assumptions and seek ways to channel that their enthusiasm and emotional commitment to broader movements for change (Bentall, Blum and Bourn 2010).

This poses the need to consider the extent to which teachers can, and should, even see their role as agents for global change, as responsible citizens for a more equitable society.

These questions relate to earlier themes raised in this chapter about agency and the considerations on the extent to which teachers are prepared to take risks, to present their own point of view and openly present a particular value base. One of the best ways of addressing these questions is to look at recent research evidence on this theme.

Evidence from Research

There have been a number of doctoral-level research studies in the United States that identify the role of teachers as agents for social change, mainly through the social studies curriculum. Cassandra Allen's study (2016) examined how social studies secondary teachers in Texas, who were supportive of their role as change agents, conceptualized, planned and implemented social justice themes in the classroom.

Her study identified that whilst the teachers she interviewed supported the concept of agency and use of reflective practice, there were noticeable differences in how to teach for social justice (Allen 2016: 103). All three of the teachers she interviewed were critical of the dominant discourses within education. However, they all felt they had autonomy in their classroom planning which came from experience, confidence and collaboration with their peers.

What was significant was that the three teachers had similar pedagogical approaches including building student efficacy, collaborative approaches to learning, inclusion and respect for multiple perspectives and encouraging a sense of social responsibility (ibid., 108).

Although their approach could be perceived as being counter-hegemonic to dominant educational practices, they did not see their approach as being overtly political. Their teaching was aimed at encouraging a sense of transformation and empowerment in the learner. Allen noted that their approach reflected Hackman's (2005) litmus test for social justice, the 'Five Essential Components of Social Justice Education: content mastery, tools for critical analysis, tools for social change, tools for personal reflection and an awareness of multicultural group dynamics' (Allen 2016: 104).

Allen's research also reflected the unease that many teachers felt about a social justice approach, in wanting to get it right when there is not one distinctive approach. She found that teachers who were supportive of a social justice approach still needed support:

> If we are to assume that social justice is both a 'process' and a 'goal' then in-service teachers need the same access to continued education and professional development that many pre-service teachers in programs devoted to social justice receive. (ibid., 120)

This recognition of the need for teachers to have appropriate support is an important issue that can be seen throughout this chapter and elsewhere in this volume.

Another thesis that addressed similar themes was Kunkel-Pottebaum's research (2013) 'Mission Possible: Teachers Serving as Agents of Social Change'. Her research looked at the formative experience of social justice teachers and the methods they used to inspire others and students to become radical educators.

Her research found that 'personal and family experiences of oppression during their youth and early adult years, childhood multicultural experiences, social activism, volunteering, and contact with adult mentors, influenced teachers to become social justice educators' (ibid., iii).

'Teachers traced their passion for social justice from experiences living and working with other cultures and social justice organizations'. This exposure and engagement with other cultures was seen to be a major factor in motivating others to 'become social justice educators and to use their classrooms to foster social activism' (ibid., 140).

Features of the evidence she identified were the themes of fostering critical thinking and what she termed 'moral action'. This was achieved through pedagogical approaches that sought to find alternative resources, emphasizing active learning, encouraging engagement in forms of service learning and community action projects and through arts, cultural awareness. Her research identified the important role that critical thinking and awareness play in raising 'social consciousness leading to moral action' (ibid., 145).

Kunkel-Pottebaum also emphasized the limitations of existing teacher training, particularly in terms of dealing with issues of social and cultural difference through multicultural approaches. Instead, she suggested that what was needed was a more overt social justice-based pedagogy that challenged teacher candidates to think critically and to be exposed to a range of voices and perspectives (ibid., 142–3). Above all, she said:

> Teaching programs need to deconstruct fundamentally the belief systems possessed by teachers with a dominant White perspective and reconstruct it with social justice attitudes, goals, and theories. Pre-service teachers need to be committed to social justice education to have the greatest impact on diverse students. The goal is to create radical teachers, teachers that examine their belief systems, understand social issues, experience multiple diverse and intercultural experiences, possess tools needed to implement social justice curriculum, provide support systems to ensure radical perspectives gain power, and feel fully committed to using their classroom as catalysts for social change. (ibid., 143–4)

This counter-hegemonic perspective outlined by Kunkel-Pottebaum again relates closely to the theme of agency and the extent to which teachers felt confident and had the space and opportunities to promote a social justice approach.

This leads on to the importance of leadership in the discussions on teachers as agents of social change. Promoting a sense of social change requires the development and implementation of skills to inspire and motivate others, to provide models of good practice and appropriate levels of support. This can be seen in the following three research studies. The first is Struve's (2019) study on: '*Anti-Oppressive Education with a "Different Kind of Rigor": Teachers' and Administrators' Perspectives of a Social Justice Education Program at an Affluent Public High School*'. This research looked at the ways in which school students from an affluent background could understand and engage with issues of power and privilege. Struve's research identified an important part of the process of engaging students to promote an awareness of, and empathy with the experiences of others, who were in a less-privileged position. Using a social justice-based approach, the research identified the importance of teacher–student relationships, the need to identify how social justice approaches could be enacted, the value of a critical pedagogical perspective and the value of ongoing professional development.

Struve found that a social justice approach can challenge students to reflect upon their own privilege and who has power and who does not in the world. Using a critical pedagogical approach, Struve identified that the 'teachers used social justice pedagogy to help the students become aware of injustice, feel more informed to address inequality, and choose to participate in social action in holistic ways using "critical compassion"' (ibid., 124).

The leadership provided by the teachers was undertaken in a form that empowered students, that encouraged them to question their own situation within the power structures that existed, and how through project-based learning all could learn together. Struve noted:

> This approach supports the expectation that all students graduate from the program with an understanding of the world around them, capable of raising awareness about current issues and addressing them head on. The teachers expect the students to act and lead the charge against injustice, inspiring change and transformation. The very existence of this program is evidence of how the teachers at the school counteract hegemony. (ibid., 128)

Ali (2015) raises similar themes in their doctoral study on '*Developing Agents Of Change: A Case Study On Preservice Teacher Leaders' Conceptualizations Of Social Justice Teacher Leadership*'. This research had its aim to 'investigate how a set of preservice teachers who have been identified as leaders in their teacher education programs conceptualize social justice teacher leadership' (ibid., 8). Like the other research studies mentioned, Ali's research supported the value of critical pedagogical and transformative learning approaches. Particular mention was made in the study of the value of democratic learning environments.

Ali's research identified an '*Evolved Social Justice Teacher Leadership Model*' through a distinctive approach and motivation:

> In this model, social justice teacher leadership is defined as intentional leadership action by a teacher that considers personal and group identity as it seeks to create social, economic, and political equity and to empower all individuals to improve the quality of their lives. Leadership in this construct can be formal or informal, which distinguishes it from traditional notions of leadership that reserve it for those in positional authority; thus, any teacher can act as a social justice teacher leader. (ibid., 185)

This model also emphasizes the importance of teacher collaboration with the aim of creating a culture centred on 'shared power' (ibid., 188).

An equally important component of this model, Ali suggests, is motivation:

> For a context where social justice teacher leadership can grow, passionate, intrinsically motivated leadership must be coupled with a formal and informal policies and procedures centered on achieving social justice. (ibid., 195)

This motivation, as noted in the research, suggests that whilst internal motivations can be built upon personal experiences, 'there may be a range of external forces that influence the practice of the teaching' (ibid.,196).

Ali identified five leadership orientations of the 'Evolved Social Justice Teacher Leadership Model':

Tasked Administrator. The Tasked Administrator is the type of teacher
  leader who uses external motivations and an authoritarian approach to
  their social justice work.
Collegial Team Leader. The Collegial Team Leader uses external motivations
  and a collaborative approach to leadership to find social justice in their
  work.
Motivated Director. The Motivated Director couples an authoritarian
  approach with intrinsic motivations to act as a social justice teacher
  leader.
Critical Collaborator. The Critical Collaborator is most likely to
  be confused with a Social Justice Teacher Leader as they use a
  collaborative leadership approach important in social justice education
  and maintain a consciousness of their and others' identities and
  experiences that found their conviction to act in the interest of social
  justice.
Social Justice Teacher Leader. The Social Justice Teacher Leader finds
  themselves in the middle region of both contextual continuums. They use
  a unique authoritative leadership approach, complimenting authoritarian
  with collaborative styles, and a critically intrinsic motivation coupled
  with a set of well-designed and diverse external mechanisms to engage
  their social justice work (ibid., 200–4).

These models were not tested out in Ali's research but pose questions and issues that need to be considered when educational leaders are considering social justice approaches. What the research shows is the value of empowering teachers, connecting to themes and approaches mentioned earlier in this chapter around agency.

The final research example is from Alison Hooper (2018), a headteacher of a primary school in the north of England, who in her master's dissertation study reviewed the impact of international school linking on school leaders in Kenya. Her research focused on the views of school leaders in Kenya on the impact of partnership programmes with schools in England in terms of deepening understanding of global issues, motivating teachers to seek social change and the broader value of such partnerships. Whilst many studies show the dangers of the potential colonial nature of such partnerships (Bourn 2014; Martin and Griffiths 2012), there is evidence to suggest that they can be an important motivating factor for school leaders, empowering them to show ways in which changes can be made within the classroom which have broader social consequences.

Hooper's research showed that for the Kenyan headteachers partnerships were important factors in 'creating a critical pedagogy to positively influence the learning process for their own school, maintaining autonomy independent of Northern hegemony' (Hooper 2018: 2).

To the teachers, a partnership provided opportunities for influencing and changing the pedagogical approaches within the school as a result of professional development through the link and the direct inputs from their partner school. Particularly important to the Kenyan teachers was the exposure they were given through the partnership to more student-centred pedagogical approaches. The partnership also had a broader influence on teachers and the schools in that it encouraged a greater opportunity to learn about and understand the lives of other people.

Above all, what the research by Hooper shows is that such international partnerships, which include an element of teacher exchange and mutual professional development, can not only be a valuable cultural exchange of knowledge and ideas; they can also become inspirations to develop new approaches to learning, broaden horizons and create a sense of being part of an interconnected world.

As other research on international partnerships between schools have shown (Edge, Frayman and Jafar 2008; Leonard 2014; Martin and Griffiths 2012), such educational experiences can present major challenges to the teachers. They may be faced with addressing their own stereotypes, to understand different cultural practices and to consider issues in different ways. That is why, as Hooper identified from dialogue with school leaders, there was the need for 'critical learning spaces' (Hooper 2018: 58).

This theme of critical learning spaces can be seen in all of the research studies and other evidence gathered in this chapter. It is when teachers have the opportunity to present their voices and perspectives, rather than just having to support learning that reproduces bodies of knowledge, that a social change approach becomes possible. It is this sense of agency, as this chapter has identified, which is particularly important within the promotion of teachers as agents of social change.

These bodies of evidence from doctoral- and masters-level studies also highlight the challenges that many teachers may have in promoting a social justice approach. They need to have the space and the appropriate skills and belief in their abilities to address difficult and complex questions in a classroom, to challenge dominant orthodoxies and to promote a sense of global social justice.

Finally, this chapter now looks at case studies of practice that demonstrate some of these approaches.

Examples from Practice

The Global Learning Programme in England and Social Change

A major theme from the literature and research on teachers and social change has been the importance of the opportunities for teachers to undertake professional development opportunities. One example of this linkage between professional development and change can be seen in England through the Global Learning Programme which ran from 2013 to 2018 and engaged over 8,000 schools[5] (Hunt and King 2015).

This programme had a clear change element with the aim of encouraging an approach to learners of moving from a 'charity mentality to one of social justice'. It supported teachers through a range of professional development and support opportunities plus a specific accreditation opportunity for teachers, called the Lead Practitioner. The elements of this were:

- Development of professional knowledge – including an understanding of both the content and pedagogical approaches of global learning and how to apply these approaches within the classroom.
- Personal skills development to enable the teacher to work successfully with colleagues, to be open to new ideas and to be able to inspire others.
- How to influence others through the development of skills such as negotiation, leading and networking.

The programme therefore included the key elements, identified by Fullan and others, about how to become a leader for change within the teachers' school and also a recognition that their own professional development is much more than just gaining more knowledge, but recognizing a different pedagogical approach. This meant a process of critical reflection, of learning to unlearn, and learning new ways of thinking, and their application within the classroom and the wider school. Bentall (2020: 360), in her study on reviewing the effectiveness of the CPD element of this programme, found that teachers regained 'a sense of purpose, the importance of pedagogy, the value of collaboration and longer-term engagement with CPD'. She found that those teachers who had engaged with professional development on this programme had a greater sense of worth in themselves. The CPD, she said, was most effective when it linked to 'individuals' motivations and sense of identity as teachers' (ibid., 361). Bentall's research also found that the most effective way of securing this motivation and sense of identity was through emphasizing the importance of pedagogy. For example, one of the most popular and effective courses on the programme was one on Philosophy for Children (P4C), which focused on inquiry-based and participatory approaches to learning.

Get Up and Goals Project

Get up and Goals! was a project financed by the European Commission that ran from 2017 to 2020. The project was co-ordinated by the Italian NGO CISP and involved twelve European countries: Austria, Bulgaria, Czech Republic, Hungary, Ireland, Italy, the Netherlands, Poland, Portugal, Romania, Spain and the United Kingdom.

The project was aimed at secondary school teachers, with a focus on themes related to the Sustainable Development Goals with particular emphasis on four topics: gender inequalities, climate change, global migrations and international inequalities.

The approach of the project was to promote education that included a plurality of viewpoints, being interdisciplinary in approach with participatory models of learning. The project also aimed to promote 'students' responsible action within their communities for a more peaceful and sustainable world' (Get Up and Goals Project n.d.). The main methods of delivery were a range of teacher training initiatives at both a national and an international level and a series of resources related to the themes of the project.

The relevance and importance of this project for the themes discussed in this chapter are the pedagogical approaches it was suggested teachers should take to engage students as potential change agents. This can be seen in the activities on climate change:

> **Stage 1 Let's get engaged**: with pair-based discussions for students on
> the following: 'Should we take action to save the planet from the worst
> impacts of climate change', followed by teachers introducing the idea
> of making a change. Videos and films are shown to the students to
> encourage their interest.

Stage 2 Be the generation of change: with the focus on student-based group discussions on the following: 'Don't ignore young people – they are the key to fighting climate change'.

Stage 3 Decision-making: using a diamond nine ranking exercise to look at the challenges facing the world.

Stage 4 Reflection on idea of activism: young people being active in leading change with the teacher helping them design an action campaign based on persuading people to change their carbon footprint.

What this activity shows is the role the teacher can play as an educator in encouraging young people to be agents of change. Using participatory learning approaches, the teacher provides a framework for the learning to take place, moving from awareness and understanding of the issues to the most appropriate forms of social action.

One UK teacher involved with the project stated that it had helped 'understand the crucial role teachers and schools have in educating pupils about how we need to live more sustainable lifestyles' and that he believed it would have a 'significant impact on future generations of pupils at our school'.

Get Up and Goals was deemed to be valuable also because it posed a different way of seeing the world, challenging existing mindsets of both teachers and pupils. Many of the themes the project addressed, such as migration, are not often discussed in the classroom, and it is this alternative approach which is at the heart of Get Up and Goals.

Role of the Teacher in Peacebuilding

Rubagiza, Umutoni and Kaleeba (2016), in their study on peacebuilding in Rwanda, show that whilst education through the teachers can play a transformative role, there are many challenges. Teachers may be expected to promote the values of tolerance and respect, but the context can often make this problematic. What the study also showed was that governments may have policies seeking change, but what was often lacking was the involvement of teachers as active participants in designing a programme and the resources to implement the changes. Professional development was recognized by the teachers as central to these goals of social change but their involvement in designing what form this training should take was not discussed with them.

There was also the problem in Rwanda, which is all too common in other sub-Saharan countries, of lack of resources and initial training for teachers. Their study concluded that whilst many of the teachers had a sense of pride and passion about their work, they needed to have the resources and opportunities to have a stake in their own professional development needs (ibid., 221–2).

Similar themes can be seen in the research conducted by Sayed (2016) in relation to social cohesion in South Africa. He found that whilst there can be calls for teachers to become agents of peace and social cohesion, they can only do so much. He stated that teachers needed the knowledge and skills to carry out the roles suggested for them. There may have been many policies in South Africa for schools encouraging social cohesion and peacebuilding, but they have been rarely translated into action.

A UNESCO study on a guide for teachers on peacebuilding notes that any form of peace education poses major questions about pedagogy. It suggests that the role of teachers needs to be redefined:

> Teachers need the disposition, knowledge, skills and commitment necessary to engage learners in critical and creative thinking and practices. Teachers must also become ethnic, religious, gender and social-class border-crossers who understand the impact of their ethnic identities and those of the learners in their classroom practices and interactions. (UNESCO-IICBA 2017: 6)

The guide further suggests that what is needed is a transformative pedagogy, that enables 'flowers to grow', to encourage teachers to be critical thinkers and aware of the world around them (ibid., 7). But what they also need are the resources and support to put these aims into practice.

Conclusion

This chapter has reviewed the literature and the debates around the role of teachers as agents for social change. The role of teacher agency is discussed and is suggested as a possible theoretical model with which to consider the theme of social change. Reference has been made to the respective roles of teachers within the classroom, the school and the wider world. Professional development opportunities have also emerged as important elements of a strategy for teachers to act as agents for social change.

What this chapter has also identified are the distinctive pedagogical approaches that teachers need to have to be effective agents of change. The references to literature and research on social justice education bear witness to the need for resources and consideration to be given by those who are seeking social change to ensure there is effective infrastructural support to teachers. The themes identified in this chapter resonate with points made in earlier chapters regarding transformative learning, pedagogy for global social justice and critical pedagogy as important components of education for social change.

Hansen (2011) refers to teachers as cosmopolitan educators, as people who have a global outlook and are open to new ideas and approaches. However, as this chapter has suggested, being an agent for change is more than just having a world outlook and a commitment to greater social justice. It means also having the skills and opportunities to influence education and learning at all levels. This means, as Pantic (2015) and Biesta, Priestley and Robinson (2015) have suggested, the concept of agency becomes relevant when considering teachers as agent of change. The spaces, opportunities and context for a teacher to try and influence educational systems and processes to secure change are of paramount importance. Teachers need also to have the confidence and belief in themselves that they can make a difference.

Sometimes the discourses around teaching and social change have tended to revert to debates about social activism or some form of ideal state teachers have to aspire to be. What has not been debated enough is the relationship between an agent for change and the learning processes that as an individual you are directly involved with. Teachers can, and do, make a difference to learners' views of the world. They can also do more than this and encourage a sense of seeking to secure a more just world. This is where the concept of 'agency' is of such importance. To be agents of change, teachers need the spaces, the opportunities and the access to professional development and support to achieve their aims.

If learning is seen as much more than the acquisition of facts and data or even the improvement of skill and a stronger values base but as a process that brings together all of these elements alongside experience and belief, then learning is by itself an agent of change.

For teachers, therefore, a direct relationship needs to exist between what happens in the classroom, the school and wider society. Teachers are agents for change within the school. But within society as a whole, any discussion on teachers as agents for change has tended to focus too much on aspects of political activism that are seen as distinct from classroom practice.

If what happens in the classroom, in the school and within wider society, is seen as part of the change process for both teacher and learner, then learning can be a real agent for not just change at individual level but also for society as a whole. As Allen (2016: 128) concludes in her research:

Public schools are meant to serve the public good. No matter what political side you may claim, at the root of public good is the concept of a more just world. With that in mind, education and schools cannot and should not perpetuate the oppressions reflected in society; rather education and schools should confront and transform the oppressions of society to create a more just world. This ideal is the foundation of social justice education. It is the hope and power of humans devoted to a more just world that will transform oppressive systems. Teachers can do this work. They can transform their own thinking, their classrooms, their students, and their schools. They can be change agents. They can empower and give voice to students, all students, to transform systemic oppressions that pervade society.

Questions for Further Consideration

- What is the difference between agents for change and being a change agent?
- In what ways can a teacher be an inspirer for social change to learners?
- Is there a danger of putting too much responsibility and expectations upon teachers as being exponents of social change?
- What are the key skills teachers need to become agents of change?

Further Reading

Bentall, C. (2020), 'Continuing Professional Development of Teachers of Global Learning: What Works?', in D. Bourn (ed.) *The Bloomsbury Handbook of Global Education and Learning*, 356–68, London: Bloomsbury.

Biesta, G., M. Priestley and S. Robinson (2015), 'The Role of Beliefs in Teacher Agency', *Teachers and Teaching*, 21, no. 6: 624–660.

Freire, P. (2005), *Teachers as Cultural Workers*, Cambridge, MA: Westview.

Fullan, M. (1993), 'Why Teachers Must Become Change Agents', *Educational Leadership*, 50, no. 6: 1–13.

Hansen, D. (2011), *The Teacher and the World*, Abingdon: Routledge.

Merryfield, M. (2009), 'Moving the Center of Global Education: From Imperial Worldviews That Divide the World to Double Consciousness, Contrapuntal Pedagogy, Hybridity, and Cross-Cultural Competence', in T. F. Kirkwood-Tucker (ed.), *Visions in Global Education*, 215–39, New York: Peter Lang.

Pantic, N. (2015), 'A Model for Study of Teacher Agency for Social Justice', *Teachers and Teaching*, 21, no. 6: 759–78.

Rubagiza, J., J. Umutoni and A. Kaleeba (2016), 'Teachers As Agents Of Change: Promoting Peacebuilding And Social Cohesion In Schools In Rwanda', *Education As Change*, 20, no. 3: 202–24.

9

Global Youth Work and Young People as Social Activists

Introduction

Young people have often been the focus of numerous policy initiatives, academic studies and bodies of practice related to social change (Furlong and Cartmel 2007; UNESCO 2014a). They have been central, for example, to the campaigns around the climate emergency. They have also been the focus of initiatives for change by various NGOs around the world on social justice themes and democracy such as in the Middle East, Hong Kong and North America. However, there is also evidence that a lot of the interest in engaging young people has had an activist rather than a learning focus. This chapter therefore reviews ways in which young people's engagement for social change can be, and has been, built upon a distinctive pedagogical approach. The challenges of the influence of social media will be discussed in terms of the extent to which it encourages an uncritical approach to engagement in global issues. Reference will be made to research looking at models of youth participation and engagement.

The chapter includes a review of research relevant to the theme of young people and social change. This includes the research on young people and social action by Pugh (2016) and the author's own research for an NGO project on Schools for Future Youth (Bourn 2016). Research by Sallah (2009, 2014, 2020a, 2020b) on global youth work will also be discussed.

The chapter concludes by looking at two examples of practice, the Woodcraft Folk and a range of initiatives with young people on the climate emergency campaign. Young people in this chapter are seen as covering the age group fourteen to twenty-one.

Impact of Globalization on Young People

Earlier chapters have identified the important impact globalization is having on the role and relationship of individuals to society. Young people experience global influences more than any other sector of society. They affect their employment opportunities, the friendship groups they develop, their use of the internet (particularly for social networking) and wider cultural influences on their lifestyle (Kenway and Bullen 2008). Young people are also the main targets of a global consumer culture (Dolby and Rizvi 2008). As can be seen from the climate emergency campaigns, many young people have a high degree of awareness and knowledge of global forces. Many of them are also conscious that it is upon their lives that the long-term impacts of climate change will be seen.

In response to the assumption that young people are merely the passive recipients of a global culture, Harvey (2003) has suggested that whilst they cannot control the speed or direction of social change, they can and do have a say on the effect such change has on their lives.

This engagement by young people is often influenced by the nature of their identity, their sense of place and the extent to which they feel they have a voice. For many of them around the world, their lives are related to school, college or the workplace and the extent to which they feel positive about their own future. Young people express their own identities shaped by an array of influences, in part as a defence mechanism in reaction to the rapidly changing world in which they are living, but also as a way of making statements about who they are and how they perceive themselves in relation to their peers and in their own community.

Young People and Social Change

The initiatives around the climate emergency have raised the need for a major re-evaluation of the ways in which young people seek social change. Whilst, as already noted, many young people are concerned about global issues and wish to see social changes, the role that education and learning more generally plays in this process of engagement needs further debate. It is evident is that many young people can gain the skills and knowledge they require to be effective campaigners on the climate emergency through the internet and social media. Training workshops have clearly been valuable but what has been different in recent years has been the ways in which young people have developed their own approaches to learning and forms of social action.

All too often in the past, structural forces have hindered effective youth engagement (Arches and Fleming 2006; Furlong and Cartmel 2007). There have been many attempts around the world to encourage and support youth participation, but time and again these are promoted in a vacuum outside of young peoples' real-life experiences. This tokenism can lead to a negative impact on young people because they could easily feel that they are not being valued (Bourn 2016).

As the climate emergency campaign shows, youth-led learning requires different skills and approaches. This also means more than merely promoting engagement through web-based initiatives.

There is a need therefore to consider what is meant by participation, engagement and social action, and it is to the literature on these areas that this chapter now turns.

Young People and Participation

I have elsewhere (Bourn 2016: 4) described participation by young people as:

> being actively involved in decision-making and taking action on issues relevant to them. Within formal education, this could be seen as encompassing a learner-centred and participative approach within both the formal curriculum and non-formal or informal learning.

For young people, participation should mean having the opportunities for their voices to be heard and the spaces to air their views. Lundy (2007) summarizes this as follows:

> Space by being given the opportunity to express a view in a safe space, free from the fear of rebuke or reprisal. These spaces should be inclusive and welcoming for all to participate.
> Voice: Opportunities to express their views, so long as they are capable of forming their own views.
> Audience: Their views must be listened to by those involved in and have ultimate influence over decision making processes. This might involve formalising channels of communication so that they could articulate their views.
> Influence: Recognition of the value of their views and acted upon where and when appropriate (Lundy 2007: 933–7; Hunt 2014).

However laudable these aims are, in practice things are often very different for young people. Spaces and opportunities for their voices to be heard are often restricted to marginal groups or framed within adult structures (Wyness 2009: 396; Bragg 2007: 344). Wierenga, Guevara and Beadle (2013: 201–202) in their research with young people in Australia and Indonesia identified the danger of youth participation being seen as tokenistic. They noticed that participation requires skills development, resourcing and support for all involved. All too often, they found that young people are not used to leading their own learning and that non-formal learning processes are often very different from formal education (ibid., 203).

The work of Mullahey, Susskind and Checkoway (1999) is particularly relevant here. They suggest that young people's work which focuses on individual learning and development, rather than on changing their surroundings, is not real participation. They propose that participation should not only give young people more control over their own lives and experiences but also grant them real influence over issues that are crucial to the quality of their own lives and of others in their communities. Through such experiences, they conclude, students learn how to use the technologies, but they also learn to understand power relationships, to be critical about assumptions, to speak the language (i.e. to use the discourse of the organizing systems), and generally, to get things done. In these learning environments, identity and agency are thus intertwined.

The evidence from the research (Bourn 2016) with young people who were engaged in a programme of learning about global issues was their awareness and sense of where they could influence change at both a local or a national level. Young people wanted to engage with issues but in ways that encouraged participatory forms of learning. Young people care about democracy but have little identification with the existing political systems and parties. To young people, social media has become one of the main forms not only of raising their views but of expressing their own identity (Trewby 2014).

This evidence also challenged the dominant European policy approach which had been that the problem was lack of youth engagement in society. The answer has been to provide representative bodies such as youth and schools councils, but their influence has been limited. Young people have, however, been far more effective as agents of social change through their use of social media and creating their own structures and ways of working (Birdwell and Bani 2014; Bourn 2016). As Gyoh (2015) has commented, young people have moved from spaces for voices to be heard to spaces where they also frame the narrative.

Youth Participation

In encouraging young people to become engaged in seeking change on global social issues, many civil society organizations have encouraged young people's involvement in their campaigns. However, research by Gyoh (2015) identified that there was a noticeable difference between NGOs which tended to seek support from young people for their campaigns and those that were clearly led by young people. Where initiatives were directly led by young people, there was also evidence of a more reflective and deeper learning process, gathering knowledge and data themselves and internalizing the value of this evidence.

This means that key to youth engagement for social change is the extent to which there is meaningful participation. In too many countries around the world where young people have had the opportunities to develop their skills, the response has been to encourage them to engage in what could be called more passive forms of social action (UNESCO 2012). This means just asking young people to sign petitions or being asked to join protests led by others.

This theme of the relationship between learning, behaviour and action has been raised by a number of academics. Young people in particular need to have positive experiences of acknowledgement, awareness and also agency, in order to give meaning to their experiences and establish linkages between the past, present and future (Jorgenson 2010). It is also a cognitive process with a complicated relationship between learning and behaviour (Bamber, Bullivant and Stead 2014) which needs to be mediated by knowledge. As Holden (2007) suggests, it is also important that the majority of young people feel they can do something to bring about positive change.

Young people's participation in campaigns such as Make Poverty History in the United Kingdom in 2005 is often cited as activities in which young people have become actively engaged. But, as noted elsewhere in this volume, such campaigning had little depth of engagement. What is meant by engagement is therefore a key question to ask.

One way of addressing this question is through looking at the example of young people's engagement in global and development issues at two levels (Bourn and Brown 2011). The first – and more shallow – level is usually seen in terms of transmitting or obtaining knowledge and information. A deeper level, and one relating learning to action, brings in a more critical understanding of the issues and suggests movement from being aware of an issue to one where there is a clear emotional attachment and willingness to do something.

However, as Asbrand and Scheunpflug (2006) have noted, there is a potential danger of what could be called an action theory–based paradigm where there is an assumed relationship between information, awareness and action.

The complex processes of learning were highlighted in the chapter on transformative learning earlier in this volume and the dangers of assuming that learning about an issue such as global poverty is going to lead to some form of social action can be seen in numerous research studies. For example, an in-depth study in the United Kingdom of sixteen-year-old to eighteen-year-old students who had taken a specific examination on World Development showed that the learning had an impact on their views about the wider world. For example, 20 per cent reported a significant impact on the conversations they had, their choice of reading material and their future plans (Miller et al. 2012: 35). There was also evidence that the learning had broadened their view of life and that they had become more aware of their actions, roles and responsibilities. Yet there was little evidence that their learning had increased their specific interest in taking further action to secure social change, to become involved in follow-up initiatives led by NGOs for example.

The relationship between learning and action was also identified as an issue in an evaluation of a UK NGO project Act Global, led by Relief International and the Citizenship Foundation. The report found that unless the project developed young people's skills to participate and take their learning forward, action was seen in rather altruistic terms or as unrelated to the learning. For example, in this project, a website was created for young people to take forward social action on issues they considered to be important. What they, in the end, took forward were issues and themes unrelated to the aims of the project that funded the website (Bourn 2012).

It is recognizing the close interplay of knowledge, skills and values and the extent to which the learner makes an emotional connection to the issue that can often be key to forms of social action. An acknowledgement of this can be seen in this European Aid–funded Global Education Project, *World-class Teaching*. This study identified the following factors to consider when encouraging young people to take action:

- Empowerment; students need to be aware of the influence they have as individuals and as a community.
- Motivation; young peoples' motivation could come from a sense of responsibility of being part of a global community.
- Capacity; ability to act and to change intentions into action (Leeds DEC 2013).

There is therefore a need to review how social action has been perceived and promoted within activities involving young people, and it is here that youth work can be seen as a valuable approach.

Young People and Social Action

One area within which the discussions on young people have moved beyond merely calling for participation has been within youth work and the promotion of 'social action'. This term is seen as 'young people taking practical action in the service of others . . . in order to create positive social change that is of benefit to the wider community as well as to the young person themselves' (National Youth Agency n.d.).

The agency noted from research they have undertaken that the most effective forms of social action come from long-term involvement and support from youth work professionals (National Youth Agency n.d.).

This approach, as Arches and Fleming (2006: 81) have commented, 'provides a valuable youth engagement strategy that emphasizes youth voice, participatory practice, and community building'.

One example in the United Kingdom of taking forward this approach is the *I Will Campaign*, which aims to make meaningful social action part of life for ten- to twenty-year-olds across the United Kingdom. To support this campaign, the National Youth Social Action research programme, conducted by Ipsos MORI, has been run annually since 2014. Its 2018 findings found:

> Young people are eager to make a difference in society; the vast majority care about making the world a better place; and believe they can make a difference. This sense of agency in relation to society is associated with higher levels of participation in meaningful social action. (Knibbs et al. 2018: 1)

The research also identified a strong linkage between 'agency within the school environment and participation in meaningful social action'. 'Meaningful social action' is defined as those who have: participated at least every few months over the last twelve months in social action or been involved in a one-off activity lasting more than a day; and recognize that their activities had some benefit for both themselves and others. There was evidence that young people continue to be interested in taking action although the level of involvement varied with only three in ten stating that it could be classified as 'committed' (ibid.).

Amongst the barriers to involvement, lack of knowledge was the most evident one particularly in terms of not knowing how to get involved. What was also noticeable from the research was that 'Fundraising or a sponsored event' were the most common forms of social action.

The support for social action within youth work in the United Kingdom has been evident for many years (Birdwell, Birnie and Mehan 2013), and the chief executive of the leading youth body in England noted:

> we know that young people are more likely to engage in social action, and to continue involvement in it if it is in something they're really interested in. Incorporating youth social action which builds on young people's interests into youth work therefore allows young people to own a project and to shape it around something that is already important to them. Doing this is a sure-fire way to increase the chances of good outcomes and long-term engagement
> – Leigh Middleton, National Youth Agency CEO. (National Youth Agency 2018)

Youth social action is seen therefore as a way of not only encouraging young people to engage in their community, but to learn about how this involvement can develop their own skills and confidence and also have an impact as a result of their endeavours.

What is less evident from the research and studies on youth social action is their connections to movements and goals of combating injustices and inequalities in the world. Where there has been engagement by young people in such initiatives, they have tended to take place outside of formal structures. This can, for example, be seen in the climate emergency campaigns. This theme is discussed further later in this chapter but beforehand, it is appropriate to consider a different approach from North America which uses a youth development methodology.

Youth Development and Social Justice

Throughout the latter part of the twentieth century and the first decades of the twenty-first, many of the policy initiatives regarding young people were related to addressing what were seen as the 'problematic nature' of young people and their lack of engagement in society. The limitations of many youth development frameworks were due to seeking short-term and quick solutions to the challenges many young people face: being marginalized, direct impact of racism, sexism and inequality in their lives and the lack of spaces to articulate their voices (Ginwright and Cammarota 2002; Thomas, Davidson and McAdoo 2008; Watts and Flanagan 2007).

Kirshner's (2008) study explores the ways in which adults work with young people to secure a sense of social justice. He identified four principles for promoting youth civic activism: start with an authentic social issue, provide meaningful exposure to well-developed civic practices, be responsive to the skill levels and interests of youth and address continuity issues in youth participation beyond the academic calendar.

Kirshner's (2009) later study showed two apparently oppositional themes of youth engagement. One being self-interest and the other being the sense of recognizing the value of working together to secure change. Whilst they do not have to be oppositional, what Kirshner further identified was that self-interest may be the starting point but through interaction with others, collective action could emerge.

This model of youth development is seen as a more holistic approach that brings together individual, interpersonal and collective well-being. It can be applied in a form that encourages young people to be active agents in not only their own personal and social development, but in their contribution to social change. But this approach, developed in the United States, has been criticized by Atkinson (2012) and others (Ginwright and Cammarota 2002) for not addressing the oppression that many young people face. A response to this, developed by Shawn Ginwright, was to posit a Social Justice Youth Development (SJYD) model that directly addresses the broader social context for youth development (Ginwright and Cammarota 2002). This approach brought in themes such as social and political competencies that could help young people to be more actively engaged in social change processes (Ginwright and James 2002).

This approach had three distinct stages of development from self-awareness related to identity formation, to social awareness where young people developed skills to critically reflect on issues that affected them and to a global level where they developed a sense of empathy and belief in social changes and a sense of international solidarity (Ginwright and Cammarota 2002; Atkinson 2012: 29).

There are other models such as Jennings et al. (2006), who identify a number of dimensions that can inform a Critical Youth Empowerment (CYE) model. These dimensions are (1) safe, supportive environments, (2) meaningful participation, (3) shared power, (4) individual and community orientation, (5) sociopolitical change goals and (6) critical reflection.

There is evidence, however, which suggests that by organizing projects themselves, young people find a safe place to participate and in engage social action. By organizing themselves, they can develop the skills on how to take collective action. This engagement can often lead to long-term commitment to social change activities, and the participation by young people can increase their educational motivations and aspirations for their future (Atkinson 2012: 37; Shah 2011).

Contribution of Youth Work as Agents for Change

Within the UK context, whilst the term 'social action' rather than youth development has been used, there is a long tradition of a more structured approach that supports the personal and social development of young people. This includes the voluntary-led uniform-based organizations such as the Scouts, Guides and Boys Brigade to more informal-based approaches located in structures such as youth clubs. One example of this, the Woodcraft Folk, is discussed later in this chapter.

However, whilst there was support and engagement for youth work having a broader social purpose in the United Kingdom, in the late twentieth and early decades of the twenty-first century, its practice, as indicated earlier, has become dominated by addressing what were seen as social problems with young people such as drugs, juvenile crime, lack of employment opportunities, marginalized groups or dealing with so-called extremism. This approach provided minimal opportunities for young people to not only challenge this model but engage in forms of social action to address their concerns and needs.

Various models were introduced in England in the second decade of the twenty-first century such as the National Citizenship Service, but this only reinforced an approach based on individual and often charitable based ways of working.

However, at a broader European level, a range of projects and initiatives have encouraged and supported youth work as agents for social change. One example is SALTO Youth, a network of resource centres funded by the European Commission that has developed a Tools for Learning website which includes resources on racism, creative approaches and game design. One of the articles linked to this initiative by Jalonen and Chaudry (2016: 1) on *Youth Workers as Agents of Change* stated:

> It is time for the youth workers to be brave again! We need to recall the radical traditions of youth work. We can support the youth to understand the unequal power structures in society and what they can do if they want to challenge the socio-political status quo. In order to do that, firstly we need to reflect whether we want to uphold the existing unequal power structures or are we ready to

challenge them? Is youth work today aspiring to those core values and ideals or has institutionalization of youth work made us servants of the state rather than change makers? Whose purpose does this serve?

They identified that there was a connection between building communities and addressing existing power structures and privileges. They learnt this particularly from a project in Sri Lanka on how to listen to different perspectives and 'help them to make sense of their realities and their role in society. Only then we can support the young people to use their power and ability to create alliances to facilitate change in their realities'.

For Jalonen and Chaudry, the core values of youth work need to include 'critical dialogue, equality of opportunity, respect' and voluntary participation. The role of the youth worker is, they suggest, to act as 'a catalyst for change and empower young people to lead and take actions on the issues that matter to them' (ibid.).

Global Youth Work

One example of an approach that addresses themes identified by Jalonen and Chaudry and provides appropriate support mechanisms, relevant expertise and potential space for young people to experiment and develop their own ideas and approaches to making a more just world, has been 'Global Youth Work'. This approach has been seen as informal education with young people that encourages a critical understanding of the links between the personal, the local and the global and seeks their active participation in actions that bring about change towards greater equality and justice. This approach emerged out of research by Bourn and McCollum (1995) and was further developed by Think Global, formerly the Development Education Association through their Global Youth Action Programme, which ran from 2010 to 2015. This programme identified a reflective practice model entitled Connect, Challenge, Change (CCC). The programme aimed to:

> help connect young people to the global issues that matter to them. We support them to make the connections between the personal, local and global, and to connect with peers who share their passions and concerns. We encourage young people to challenge themselves, to gain a more critical understanding of the world around them, and to challenge inequality and injustice. We support young people to plan and take action to bring about positive change towards a more just and sustainable world. (Williams and Edleston 2010: 3)

This approach to youth work was further developed by Y Care International and through a range of articles by Adams (2014) and Sallah (2009; 2020a, 2020b). Sallah (2014) grounded global youth work on the following:

- Concern with how the concept and process of globalization impacts on young people's realities.
- Based on the principles of informal education and youth work.
- Located in young people's realities.
- Challenging oppression and promotes social justice.
- Promoting consciousness and action.

Reflecting the influence of Freire and others, Sallah (2014: 80) suggested that global youth work should:

> provoke young people's consciousness. It is not about analysing and giving young people a to-do list but rather a dialogical approach where both practitioner and young people are teachers and learners, actors and doers symbiotically and simultaneously. It is one with the object of synthesising young people's existence with their lived realities.

The value of this approach is that it combines learning with forms of social action and locates its methodology from a starting point of the interests and concerns of young people. It does not try to preach a particular perspective but aims to encourage young people to reflect on their situation, views about the world and personal experiences. From further learning and engagement with issues, the young people could identify ways they could take action. It is an approach that brings together the social action and youth development social justice model outlined earlier but within the context of youth work.

Young People Taking Action for Change

As a result of the social movements led by young people and the profile many of these youth-led campaigns have had during the second decade of the twenty-first century, it is not therefore surprising that the focus of the 2020 International Youth Day on August 12 was celebrating 'Youth Engagement for Global Action'. This day encouraged action at local, national and global levels (United Nations 2020).

The combination of the impact of the climate emergency campaign and the use of social media have shown that young people can not only create their own methods for raising awareness and understanding; the role and relationship they might have to adult-led movements has to change. It has been estimated that in the United Kingdom today over 90 per cent of young people between the ages of fifteen to nineteen use social media every day. Most of them are members of various social media platforms, and it is through them that they get most of their knowledge about current affairs and issues that might encourage further involvement. It is also a place where they can freely express their views and join relevant interest groups (Bullies Out 2019).

What this and various other initiatives in recent years have emphasized is the potential importance of the youth voice which has begun to move on from the themes and comments made earlier in this chapter. What has also been evident is the ways that a number of these initiatives have connected to broader movements against social oppression, be it against people of colour or of a different sexual orientation or gender:

> Social change is about shifting negative dynamics, and it's important to remember how issues are connected. Oppression takes place whenever one group has power over another, and often includes inequality, silenced voices, and abuse of power. Oppression can be based on race, gender identity or expression, sexual orientation, abilities or disabilities, age, education or income, or other parts of people's identities. Working toward positive social change means challenging oppression. (NSVRC 2014: 2–4)

As outlined in earlier chapters, linking social change with combating oppression has been a theme of numerous initiatives involving young people and that connects to themes such as liberation and social justice. However, what is often missing from these calls for action by young people is the research and evidence on the processes of their engagement in global social issues, the learning journey they have been on and the extent to which their views are heard.

Research on Young People and Social Change

Three examples of research on young people and social change are now considered from very different perspectives. The first is Katherine Pugh's master's-level study on youth-led initiatives for social action which compares two examples from the United Kingdom with two from Brazil. Secondly, there is Trewby's doctoral study, which takes a narrative-based approach with young social activists, on 'Journeys to Engagement'. Finally, there is Son Gyoh's doctoral research, which looks at how knowledge is constructed and applied within a number of NGOs including youth-led organizations, and it is these organizations that are here reviewed.

Pugh's study (2016) was on: 'To what extent does participation in social action projects enable development of global skills in young people in Brazil and England?'

The research examined what Pugh termed 'Meaningful Social Action' projects across Brazil and England. The two in Brazil were Engajamundo, which is a national advocacy network with more than 600 young people campaigning and raising awareness about social and environmental challenges, and Favela Street, which uses football as a forum to tackle local challenges and injustices. In the United Kingdom, one of the projects was 'Find Your Smile' run by Fixers. This organization, which sadly no longer exists, facilitated individuals to have a positive experience and address the challenges surrounding them. The other was OxCoop, which exists under the umbrella of Student Hubs, and enables students to tackle social challenges and create a positive change with the skills to become active citizens.

Pugh's research with youth projects in Brazil and the United Kingdom found that social action had to be 'meaningful' and relevant to the young people's own experiences. She found skills development to be an important component of young people's learning journey. She found that young people saw meaningful social action as part of their desire to change the world, to fight injustices and promote positive solutions. For young people to be effective agents for change, Pugh suggested they needed the training and opportunities for skills development. She notes:

> Social action refers to a multi-step process whereby citizens address an issue they are passionate about, grow in understanding and seek solutions to solve it. In recent times, as digital technology has become more widely available worldwide, citizen movements have grown significantly as a means to engage activists. (ibid., 8)

From Pugh's research, a number of themes emerge, which are relevant to debates in this chapter. First of all, the evidence identified the passion and enthusiasm from the young people to secure social change: 'I felt I should stop this injustice that is happening' (ibid., 29). What she also identified was the different perception of young people she gained compared with that of the media:

> The young people in my research utilise their interests and expertise for the greater good and help dispel the widely accepted opinion painted by the media, who often portray young people as lazy and a nuisance. (ibid., 29)

Motivation, as noted earlier in this chapter, was a key factor in securing high levels of participation. To the young people, meaningful social action meant social development, having a voice, securing change and fighting injustice. A focus of Pugh's study was skills development needs, and in this she found *decision-making, problem-solving, personal social responsibility, communication, teamwork* and *leadership* as most important.

Participants in Pugh's research stated that 'they wanted to make change happen which inspired them as young people to contribute to and combat global challenges. In so doing, the projects provided them with the opportunity to both influence and create change' (ibid., 38).

To summarize her approach, Pugh produced a diagram, entitled River of Transformative Participation, which highlights that through a combination of truly Meaningful Social Action and young people's skills development, young people are equipped to deal with a number of global challenges and, in some cases, contribute to the journey of other participants. It is clear that the skills prioritized by young people and displayed during their activities are similar to those valued by employers and policymakers.

In conclusion, what was evident from Pugh's research was the clear focus from the participants on wanting to change the world. The research also identified the ways in which young people were able to develop wider community empathy, and she noted 'that the participation in social action helps the young people

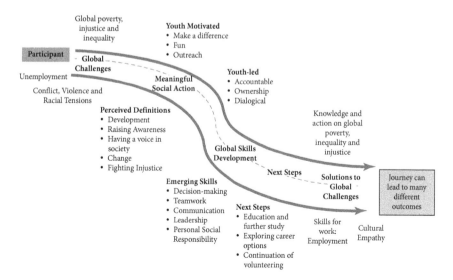

Figure 9.1 River of transformative participation.

to look outward, regardless of their initial motivations, and establish a greater cultural awareness, locally and beyond' (ibid., 44).

Trewby's (2014) doctoral research explores how a grouping of individuals in the United Kingdom came to, and sustained engagement with, global justice issues. His thesis developed a new conceptual framework for understanding forms of engagement and summarized knowledge about individuals' journeys to engagement. A feature of his research was the ways in which the young people acted as multipliers of engagement.

The relevance of Trewby's research to the themes outlined in this chapter is primarily twofold: firstly, his approach to what is meant by engagement and his theoretical approach to 'journeys to engagement'; secondly, the stories from the young people and the differing and complex ways in which they become involved in forms of social action and changed their plans.

With regard to 'forms of engagement', Trewby notes that there is no set model or boundaries of forms of engagement. He did however note that some form of continuum might be useful in terms of areas such as low cost and high cost; low risk and high risk; non-political and political; conventional and unconventional; individual and collective.

A key interest for Trewby, and one that has already been raised in this chapter, is that of motivation, to understand young people's reasons for engagement. From his review and analysis of the literature, and reinforced from the interviews with the young people, were the following pre-conditions. The first identified was knowledge of injustice. But as Trewby notes, this does not guarantee behaviour change and action. He noted, however, an important caveat that knowledge of the issues could be interpreted as 'belief in the existence of the issues'. The second precondition Trewby identified was 'an individual's belief that they are able to become engaged' in forms of social action (ibid., 36). The third is that becoming engaged would make a difference, that 'yes we can'.

What was evident from Trewby's research was that although education can play an important role in the construction of these beliefs, the reality was much more complex and involved a range of personal, family, cultural and experiential factors. Role models, current fashions and the influence of celebrities were factors that also need to be considered. In taking on a deeper form of engagement, Trewby saw the importance of an activist identity and how this influenced the nature and the long-term commitment a young person had towards campaigning for social change.

An important part of Trewby's evidence for the themes outlined in this volume is that his interviewees provided a number of examples of 'learning through doing'. Whilst all of Trewby's research was looking at individual journeys to engagement, a feature of the forms of social action the interviewees took was that it tended to be part of some form of collective and group-based movement. Exposure to broader social experiences, particularly if they were overseas, was seen as significant in terms of their personal development. This could take a variety of forms and take place at different times in their lives but there was evidence from all of them of a process of reflection and questioning assumptions. This relates to a broader theme from Trewby's research of the need by all of the interviewees for having the space to take 'time out', to reflect and to develop their own individual learning.

Trewby's research also raises questions about the role of identity in the construction of journeys to engagement. Every person has a different biographical story to tell but what was evident from the research was that identities related to opportunities and choices for what and how to engage.

Finally, what Trewby's research also showed was the value of his theoretical model of a continuum of risk and forms of engagement rather than overly simplified dichotomies. He found that engagement in 'low risk' activities such as fundraising might play a part in developing commitment and a sense of empowerment.

Son Gyoh's research looks at international NGOs and student-led movements and the ways in which they gain the knowledge to implement their campaigns and the role that a process of learning has. His research with student-led organizations was focused on People and Planet, a campaigning organization with a focus on global social justice and sustainability issues and Medsin, a network of young health professionals with a focus on global matters which is now called Students for Global Health.[1]

His research identified some themes that showed the distinctive ways students engaged with their organization as compared with being part of an International NGO. One of the distinctive features of the activities of these student-led organizations can be seen in this quotation from Gyoh's research from a member of the People and Planet management committee:

> I think involving young people empowers them in the decision process . . . other big NGOs concentrate on training people on how to do campaigns, but we get young people involved in all the processes. If you are to generate their ideas, it will help them get more confidence in life. (ibid.,133)

The research also identified that the young people who became involved had a passion and enthusiasm for global social justice. For many of the young people involved with the organizations, Gyoh found that they saw a close relationship between education and advocacy. 'In running the campaign, you need to educate members on the issue before they engage in advocacy.' What was also significant about People and Planet was that decision-making on campaigns was decided democratically through their annual meetings.

Another distinctive feature of his research was the identification of how knowledge was constructed and used. As one student said, 'we want to empower the activist with the knowledge to be knowledgeable' (ibid., 168). This meant that what they undertook was knowledge-based advocacy. This means that rather than directly trying to change policy, the role of the organization was to influence the forces that have an impact on policy formation. This meant that the role of the organization was to act as mediators, to provide their young campaigners with the tools to act as knowledge producers.

As Gyoh noted:

> The student-led organisations . . . framed their campaigning on social justice rather than humanitarian compassion and used protest images to provoke deliberation and questioning. Campaigning was also seen as nurturing and sustaining a network of activists that can influence their peers and by extension, public perception. (ibid., 141)

His research also noted the power and influence of the internet and the role social media played with the organizations.

Gyoh identified that for the student-led organizations, campaigning was considered as a 'form of advocacy that enables pluralism and the collaboration between knowledgeable actors. Campaigners were seen as repertoires of knowledge on the conflict issue, and were therefore, involved at the different levels of framing and communicating the knowledge' (ibid., 149).

The research by Gyoh is significant for the themes addressed in this chapter because they demonstrate how young people saw the connection between learning and action. In addition, the evidence also reinforced the themes addressed earlier regarding the importance and value of the independent youth voice. It is clear from Gyoh's research that, by maximizing the young people's commitment and enthusiasm for global justice issues, knowledge-based advocacy can be effective.

Each of these research studies, Pugh, Trewby and Gyoh, identified the complex relationship between learning, experience and social action. What they showed was that education for social change has to include a recognition of the different and multifaceted journeys young people make that might lead to forms of social action. Their research also showed that campaigning and advocacy has to be built upon a strong knowledge base that can empower young people to take their learning forward.

Case Studies

There are many case studies that could be taken as examples of good practice with young people and social change. The rationale for the two taken here is that the Woodcraft Folk, probably longer than any other youth organization in the United Kingdom, has had education for social change as part of its aims and principles. Secondly, the initiatives around the climate emergency demonstrate the ways in which young people are now taking ownership themselves of how to secure change rather than looking directly to adult organizations.

Woodcraft Folk

One of the leading youth organizations in the United Kingdom that has put into practice the concept of global youth work and relating it to seeking social change has been the Woodcraft Folk. This organization, for whom I worked between 1977 and 1990, was formed in 1925, and although it has remained rather small in comparison with similar bodies such as the Scouts and Guides, it has consistently put the promotion of learning for a more just and sustainable world at its heart (Palser 2020). It has had clear educational principles which emphasize social change:

> We seek to develop in our members a critical awareness of the world. We will work to develop the knowledge, attitudes, values and skills necessary for them to act to secure their equal participation in the democratic process that will enable them to bring about the changes that they feel are necessary to create a more equal and caring world. As an educational movement, we believe that equal opportunities should extend to all aspects of activity and participation in the Woodcraft Folk. We will combat oppression or discrimination in our movement, whether on grounds of age, class, gender, race, sexual orientation or for reasons of disability. We will educate our members so that they may take these issues into the wider community. (Woodcraft Folk 2013: 3)

Its aims and principles also include the following:

a co-operative and sharing attitude to life; international understanding; the rights of the child; one world; a world at peace. Central to all of the activities of the Woodcraft Folk 'is the cultivation of a world outlook'.

The organization is based around locally run groups for different ages between four and sixteen. It is co-educational, non-religious and based around weekly group nights and outdoor activities such as camping. Through these activities it aims to help its young people:

- Understand important issues like the environment, world debt and global conflict.
- Develop activities focused on sustainable development.
- Encourage children to think, hoping that they will help build a peaceful, fairer world (Woodcraft Folk n.d.).

Putting these social change goals into practice could appear to be idealistic. But as can be seen from the following examples, the organization is conscious of grounding these aims within relevant age group activities:

- Six- to nine-year-olds: including learning about how to participate in making decisions by voting on which game to play at the end of the session and discussing the world critically through news at circle time.
- Ten- twelve-year-olds: including understanding the nature, needs and challenges of their community by choosing a local cause to support through fundraising.
- Thirteen- to fifteen-year-olds: including initiate and lead social action activities by running their own campaign to lobby their local council for better facilities for young people; also to have a positive impact locally and globally by volunteering to support asylum seekers in their area (Woodcraft Folk n.d.).

A feature of the Woodcraft Folk's educational priorities has been to empower 'children and young people, supporting them to engage in decision-making at all ages as well as enabling them to have their voices heard on the issues which matter to them'. This reflects some of the themes around youth engagement identified earlier in this chapter. This includes to 'take action on issues important to young people' and to 'demonstrate international solidarity'.

Reflecting themes mentioned earlier in this chapter regarding social action, the Woodcraft Folk uses the term as a way of encouraging the value of collective endeavours, 'social action makes us feel less powerless' and meet 'other people who share our same values and who had similar experiences as us', 'learn new things and change perspectives' (Woodcraft Folk 2020).

It is an organization that provides a progressive alternative to many dominant societal views. Above all, its encouragement and support for young people participating in campaigns comes out of the educational activities it provides and the whole ethos upon which it organizes all of its work.

Young People and Climate Action

Undoubtedly one of the major movements for change led by young people in 2019 and 2020 has been for action on climate change. Inspired by the practices of the Swedish activist Greta Thunberg, hundreds of thousands of young people around the world have been mobilized to encourage policymakers to directly address the emergency of climate change. The year 2019 was regarded as the year of young people taking action for the climate, with millions of them around the world taking to the streets for the Global Climate Strike.

The range of initiatives on climate change have also posed questions about the relationship of awareness-raising to learning and building an informed constituency of support and engagement that can influence policymakers. An initial reading of the campaign could suggest that what has been important in this campaign has been the use of simple messages, the power of social media and the value of gathering an emotive response from young people.

Walker (2017) had raised some of the issues around the dangers of seeing such initiatives in a simplistic way. She noted that in too many campaigns for social action there had been too much of an emphasis on relating awareness-raising to behavioural change – called the ABC model where A stands for Attitude, B for behaviour and C for Choice (see also Shove, Pantzar and Watson 2012: 2). The limitations of this mechanistic approach to learning and action had also been criticized by a range of academics (Hobson 2013; Middlemiss 2014; Kollmuss and Agyeman 2002).

What is suggested here instead is the need to look more closely at what the climate justice campaign tells us about young people, learning and social change. It has been noted for more than a decade that many children and young people have greater awareness and understanding of climate change themes than other sectors of society (UNICEF 2008: 29), and this has had an effect on their parents and peers (Bartiaux 2009; Percy-Smith and Burns 2013: 333; Walker 2016).

In many societies, young people have also been at the forefront of using social media not only for personal friendship groups but as a way of engaging their peers in social causes. In societies where young people have instant access to the internet and social media, they are capable of mobilizing and engaging many thousands of their peers in social action, as can be seen through their endeavours around climate change. Alongside this use of social media has been their ability to make use of educational resources that have been produced to facilitate their social action. Some of these resources have been produced specifically for the school classroom (Centre for Alternative Technology 2020), whilst others are related more to enabling young people to be more effective in their campaigns (British Youth Council 2020).

These examples show the close relationship between young people's interest and enthusiasm and their learning, which can help them develop their knowledge and skills to take their engagement further. What is evident is that the campaigning of Greta Thunberg and others have not only raised the profile of climate change, they have suggested forms of social action in a way that responds to and empowers young people.

An example in the United Kingdom that shows this change in approach is how UNICEF UK has supported young people on the issue of climate change. Whilst the organization internationally had developed a web platform 'voices for youth' (UNICEF n.d.), this was taken a step further in the United Kingdom through its Outright initiative. This initiative supported school children and young people to engage in campaigns around climate change. It has a particular focus in the calendar year from September to November. What is significant about the approaches taken within Outright has been that, unlike climate change initiatives by some other organizations, UNICEF UK have encouraged a more enquiry-led approach, offering suggestions and posing questions, such as: What changes would you like to see made? This approach is also aided by UNICEF's primary focus which is children's rights, and, as suggested in other chapters in this volume, this is valuable in enabling a more educationally based campaign (UNICEF UK 2020a).

Alongside this work, UNICEF developed a more generic Youth Advocacy Toolkit, which is about 'supporting young people to speak up and helping them actively take part in the decisions that affect them'. This toolkit has the following pedagogical approach:

Explore: identify the problem in terms of what needs to change. Outline your vision and research and analyse the issue.
Think: what steps need to be taken to progress the issue and identify who has the power and who can make a difference.
Act: what do you need to do and what do you need to say and devise an advocacy plan.
Evaluate: what were the lessons from the actions? (UNICEF UK 2020b: 3)

Another example that demonstrates what a youth-led movement means in practice is SustainUS,[2] based in the United States, who have trained several thousand young people to be advocates for global environmental justice. This organization clearly links campaigns around climate change to broader social justice issues for global change as can be seen from their Sustaining Our Resistance network:

> Sustaining Our Resistance is a collective of SustainUS members that offer peer-to-peer, popular education trainings for youth activists and organizations seeking skills and processes to further their social change goals. Our purpose as a collective is to support one another in delivering empowering, transformative training experiences for youth activists in line with the SustainUS principles. (SustainUs 2020a)

This network frames its activities around climate change not only around social justice but as part of global social movements against oppression and inequalities around the world.

A feature of the network is to lobby international bodies such as the UN from an informed position. They put a lot of emphasis in their network to training and support for young people using particularly arts-based approaches and understanding concerns of indigenous communities. This Sustaining Our Resistance approach aims to empower young people through transformative training experiences to be activists for social change (SustainUs 2020b).

Finally, the third example of models of youth engagement is the Student Climate Network in the UK (UKSCN). There are many similar models to this elsewhere in the world but what UKSCN demonstrates is a clear connection in their activities between education and campaigning. Its demands include not only calling to 'save the future' but also 'teach the future' and 'tell the future'. But like other networks and themes identified throughout this chapter, the Student Climate Network's fourth demand is 'empower the future' by calling on young people to be included in policymaking (UKSCN 2020a).

Reflecting themes from SustainUs, UKSCN relates campaigns on climate change to broader social justice issues, challenging oppression and recognizing the need to be inclusive to all who share the aims of the Network. The aims of the network also reflect the importance of critical thinking and listening to different viewpoints:

> When we are challenged we agree to listen and reflect on what we are being told, even if we disagree.
>
> We work to create an environment where it is okay to ask if we don't understand something, and where a wide range of different ways to learn are available. We

are all responsible for our own education and for sharing what we have learned with others. (UKSCN 2020b)

An example of the impact of the climate campaign and the strikes many young people have undertaken can be seen from this blog from Emily, who comes from a small English town, Matlock in Derbyshire. Like many young people who became involved in the campaign, she said she had always had a passion for environmental matters but had never considered herself 'confident or rebellious enough to protest'. She took part in a march in London, and this became 'one of the most empowering experiences of my life. Although I was only one of thousands, I felt like I could really make a difference and help change the world for the better'. From this she set up a local group in her home town and started to influence local policymakers (UKSCN 2002c).

What is clear from these examples around climate justice is that with young people's engagement in social issues, if it relates closely to their own experiences and interests and is led by them, there is a likelihood of not only greater impact but a more informed young populace.

Conclusion

These examples reinforce themes discussed elsewhere in this and other chapters in this volume about the relationship of lived experiences to learning and social change. What is also significant from these case studies and the evidence from the research is the role that education and learning in its broadest sense has played in the process of their journey to engagement and social action.

This chapter has reviewed the research and examples of practice of youth involvement in initiatives for global social change. It has identified that key questions to consider are what is meant by participation and social change. The evidence from the research also suggests that where learning and skills development are central to any campaign or initiative, then it is likely to have more lasting impact.

The role of youth organizations, and particularly organizations supportive of the concept of global youth work, can provide some valuable models of practice that could be applied more widely. Finally, the campaigns around the climate emergency have clearly, in some organizations, led to a fundamental rethink as to their role in working with young people, moving from a top-down approach to a facilitating and empowering model.

Questions for Further Consideration

- What are the prerequisites for young people's engagement in campaigns for global social change?
- What are the lessons from the evidence of the research on youth participation in Europe?
- What is the relationship between participation, social action and social change?
- In what ways can global youth work contribute to youth initiatives for global social change?
- What is significant about the youth-led campaigns around the climate emergency for the discourses around young people and social change?

Further Reading

Birdwell, J. and M. Bani (2014), *Introducing Generation Citizen*, London: Demos.

Ginwright, S. and J. Cammarota (2002), 'New terrain in youth development: The promise of a social justice approach', *Social Justice*, 29, no. 4: 82–95.

Lundy, L. (2007) '"Voice" is not enough: conceptualising Article 12 of the United Nations Convention on the Rights of the Child', *British Educational Research Journal*, 33, no. 6: 827–942.

Sallah, M. (2014), *Global Youth Work: Provoking Consciousness and Taking Action*, Lyme Regis: Russell House Publishing.

UNICEF UK (2020), *Youth Advocacy Toolkit*, London: UNICEF UK.

Walker, C. (2017), 'Tomorrow's Leaders and Today's Agents of Change? Children, Sustainability Education and Environmental Governance', *Children & Society*, 31: 72–83.

10

The Role of the Academic Tutor

Introduction

In 2015, Professor Peter Scott from UCL in the United Kingdom stated that universities were increasingly losing their 'sense of public responsibility and wider social purpose' (Scott 2015). Whilst there may be some truth in what Professor Scott has said, the purpose of this chapter is to look specifically at where universities, and in particular academics within them, are addressing a social purpose and where this relates to consideration of education for social change. The focus in this chapter is therefore on the academic in terms of their role primarily as an educator, a tutor for students, be it at undergraduate or postgraduate level, and their contribution to broader university life and policies that are relevant to changing needs of societies.

The chapter begins by reviewing the changing nature of higher education and the role of academics therein. It then discusses the extent to which universities and academics have, and can promote, a sense of social justice and how this relates to debates around the concept of 'public good'. The role of the academic tutor as an agent for social change is then reviewed particularly in the context of their pedagogical role. The chapter surveys evidence from literature, policy and research on sustainability and global citizenship within higher education and how this relates to transformative learning and social change. The chapter then looks at specific examples from research, taken from doctoral theses of students I have supervised, in terms of the personal biographies and outlooks of individual academics and the nature of a curriculum for global citizenship. With regard to examples of practice, the chapter reviews two examples which demonstrate a change element. The first looks at the range of initiatives and approaches at Walden University in the United States and the second is from the National University of Agriculture in Slovakia.

Changing Nature and Role of Higher Education

Higher education institutions around the world have grown in number and size in response to societies increasingly emphasizing the importance of the 'knowledge economy' within the evolving globally hegemonic influence of neoliberalism. This has meant not only an increase in courses, staffing and students, but posed questions as to what the purpose of the university is. No longer are universities in most countries around the world places for a very small, privileged elite. Their role in relation to the needs of the economy, intellectual development and expanding students' learning experiences have changed. Whilst universities have tended to follow the three common characteristics of teaching, research and community engagement, what do these three elements mean in practice and which are given greater prominence and recognition?

McCowan (2019: 62–4) identified four types of universities: Medieval, Humboldtian, Developmental and Entrepreneurial. The Medieval type is seen as one based around transmission of knowledge and belief in the value of study in itself. The Humboldtian, reflecting traditions from the European Enlightenment, emphasized knowledge in terms of the pursuit of truth and academic freedom. The Developmental has as its main focus the relationship of learning to economic development with an emphasis on vocationally based degrees. Finally, Entrepreneurial is seen as a direct response to neoliberalism with an emphasis on competing in a global marketplace of higher education with close linkages to the corporate world.

Universities, regardless of the above categorizations, have also seen their role change in ideological terms. They have remained places that reproduce dominant bodies of knowledge, educate future elites and 'leaders' of society and train the future workforce (Castells 2001). But they have also become sites of ideological and cultural struggle. This has meant that universities have allowed and encouraged dissenting voices which have as a result posed ideological contradictions (Torres and Mitchell 1998). Case (2017) notes there are examples that demonstrate how academics have made a conscious decision to promote social justice as an antidote to the dominance of neoliberal and marketization influences.

Many universities around the world are conscious of these tensions, and debates on these issues pose questions as to the extent to which they aim to have a social change agenda. As Rouse suggests (2011):

> as our socio-political and socio-cultural societies attempt to coexist in an
> equitable world, higher education must be called upon, as transformative agents,
> to lead this social change endeavour. (p. 51)

She further suggests that when academics make use of a critical perspectives approach, they can not only critique existing social issues but provide a transformative agenda that encourages social change (ibid.).

What is more evident within many universities, however, is the way in which this social purpose is reframed in terms of 'public and common good'.

The University's Social Purpose and Search for Common Good

The term 'public good' has been promoted as a way of posing the need for universities to consider their wider societal role related to participation and challenging social inequalities. Marginson (2016) notes it has been used with an economic slant with universities playing a role in improving local or national economies. Instead Marginson suggests using the concept 'common good': 'providing equal opportunity for as many as possible in the interest of a more rights-based, egalitarian, and cohesive society'. He further suggests that this term should also be seen as a 'global common good', as universities have to operate within the context of globalization (UNESCO 2018).

A number of universities and colleges, in promoting this theme of the common good, often relate it to contributing to positive social change. Examples from the United States include Boston University in the Northeast United States, which has proclaimed, 'Changing the world is part of our identity' (Boston University n.d.), and Stanford University (2017) in the West, which identifies amongst its purposes 'to promote the public welfare by exercising an influence in behalf of humanity and civilisation'. As Yob (2018) has noted, although there are cultural differences in the motivation for social change and the context for becoming engaged, many institutions of higher education around the world have embraced similar purposes and missions.

This has meant that the promotion of the term 'the common good' is seen to include not only knowledge development and research, but also ensuring it contributes to addressing the societal issues of the day.

Brennan (2008), in discussing the term 'common good', identified societal roles for higher education institutions as constructing a knowledge society that is just, stable and critical. Concerning the last point, the issue is the extent to which universities recognize and enable dissension and competing voices and provide the 'critical space' for controversial ideas.

An important voice on these questions is Henry Giroux. He has written extensively about the dangers of economic influences within higher education, what he has called its 'vocationalisation' (Giroux and Bosio, 2021). He has stated that the 'incursion of corporate and military culture into university life undermines the university's responsibility to provide students with an education that allows them to recognize the dream and promise of a substantive democracy' (Ibid., 8). Giroux calls for educators to 'rethink the space of the social and to develop a critical language in which notions of the public good become, public issues, and public life become central to overcoming the privatizing and depoliticizing language of the market' (Ibid., 9). This theme of the broader social purpose of higher education is one that Giroux has highlighted for many years, including the ideological and political struggle within which universities operate. To Giroux, 'education is not only about issues of work and economics, but also questions of justice, social freedom, and the capacity for democratic agency, action, and change as well as the related issues of power, exclusion and citizenship' (Giroux, 2006 : 270).

This space for academic freedom and a recognition of the social and ideological role universities play is therefore central to any discussion of the role of the academic as an agent for social change. However, this desire for challenging dominant orthodoxies needs to be framed and seen within the context of the influence of neoliberalism. There may be many academics around the world who seek to challenge this 'entrepreneurial university' which is now so dominant around the world. It is the extent to which they feel confident, and have the spaces and opportunities to promote learning that questions neoliberalism, that is perhaps one of the biggest questions of today within higher education. Academics may have more freedom and space than schoolteachers but many of them are finding their roles becoming increasing narrowed, with the emphasis on assessment and pressure to produce 'high quality' research outputs.

Academic Tutor as Agent of Social Change

Whilst recognizing the constraints academics face, they can and do play a role as a change agent. They contribute to research and advancement of knowledge, and at the broadest level as educators they are involved in the personal and intellectual transformation of learners (Ramsden 1998). The approach of Ashwin (2019: 6) is particularly relevant here. He suggests that academics should:

> design curricula that are focused on providing students with access to knowledge that will transform their sense of who they are and what they can do in the

world. To do this we need to have a clear sense of who our students are, how the knowledge we will give them access to is powerful, and who it will enable them to become in the wider lives as well as in their careers.

Rather than focusing on labour market outcomes, Ashwin suggests academics should design degree programmes that give 'students access to powerful knowledge' (ibid.).

It is this suggestion that establishes the role of the academic as an educator and an agent for change that is particularly significant. It is all too easy to focus on the role of the academic in terms of their research and publications outputs promoting a different world view. What is being suggested by Ashwin is that this transformative role can be part of the academic's teaching.

Doring (2002: 143–4), goes even further and suggests that to be effective agents for change, academics need to have a 'personal commitment, motivation, time and resources'.

Higher Education and Social Justice

Higher education institutions around the world have had to respond to changing social, economic, cultural and political forces. In recent years, this has included specific issues such as climate change, Black Lives Matter or the impact of Covid-19. These themes reflect wider social issues such as inequalities within society and the need to embrace the principles of sustainable development. They also pose questions as to what and how universities can address these challenges. Some of these trends are, of course, not new, and Rouse (2011: 15) has noted:

> Many [American] institutions have embraced social justice ideologies such as diversity, multiculturalism, and inclusion as key initiatives to support cultural difference, promote equity, and encourage social change. For example, several institutions are making global learning and social justice education an integral component of the undergraduate curriculum as a way to foster students' understanding of social responsibility in local and global citizenship. By educating for and promoting social justice ideologies, higher education may invite and engage multiple perspectives . . . [that] help [to] influence and facilitate a more inclusive institutional culture.

These advances and evidence of engagement in broader social issues has, however, tended to have come as a result of ideological and political struggles either within the institution or society more widely.

Whilst most universities would recognize and support that they have a responsibility to equip their students with different viewpoints and encourage critical thinking (Coll and Zalaquett 2007: 275), there is always the danger that this could be tokenistic. It is where academics have consciously promoted, supported and implemented initiatives that seek lasting change that there is evidence of forms of social transformation. One area that brings some of the questions open to further discussion and analysis is the role and support given to sustainable development within institutions and by academics.

Sustainable University

What is evident from numerous studies is that higher education in many countries has played a leading role in encouraging societal changes to a more sustainable world (Sterling, Maxley and Luna 2013; Wals et al. 2016).

This has taken many forms from focusing on encouraging changes in environmental behaviour patterns, to building evidence from research and providing models of good practice through specific courses. However, whilst there have clearly been many innovative examples, there has been a tendency in many countries to focus on changes within the life and activities of university campuses and then use this as an exemplar for wider societal engagement.

There are, however, examples of more systematic approaches that aim to have broader social relevance and a transformative component. These include the concept of eco-social innovation (ESI) outlined by Wals et al. (2016). To them, ESI:

> implies a process of transformation and, indeed, a profound transformation of the way people think and operate, in the use of assets and resources, in production and consumption patterns, in social structures, etc. We suggest that such social transformation, fuelled by current challenges, can be a vehicle towards a values-driven socio-ecological oriented sustainability. (ibid., 30)

Reflecting debates on transformative learning, Wals et al. suggest an approach that could be summarized as 'walk the change' through a cyclical journey of reflection and action:

> which engages learners in understanding why things are the way they are (current state), what keeps them from changing (maladaptive resilience), how things should be (more desirable state), what needs to be done to bring about

change, trying out new ways of doing things, learning from the experience and re-entering the cycle until a more desirable state is reached. (ibid., 30–1)

It is here that the influence of Mezirow can be seen through the need for the learning to go beneath the surface and open up the minds of the learner to new views and possibilities.

The proposals outlined by Wals et al. also suggest that an important aspect of ESI is social change. In this, they found the work of Heifetz (1994) and Heifetz, Linsky and Grashow (2009) particularly valuable. Heifetz developed this concept of adaptive leadership where there are no clear boundaries or ready-made solutions. This means that, 'rather than seeking technical solutions, adaptive change comes through a process of experimentation, sensitivity to the context and an attitude of curiosity and discovery' (Wals et al., 33). What this suggests is that social change can be related to people's motivation and desire for change, their sense of agency.

This emphasis on agency suggests that key to the development of a sustainable university is the commitment, enthusiasm and expertise of the individual academics. This has been noted by Thomas (2016), who also highlighted the quality of the teaching academics provide. A constant challenge for many academics is that whilst they may be sympathetic to the ideas of sustainability, they may feel they lack the expertise to include the subject within their teaching. This is where the commitment and support of the university and the broader higher education policy context are relevant. Thomas (ibid., 67) noted the following areas that need to be understood by and for the academic: personal values, pedagogy, professional culture, information sources, sense of self and reflective self-learner. The external policy context is important, not so much for setting out policy statements, but broader more informal guidance and, in some cases, resourcing to test out sustainability approaches within universities. This, for example in the United Kingdom, has meant at various times funding for projects, promotion of award programmes and engagement of student bodies (Sterling, Maxey and Luna 2013).

The second area to review in terms of the role of academics as agents for sustainable change is with regard to changing course content, the curriculum. One of the challenges for sustainability within the higher education curriculum is that the term can be easily applied as a body of knowledge within a range of subject areas be they geography, natural sciences, engineering, architecture and design. But if education for sustainable development (ESD) is seen as more than a body of knowledge but as a distinctive pedagogical approach that is transformative, then this implies a more interdisciplinary approach that requires more innovative styles and approaches to teaching and learning. Some have suggested the use of the term 'literacy' (Stibbe 2009), which emphasizes skills development. However, this can lead to an approach towards learning of working towards some form of ideal, completed full literacy state rather than seeing sustainability as a complex, more processed focused term.

Finally, how do academics themselves perceive sustainable development and to what extent do they see the term as encompassing social change? Research by Christie and Miller in Australia (2016) found that teaching academics welcomed, or wanted to see, more education for sustainable development (ESD) within university courses. Their research also found limited understanding of what the terms meant, and there were clear differences between different disciplines with, surprisingly, science academics less familiar with what the term meant.

Numerous universities make claims to be change agents for sustainability at strategic and operational levels. However, many of these claims remain at a higher-order level within the institution and do not always trickle down to teaching and learning and the practices of individual academics. It is certainly possible that universities through the practices they promote can help to change behaviour patterns in both academics and students. But it is the extent to which this is meaningful and long term that perhaps needs closest scrutiny. Stephens et al. (2008) in their study identified five questions that are critical for the extent to which sustainability is supported and embedded within an institution. They are: the dominant sustainability challenges of the region; the financing structure and independence; the institutional organization; the extent of democratic processes; and communication and interaction with society (ibid., 321).

These questions, however, pose wider points such as what and whose finances, ways in which the university engages with environmental issues from the surrounding area and its general interaction with local communities. In what ways can academics themselves promote a sense of sustainability that is in itself about social change and have the spaces for engaging their peers and their students? Moreover, how do the debates within the university relate to the needs of the wider society, not only local to the institution but also beyond and into the wider world? This is where and how the concept of global citizenship is used and seen by both individual academics and institutions in general.

The Global Citizenship University

The term 'global citizenship' or variations of it, such as 'planetary citizenship' or 'global learning', have become an important feature of the landscape of many universities around the world. There is clearly a connection between the ways of global citizenship within higher education and the wider higher education policies and programmes around internationalization. The area of internationalization of higher education has been most closely associated with the international marketization of courses, recruitment of international students, although it has in many institutions also been interpreted as a way of encouraging a more diverse, culturally sensitive and broader curriculum. Promoting the term 'global citizenship' has therefore been used in some instances as a direct outcome of internationalization strategies (Kraska, Bourn and Blum, 2018).

The literature around global citizenship in higher education is extensive (Shultz, Abdi and Richardson 2011; Shultz 2011b; Goren and Yemini 2017; Pashby 2011; Clifford and Haigh 2018; Gaudelli 2016; Jorgensen and Shultz 2012), but particularly relevant for the themes outlined in this chapter is the research that specifically looks at the role of academics within the universities' policies, practices and broad discourse around these themes.

For many universities, the use of the term has become linked to the concept of 'global graduates', students who are seeking skills that could help them live and work anywhere in the world. As Sundaram (2018: 411) notes, if the role of a university is to shape future citizens for a pluralistic global world, then a core aim for higher education 'might be to educate global citizens, students who can critically reflect on their own positions in a global framework'.

But global citizenship can also be seen as an approach to encourage a more globally responsible graduate with the role of the academic being to provide the teaching and leadership to encourage learning and active engagement in society for social change.

These different interpretations of the use of the term have led to what Moraes (2014) has called being a 'floating signifier', open to a range of possibilities as how it could be used. For some, global citizenship is seen as an attribute covering areas such as awareness, responsibility, participation and cross-cultural empathy, achievement and international mobility (Rhoads and Szelényi 2011; Schattle 2008). This awareness and sense of place in the world could, as some have argued, lead to a sense of global responsibility and action for change. However, within universities there has been a tendency to promote the term in relation to equipping graduates for working in the global economy or as someone who has a sense of global social responsibility. The former could be said to be located with neoliberal discourses and the latter in more liberal, humanistic and cosmopolitan discourses.

Hammond and Keating (2018) make a useful distinction between these economic (global worker) and humanistic (global citizen) agendas. They see a global citizen as someone who assumes and exercises their civic rights, whilst a global worker is someone who has the skills and knowledge to be productive in the workplace.

There is, however, a third interpretation of global citizenship within higher education and that is where academics have encouraged and promoted an approach in their teaching that is located in a more critical pedagogical approach, that emphasizes power and inequalities in the world and sees the role of universities to challenge dominant orthodoxies in society and encourage anti-oppressive practices (Kraska, Bourn and Blum 2018).

These three interpretations are now looked at in detail.

Neoliberal Perspectives

Jorgenson and Shultz (2012) noted that the promotion of global citizenship is often closely related to marketing strategies to attract students who seek a global experience in preparation for working in a competitive global workforce. Higher education is seen as a commodity, and the role of the academic is to work within this framework and equip students with the skills they require to secure meaningful employment.

Global citizenship is therefore often equated with global leadership and maximizing the opportunities globalization provides. For academics, this can often mean being encouraged to offer courses that 'emphasise leadership skills and learning economically useful languages' (Marshall 2011: 8). As Rhoads and Szelényi (2011: 271) suggest, this approach to global citizenship education can also be called globally informed individualism, which comprises educating global citizens 'who are informed by global understandings but enact them in their self-interest and, by extension, in the interest of their immediate families, on a local or global stage'.

One of the challenges for many academics is that whilst seeking more liberal or critical approaches to global citizenship, the dominant culture and ideology of the institution might result unwittingly in them following an economic outlook.

Liberal-Humanistic Perspectives

From a liberal-humanistic point of view, the purpose of universities and course curriculums comes from an individualistic perspective, equipping students to understand the world in which they live, creating spaces to encourage debate and develop students' sense of place and role in the world, leading debates on a range of issues, and developing in graduates a sense of the wider world. There is a recognition of the importance of critical thinking and the promotion of civic values and skills for life (McCowan 2012; Balarin 2011).

Within some of the viewpoints from this perspective, there is an emphasis on the promotion of a global moral consciousness and a cosmopolitan outlook (Hansen 2011). This means being open to other perspectives, but at the same time viewing the world as a totality and encouraging common values bases. This means the academic has a moral purpose (Nussbaum 2002; Benhabib 2002). This can be summarized by Dill (2013: 2) as 'an awareness of other perspectives, a vision of oneself as part of a global community of humanity as a whole, and a moral consciousness to act for the good of the world'. Dill sees this global moral consciousness as ensuring a sense of responsibility and empowering humanity to make a difference.

Critical Perspectives

The critical pedagogical approach, influenced by the work of Freire and Giroux, starts from questioning the dominant ideological nature of higher education with global citizenship and the promotion of a pedagogy for global social justice. Shultz (2010) suggests that global citizenship can provide a space for 'dealing' with difficult knowledge and difficult justice, and for managing diversity, all of which are inherent in today's world. This means challenging the dominant Western-based ideologies within higher education with the role of academics to promote not only a plurality of perspectives but to do so within the context of equipping learners with the knowledge and skills to seek social change. Key proponents of this approach are Andreotti (2006), Torres (2017), Pashby (2011) and Stein (2020). There is a major emphasis within this approach on addressing the influence of colonialism through higher education, to identify its impact on reinforcing stereotypes and the dominance of Western thinking and the need to pose alternative perspectives.

Torres (2017) presents a slightly different approach, emphasizing the impact of globalization and power relations from an ethical values base of social justice and equity. To Torres, this caring ethical perspective is central to global citizenship education.

The area of decolonizing the curriculum and the influence of critical race theory and addressing the lack of feminist thinking within higher education should also be included within these critical perspectives. With regard to decolonization, some of the major initiatives in this area have been in South Africa (Bhambra, Gebrial & Nisancioglu, 2018) and in countries where indigenous communities were marginalized or ignored within many courses (Shultz, 2018). More recently, influenced by critical race theory, questions are being asked in a number of universities in both Europe and North America as to 'Why is my curriculum white' (Begum and Sani, 2019). With regard to feminist perspectives, the debates relate to only access of women to appropriate spaces as well as both the content of the curriculum and approaches to teaching and learning (David, 2012). An important figure in linking feminist theory to critical race theory and critical pedagogy has been bell hooks, who has been discussed in more detail in other chapters in this volume (hooks, 1994).

An increasingly influential variation on this approach is the reference to the environment and linkages to themes in the earlier section of this chapter. This eco-critical perspective acknowledges the variations that exist ecologically between intelligences and cultures and the culture of the individual and those that dominate humanity (Bosio 2020). It aims to bring together environmental, social and cultural approaches that aim to combat injustices (Lupinacci and Happel-Parkins 2015). This approach aims to connect with how humans relate to the non-human environment in a 'harmonious, respectful, and pragmatic manner' (ibid., 55). A variation on this approach is that promoted by Misiaszek (2015), who advocates an eco-pedagogy of global citizenship education that connects human to non-human relations through an education for and through social and ecological justice. More recently, Pashby et al. (2020) have recognized the dangers of their approach being seen as too binary and not acknowledging the potential overlaps and linkages between the different perspectives.

The work of Andreotti (2006, 2011) and also that of Shultz (2007, 2010, 2011a) have also identified the relationship between debates on critical global citizenship with that of de-colonizing the curriculum. Stein and Andreotti (2016), for example, suggest that postcolonial studies can contribute to asking questions about the universality of the being a global citizen and the need to include reference to race, gender and class. Shultz (2018: 252) suggests that global citizenship education can address conditions of inequality and injustice in the world, 'by engaging with the histories and legacies of colonialism'.

What this discourse around global citizenship identifies are wider questions posed in this chapter about the broader global social purpose of universities and the extent to which there are spaces, opportunities and places. This is where some of the recent research on this area is particularly helpful.

Research on Academics within Faculties and Education for Social Change

As this chapter has identified, there have been numerous studies on the role of academics as agents for social change but there have been very few in-depth research studies. Therefore, the two research studies discussed here, both based on doctorates that I have supervised, provide important new additions to the discourse. Maureen Ellis' research (2013, 2016) applies a critical realist approach, using an interview schedule grounded in Cultural Historic Activity Theory (CHAT) to review the global education and sustainable development perspectives of over 500 academics, teacher educators, teachers and NGO practitioners. The second is the doctoral study by Emiliano Bosio (2020), whose thesis is on academics within universities engaged with global citizenship in the United States, Japan and the United Kingdom.

Here the focus is on Ellis' (2013, 2016) research with academics and the ways in which they practised their ideas. It used reflective autobiography, inspiring biographical accounts and critical theory. A feature of their personal journeys was the influence of international travel, being marginalized and relating their own disciplinary expertise to broader professional practice. Several referred to their early professional practices, be they in education or social work, which led them to rethink their ideas and to question particularly Anglo-centric perspectives. An important element of these influences was the breaking down of the theory/practice divide. Freire was seen by several of them as an important influence. Their commitment beyond university life to broader social and political action and the bringing together of all these experiences were regarded by them as transformational to both themselves and their influence on students.

Themes such as encouraging collective transformation in the learners with an emphasis on critical literacy were evident from the interviews. One academic Ellis interviewed noted the importance of giving their students the opportunity to have their voice heard:

> when you give people permission to take their own story seriously, they will make very critical statements about society . . . it's almost transgressive to do so, it's almost like you can feel them crossing a threshold . . . because they are having to go against everything they have been told, all the silencing, all the people . . . telling them shut up . . . and their own internal voice telling you you've got no right to say, because who do you think you are? (Ellis 2016: 148)

A theme from her research was how academics addressed the contradictions they were faced with, operating within a neoliberal context but yet finding spaces for promoting radical voices. Academics, she said, spoke about 'freedom by default' (ibid., 150). They referred to the course validation processes as tick box exercises which bore no relationship to what they actually taught. Some teacher educators were, however, more cautious, reflecting the constraints within which they have to operate. There was, above all, a recognition of the need to be careful about how they might wish to mobilize and support students for radical action but yet at the same time seeing themselves as wanting to 'politicise students' (ibid., 172).

Some of the academics were open about how they saw their role. One asserted, 'So I try to ride two horses. I'd definitely say I've got a political agenda' (ibid., 153). A teacher educator noted that their role could not be neutral:

> I would hope that it [ethics] comes up through the whole thing, that you can't be neutral, that you may have a view that you think isn't ideologically driven, but actually it *is*, and it's trying to uncover where you've got your ideology from. No, I think that goes right through . . . It's more political, more ideologically driven. (ibid., 154)

Ellis however found that despite this awareness of their roles and sympathy for critical pedagogical perspectives, there was often little recognition, particularly by teacher educators, of what could be the routes for systemic change.

Reflecting themes in this chapter and elsewhere in the volume, Ellis found that the academics encouraged their students to address global organizations and institutional change, to look at the broader context of their learning, to be self-reflective and consider their own sense of identity. As one teacher educator said to her, criticality was 'the whole purpose of education' (ibid., 165).

This evidence from Ellis demonstrates that whilst many academics see a broader social and perhaps transformational approach to their teaching, they were aware of the constraints and challenges they faced. These academics felt they had opportunities to bring in critical pedagogical perspectives and saw a key part of their role to be to challenge students to question their assumptions and to provide them with the knowledge and skills to take their learning further into society. The academics Ellis interviewed were also conscious of the role of social media, to encourage critical literacy and develop different forms of assessment.

Bosio's thesis (2020) is relevant to the themes of this chapter for three main reasons. Firstly, in relation to the discussions on categorization of universities, he suggests that whilst the distinctions of neoliberal, humanistic and critical are useful, he found that value creating was an important additional category to consider, emphasizing more the spiritual side of global citizenship. He also found that there was a need to have a meta-analysis to show the linkages between the different categorizations and also to see the particular relevance of a specific approach.

Secondly, his research identified ways in which academics perceive global citizenship education and the extent to which they see the use of the term as an agent for change. Bosio found that in Japan a more economic and individualistic interpretation was evident than in the United States or the United Kingdom, although there was a general consensus on the potential transformative power of the application of the term. Whilst each of the case studies Bosio investigated identified some important themes, particularly relevant for this chapter are the examples from University of California at Los Angeles (UCLA) and Liverpool Hope University. The other two case studies, Columbia Teachers College based in New York and Soka University in Japan, whilst different in context and philosophy, focused more on individual learning attributes.

From the evidence gathered at UCLA, Bosio identified eight themes from the academics he interviewed:

> (1) Global Citizenship Education (GCE) must essentially be critical; (2) it must aim at removing the divisive and authoritarian barriers between academics and students through critical dialogue; (3) it must develop students' critical identities; (4) it must support students to develop a critique of neoliberal forms of globalisation; (5) it must engender students' critical reflection on global issues; (6) it must empower students to have a self-belief that they can be agents of social change; (7) it must be conceived in a classroom that is a critical forum where students can discuss global/local issues; and (8) it must include a list of critical core-values that foster students' critical awareness. (ibid., 116)

Bosio further noted:

> The UCLA academics approached Global Citizenship Education (GCE) in the classroom as a way of confronting neoliberalism and combating increases in social injustice. They believe that neoliberalism and populist authoritarianism provide serious stumbling blocks that can have an adverse influence on all GCE models in higher education (HE) in the United States. (ibid.)

Reactions to the influence of globalization and neoliberalism were seen as important motivators for the academics. Bosio identified that the academics were of the opinion that 'critical GCE (could) be interpreted as a "pedagogical-agent for change" aimed at questioning neoliberal forms of globalisation' (ibid.,119).

Thirdly, Bosio identified some of the challenges and opportunities that exist for higher education tutors in the ways in which they might interpret and apply global citizenship within the courses they are responsible for. At UCLA, for example, Bosio found that academics saw one of the major challenges for implementing GCE was the 'divisive and authoritarian barriers between academics and students'. This was aimed to be addressed through a process of praxis, of thinking, making and doing (ibid., 117). Also, what was regarded as being equally important was making the programmes provided relevant to the lives of students. A theme that emerged from Bosio's research with his interviews at UCLA was their conceptualization of GCE as a 'dedication to the common good'. Which is seen by them as a 'form of humanistic concern that fits the model of solidarity' (ibid., 118–9).

To support this, Bosio identified that at UCLA the academics were of the view that GCE must 'empower students to have a self-belief that they can be agents of social change'. This means supporting students:

- To be conscious of their role in the world now and in future.
- To have the confidence to transform themselves and their society.
- To learn from their knowledge of the world.
- To reflect on such knowledge.
- To believe that they have the capability of becoming agents of change (ibid., 121).

The other case study Bosio identified was Liverpool Hope University (LHU) and its Wider Perspectives in Education (WPE) programme within their BA Primary Teaching undergraduate degree. It proposes dedicated modules that are designed to introduce trainee teachers to global citizenship and the benefits of serving others. Through this initiative, LHU aspires to foster globally minded future teachers who have a strong sense of civic responsibility and regularly contribute to beneficial community projects within their capacity as global citizens (ibid., 153). The programme offers opportunities such as exchange projects with students in other countries and a focus on rights and responsibilities. As Bosio notes, global citizenship principles were implemented in the programme through three distinctive pedagogical approaches:

- Encouraging future teachers to participate in, and reframe, societal change within a more knowledgeable context.
- Encouraging students to compare their personal values as future teachers before and after engaging with the WPE.

- Encouraging students to strengthen their commitment to becoming the teachers of the future (ibid., 154).

A feature of this programme was the influence of transformative learning theories and practices, encouraging students to make a distinction between charity and social justice and promoting a sense of social responsibility. What is significant about the evidence gathered by Bosio in terms of the themes of this chapter is the emphasis academics put on encouraging personal change in the students. He notes it 'does not relate to the student merely thinking about something in a new or different way; it also involves having a personal connection to the issue and taking decisions for action' (ibid., 155). Bosio however found that some of these goals were difficult to realize, such as getting students to having broader worldviews or a greater sense of social justice (ibid., 156). However, as one academic commented to Bosio, 'students must learn that it's not enough just to find out about global situations, action must also be taken to implement change' (ibid.).

What the evidence from Bosio's research demonstrates is that there is a clear connection between how the academics perceived global citizenship and their sense of social change. The views and outlooks of individual academics were clearly significant, and there was a strong sense of social justice educational perspectives in their approaches. But as the example from Liverpool Hope notes, whilst many of these ideals might be reflected within courses, they were much more challenging to get fully implemented.

Case Studies: Examples of Academic Engagement for Social Change

The following case studies have been chosen because the theme of social change is clearly evident, and they bring in themes already identified in this chapter related to creative spaces, the specific influences of education for sustainable development and global citizenship and, finally, relevance of curriculum change. As the case studies in the following paragraphs will also demonstrate, there are numerous ways and examples of academic-led initiatives within universities for social change. Some such as Walden University in the United States have a strong social change ethos and have developed an innovative staff professional development programme to support their vision for degree courses. The second example from a university in Slovakia shows the value of having a committed enthusiast to lead initiatives for change within the university and having external support from funders to put her ideas into practice.

Walden University and Curricula for Global Social Change

Walden University is a for-profit university in the United States focusing on distance learning programmes for career professionals with the 'opportunity to transform themselves as scholar-practitioners so that they can apply what they've learned to effect positive social change' (Walden University 2017). As the university operates outside the framework of state-funded universities, Walden has potentially more creative space than other institutions. Its mission of social change encourages all members of the academic community to strive for positive social change. It does this through a range of initiatives at local and international levels as well as producing regular social change impact reports, an academic journal, *Journal of Social Change*, and professional development support for academics.

In 2015, the university had developed a five-year strategy of *A Vision for Social Change*. The goals for this vision included the following:

- Leveraging Walden research capacities, expertise, networks, and curricula to serve external organizations and communities in the application of social change.
- Strengthening the impact of Walden curricula to educate agents of social change across all of our programs.
- Raising the social change consciousness, skills, and knowledge of Walden's internal communities.
- Continuing to improve how we support ongoing social change initiatives that engage current students, faculty, alumni, and our partner communities (Walden University 2020).

A feature of the way academics based at the university engage with social change themes has been to develop a specific curriculum to address these areas for the whole institution. In 2006, the definition adopted for social change by the university had been 'a deliberate process of creating and applying ideas, strategies, and actions to promote the worth, dignity, and development of individuals, communities, organizations, institutions, cultures, and societies' (Yob et al. 2016: 206).

In deciding to review this definition, a task force within the university identified that there was not strong support for having one definition of social change or that there was no consensus as to what it meant.

After several presentations of different definitions, the group decided to abandon the idea of narrowing down the concept of social change to its key essence. Instead, the task force chose to break open the concept to explore what it might consist of if expressed in functional terms. This line of inquiry led to a set of features of social change the group considered essential in an educational programme preparing students to be social change agents. In brief, the task force identified eight features of an education for social change, given as follows.

In the cognitive domain:

- Scholarship: application of research and theory to real issues and challenges in the community.
- Systemic Thinking: the examination of the multiple causes, contributing factors, and solutions needed for complex social problems.
- Reflection: personal and group reflection during and after a phase in a social change project to enhance practical and theoretical knowledge of the issues involved.

In the skills domain:

- Practice: the ability to plan, execute, and assess a social change project in the real world.
- Advocacy: the ability to raise awareness of an issue through education and advising.
- Collaboration: identification of likely partners and the ability to work in and/or lead a team of change agents.
- Political or Civic Engagement: the ability to engage in the process of developing or reforming policies and laws to support a social change initiative in the community, institution, profession, or wider society.

In the values, attitudes, and ethics domain:

- Humane Ethics: commitment to promoting the good of others, including the ecosystem (Yob et al., 2016).

Yob (2018), in outlining this, suggests ten competencies that can provide the conceptual framework for curriculum building for social change: three in the knowledge domain (scholarship, systemic thinking and reflection), four in the skills domain (application, advocacy, collaboration and political engagement) and three in the affective domain (ethics, commitment and courage).

These concepts mirror themes outlined elsewhere in this volume but what is significant about them is that they reflect broader pedagogical approaches related to themes such as transformative learning and social justice.

A follow-up faculty task force, tasked with implementing these eight features, created the Curriculum Guide for Social Change, which provided a matrix for mapping social change in courses

The model they developed reflected a process of moving from the individual development of the student towards a sense of being an agent for social change to one that had wider circles related to wider societal influence and engagement. This guide was seen as a 'mapping tool' to help identify gaps within courses in the university and how to revise existing programmes and develop new ones.

The evidence gathered as to where and how social changes themes were being reflected in programmes identified that they were strongly reflected in terms of advocacy and systematic thinking. However, there was less evidence in the scholarship area covering research and theory.

This example demonstrates how a university which has as its purpose a clear interface between learning and society can use the term 'social change' as a tool for inspiring academics and engaging students.

Example from Slovakia

An example of identifying a social change goal within courses at a university can be seen in the Slovakia University of Agriculture (SUA) at Nitra. It is one of the leading universities in Slovakia and provides education in the field of agriculture and related research areas such as food technology, sustainable development, economics and management, international trade and tourism. The Faculty of Economics and Management, where the example outlined below was developed, has a strong international focus, co-operating internationally with forty-seven educational and academic institutions in Europe and beyond.

With funding from the Slovakian government, and in partnership with the Pontis Foundation, the Faculty of Economics and Management (FEM) at SUA developed a number of projects to bring global themes and elements of social change more directly into their teaching and learning between 2012 and 2016. The main aim was:

> to develop the critical thinking of students through the appropriate incorporation of individual global issues in the existing curricula of economic faculties, using appropriate methods, with the aim of supporting students' motivation

to become actively interested in the problems, risks, and threats of the current world. (Mravcová 2016: 65)

This project aimed to bring themes of global citizenship into a range of courses and to provide students with a wide range of global skills. A feature of the initiatives developed were the production of a special publication to support these changes (Svitačová and Mravcová 2014).

Up until the launch of this initiative, global citizenship and global education themes had not been common within Slovakia. There was very little existing literature or examples of practice to build on. The first stage of SUA's engagement in this area was through funding from the Slovak Ministry of Education in 2012. This was followed by further initiatives, this time funded by SlovakAid and co-ordinated by the Pontis Foundation. The aim was that, as a result of piloting initiatives at SUA, they could be later replicated in other universities.

The main objective was to establish conditions for the implementation of global issues into the curricula of SUA. The focus of this was on developing the professional capacities of academics to teach global issues and to build a constituency of support for this field amongst both teachers and students.

Using a range of participatory training methods, a pilot course on Development Education was introduced which secured engagement from academics across several faculties. One of the questions the academics discussed was whether the themes should be reflected within a stand-alone course or across programmes. What was agreed was that global and development themes should be included across a range of courses but what was seen as equally important were the pedagogical approaches with the need for greater attention to be given to more co-operative forms of learning, the use of role plays and the involvement of external speakers. This led to the introduction of a new, accredited programme on global and development issues. In addition, global citizenship themes became part of a number of existing courses as a cross-cutting theme. To ensure the sustainability and wider applicability of these initiatives, publications were produced to demonstrate how global citizenship themes could be part of university courses.

The Faculty of Economics and Management saw the need to promote an understanding of the influences of global forces, the need for sustainable development and the inequalities that exist in the world. The areas around global citizenship were seen as particularly important to the faculty because they provided opportunities for addressing questions around inequalities in the world. Many of the graduates from this faculty planned to work for multinational companies, and the area was seen as relevant to business- and agricultural-related sectors.

As part of the development of these initiatives at SUA, co-operation was developed with a number of foreign educational institutions through internships and sharing of professional experience. A feature of these partnership was the collaboration developed with the Jomo Kenyatta University of Agriculture and Technology in Kenya.

SUA, as a consequence of these initiatives, became more of a global university. As a result of the leadership of a small number of academics, particularly Anna Mravcoca, there is a recognition of the importance of global topics within many courses (Svitačová and Mravcová 2014). She played a key role in introducing global citizenship as a cross-cutting theme into a number of degree courses. What she found through her dialogue with students was the need to include a range of interactive and participatory methods to encourage the development of their own views so that 'they can find inspiration, feel emotions, create their own opinions, see the connection with their own life, and see the opportunity for action and change' (Mravcová 2016: 75).

Conclusion

This chapter has outlined the role that academics within universities can and have played in promoting themes of social change within their teaching and learning. It has shown that a key challenge is the extent to which this promotion of change can be undertaken within the dominant influence of neoliberalism. There is evidence to show that, using the lenses of sustainability and global citizenship, curriculum development is possible that encourages a broader social purpose to the learning being undertaken.

Reference has been made in the chapter to the different types of universities and the extent to which they perceive themselves as having a broader social remit. The evidence from the research by Bosio shows that an important driver is the social and political outlook of individual academics. Ellis's research identified the contradictions within which many academics have to operate but, to many of them, there was a clear social and political purpose to their work. Finally, the evidence from the Slovak University of Agriculture shows the role academics can play as drivers for change and the need to secure institutional buy-in to a broader social change agenda.

As this chapter has outlined, there are a number of terms and themes that universities have used to promote their social remit including 'common good' and 'public good'. The extent to which they are valuable is an area that perhaps needs further debate. Global citizenship and sustainability were suggested as key areas which could move beyond these discussions and provide an approach that could not only challenge dominant ideologies within society, but act as the opportunities for academics to be agents of change through both their research and teaching.

Questions for Further Consideration

- In what ways can academics in universities play a role within their institutions as agents of social change?
- In what ways can sustainability strategies within universities play a broader role in encouraging wider social change?
- What are the strengths and weaknesses of academics focusing on global citizenship as a mechanism for seeking broader university engagement in seeking social change?
- What is the value of the concept of the common good as a way of interpreting the role of higher education institutions as agents of social change?

Further Reading

Ashwin, P. (2019), 'Transforming University Teaching', *Centre for Global Higher Education working paper series* no. 49.

Brennan, J. (2008), 'Higher Education and Social Change Higher Education and the Future of Higher Education Research', *Higher Education*, 56, no. 3: 381–393.

Hammond, C. D. and A. Keating (2018), 'Global Citizens or Global Workers? Comparing University Programmes for Global Citizenship Education in Japan and the UK', *Compare: A Journal of Comparative and International Education*, 48, no. 6: 915–934.

Marginson, S. (2016), *Higher Education and the Common Good*, Manchester: MUP.

McCowan, T. (2019), *Higher Education For and Beyond the Sustainable Development Goals*, London: Palgrave.

Yob, I. M. (2018), 'Conceptual Framework for a Curriculum in Social Change', *Journal of Social Change*, 10, no. 1: 71–80.

11

Civil Society Organizations as Agents for Change

Introduction

Civil society organizations (CSOs), including international non-governmental organizations (NGOs), have played a major role in promoting education for social change around the world. Their importance has been stressed by policymakers such as the former United Nations secretary general Ban Ki-moon, who highlighted the contribution of non-governmental organizations to achieving the Sustainable Development Goals: 'I am such a strong believer in NGOs, I constantly call on governments to expand space for you to operate,' and he 'urged freedom for civil society organizations' (United Nations 2016b). The European Commission includes civil society organizations within all of their consultation processes around governance and proposals for law changes.

Yet, despite this rhetoric and goodwill for the voices of civil society in many regions of the world, the spaces for their organizations to influence policy or ensure more pluralistic perspectives has become more limited. Some of this has been the result of civil society organizations in some countries developing as little more than the arm of the state. But in other countries, even in some of the leading industrialized countries in the world, independent voices have been muted.

This chapter reviews the evolution of civil society organizations in terms of their role as agents for change. Throughout the chapter, the terms 'civil society organizations' (CSOs) and 'non-governmental organizations' (NGOs) will be used. For the purposes of this chapter and volume, the term CSOs will be used to cover a wide range of bodies that are not part of national, local or supra state structures or organizations. NGOs in this context will be interpreted as primarily organizations that are either local or national bodies with a specific focus related to environment and development issues.

The chapter reviews some of the academic debates around their changing role and looks at their relationship to the Sustainable Development Goals. Building on themes outlined in earlier chapters in this volume, specific consideration will be given to the role of civil society voices and organizations within the policies and practices around sustainable development and global citizenship. Like other chapters, there is a specific section dedicated to evidence from research. Finally, the chapter will review specific examples of types of civil society organizations and their role in the themes identified. This includes a leading international NGO, CAFOD; a body that focuses primarily on social media as its main approach to social change; and a grassroots organization from development education in the United Kingdom.

Civil Society and Civil Society Organizations

Within and around the discourses on social change, the role of civil society is regarded by many policymakers and practitioners as being central to securing social transformation. Civil society is usually defined as the areas and forms of social action outside of the state. The African Development Bank states that civil society is the voluntary expression of the interests and aspirations of citizens organized and united by common interests, goals, values or traditions and mobilized into collective action (AfDB 2012: 10).

Civil society is usually seen as covering a wide range of bodies, non-governmental organizations and non-profit organizations that have an organized structure or activity. They could also be said to include trade unions, religious organizations and informal social movements. Edwards (2011) defined the area as 'the sphere of uncoerced human association between the individual and the state, in which people undertake collective action for normative and substantive purposes, relatively independent of the government and the market' (p. 4).

One of the major issues within the debates around civil society is the extent to which it contributes to, or challenges, the status quo within economies and communities, including whether it acts as a substitute for the state or as a conscious alternative to it. This means the extent to which civil society roles include the following:

- Being service provider
- Being advocate/campaigner
- Being watchdog

- Building active citizenship, motivating civic engagement at the local level and engagement with local, regional and national governance
- Participating in global governance processes (Cooper 2018: 2).

There is a recognition by many international bodies that civil society could be said to cover small, informal and localized forms of social engagement as well as highly professionalized international non-governmental organizations (INGOs) (Kreienkamp 2017: 1). For example, the World Bank defines civil society as:

> the wide array of non-governmental and not for profit organisations that have a presence in public life, express the interests and values of their members and others, based on ethical, cultural, political, scientific, religious or philanthropic considerations. Civil society organisations therefore refer to a wide array of organisations: community groups, NGOs, labour unions, indigenous groups, charitable organisations, faith-based organisations, professional associations, and foundations. (World Bank n.d.: 1)

The European Union defines civil society organizations as 'an organizational structure whose members serve the general interest through a democratic process, and which plays the role of mediator between public authorities and citizens' (European Union n.d.).

For the purposes of this chapter, the focus of civil society organizations is on independent voluntary bodies be they local, national or international. This chapter therefore does not directly discuss the role of trade unions, religious organizations or professional bodies.

There is, however, a need to make a distinction if 'civil society organizations' is seen as an umbrella term between non-governmental organizations, grassroots organizations and more informal social movements. NGOs are bodies that have a formal and legal basis and are non-profit and outside of government and other public bodies. Grassroots organizations are usually bodies that have emerged as a response to needs of local communities and wish to see some form of change be it at local, national or global level.[1] More informal social movements could well be groupings of people who have come together for a specific social purpose but have no formal organizational structure.

An important dimension to civil society organizations that has particularly become important in the twenty-first century has been global networks and bodies. As social and political change has increasingly been affected by global forces, the role and need for civil society bodies to have a broader perspective has become essential. This means not only international NGOs who have always had this global focus, but bodies concerned with issues such as racism, gender inequality and campaigns for greater democracy. The Black Lives Matter movement, whilst it emerged in the United States, quickly became global. The same can be said about the 'Me Too' movement. Finally, with regard to specific calls for greater democracy in certain countries in the Middle East, it was civil society bodies who quickly encouraged neighbouring countries to follow suit.

Civil society organizations can both provide immediate support to help the needs of groups and promote longer-term transformative change. They can provide mechanisms for bringing together special interest groups, opportunities for participation in the decision-making process and the fulfilment of identified goals. They can play a particularly valuable role in enabling groups who have been marginalized or excluded from formal decision-making processes to have a voice.

If it is often assumed that civil society organizations can bring critical voices to social and political debates. Whilst this can be the case, there is also the criticism that they have become too close to the state and have compromised their independence. Tarozzi notes that on the one hand NGOs, for example, could be seen as potentially flexible and open to change and 'bring in innovative, values-based and transformative approaches particularly in education' (Tarozzi 2020: 143). But on the other hand, some NGOs tend to focus too much on their own image and link learning to fundraising (ibid., 144).

Van Dyck (2017) has argued that there is a growing gap between organized civil society and the constituencies they represent (p. 2). This includes growing public distrust and uncertainty about their relevance and legitimacy, organizations failing to uphold their mandate in the face of adversity, and organizations 'following the money' by accepting money for programmes and initiatives that are not aligned with their core mandate (ibid.).

New actors are bridging the divide between the people and organized CSOs through their mode of engagement, tools and approaches, which have democratized the advocacy space (ibid., 3). This changing space is being increasingly filled by informal networks who through forms of social media are able to raise awareness, galvanize, enthuse and give clear guidance for action to many thousands of people (Rutzen 2015).

Civil Society and Social Change

Allen, McAdam and Pellow (2010:1) pose the question: What is the role of civil society in social change? To them, the goal is to enable it: 'to act as a force for fairness and justice for all the world's citizens'. They suggest that as well as providing services to support groups in society, civil society groups can play a major role 'at the local, regional, national and international levels' to 'solve problems in a sustainable way'.

It is often social movements and civil society groups who have been the drivers for some of the major societal changes such as women's suffrage, the abolition of slavery or access to education. Allen, McAdam and Pellow suggest that simple changes in individual behaviour or national legislation is often insufficient and that social movements can help to ensure long-term cultural shifts.

Whilst earlier chapters have made reference to social movements, it is important to note here the relevance of the work of Manuel Castells (2009) and his concept of 'the Network Society'. To Castells, the role of social media, particularly the internet, has enabled the democratization of access to knowledge. However, he has gone further and seen social media as a potential resource against the more oppressive forces of globalization. Social movements, to Castells, have been seen as key here because they can be places where values for change could be developed through forms of collective social action.

Korten (1990) posed that many developments of NGOs moved from being small scale and welfare-focused to being more self-reliant, acquiring greater expertise and knowledge to being actors for change. Whilst this could well have been the case in the late twentieth century, it could be argued today that there is no longer a need for civil society bodies to go through these stages. As a result of access to knowledge and information through the internet and the opportunities social media provides, some may even start with action and change focus. Others will be able to gather expertise and knowledge from external bodies or through the use of social media.

Michael Edwards, one of the leading commentators on NGOs, has questioned the extent to which civil society groups are having the impact on influencing social change that they may have had twenty or thirty years ago. He suggests that 'civil society groups are increasingly divorced from the forces that drive deeper social change'. Edwards suggests that only if these civil society groups and movements have deep roots in society will they be able to secure lasting change. He notes:

> civil society is like an iceberg, with the peaks of protest rising above the waterline and the great mass of everyday citizen action hidden underneath. When the two are connected – when street protests are backed up by long-term action in every community, bank, business, local government, church or mosque, temporary gains in equality and diversity have more chance of becoming permanent shifts

in power and public norms. In that respect it's not the Arab or any other 'Spring' that really makes the difference, but what happens in every other season, of every other year, across every generation. (Edwards 2014: 1)

Edwards notes that there has been a move away from large membership-based civil society organizations to more specialist interest groups. What he does, however, note, is that social media has transformed the forms and nature of civil society engagement for social change. But he also notes that a lot of the actions which are social media-based are rather 'thin' in terms of levels of engagement and often have less impact on transforming society.

Similar comments have been made by Lang (2013) concerning the ways in which movements and organizations have become depoliticized as a result of their engagement in public policy, funding and practice. Lang calls this the 'NGOisation' of civil society in which social movements have become bureaucratized that 'focus on generating issue-specific and, to some degree, marketable expert knowledge or services' (Lang 2013: 64).

However, in 2019 and 2020 there have been two social movements from civil society that have perhaps challenged some of these perceptions. The first movement is the climate emergency movement, led by young people, which has not only engaged large numbers of people but has forced many civil society organizations to put climate change and sustainability issues at the forefront of their agenda. The second is the Black Lives Matter movement, which began in the United States but has led many civil society organizations to review their internal structures, examine the extent to which they give opportunities to people of colour and address the continuing influence of colonial practices.

What both of these initiatives demonstrate is that civil society can play, and continues to play, a role as an agent for social change but often it is the organizations that aim to represent civil society that need to have a closer relationship with the views and outlooks of people.

Edwards' ideas are, however, relevant in that 'civil societies' have a transformative potential, 'to find ways for people to come together *across* their differences and hammer out some common ground. That common ground then gets translated formally into laws and policies by voting in reforming governments, and informally into the norms of public opinion that help to set some sense of direction for society' (Edwards 2014).

These observations reflect a general observation that civil society has been compromised by commercial forces and a decline in funding by the neoliberal state.

In terms of the relationship between civil society organizations and campaigns for social change, what is evident is the need to mobilize resources and build movements and networks for action. They also need to effectively play a role in raising the consciousness of relevant groupings of people in society. They often have also to provide a route map for resolving the issue they have raised, have a strategy for influencing others and take advantage of political opportunities

Policy changes may often be the goal of many civil society organizations today, but their effectiveness can frequently depend on resources. This has brought many of them into a dilemma about accepting public funding whilst at the same time retaining an independent voice.

Forums for Civil Society Organizations

Reflecting the global nature of social action in the twenty-first century, a feature of initiatives around the world by civil society organizations has been to establish networks and forums that have a distinctive goal of social change. The most well-known of these is the World Social Forum, which is an annual gathering of civil society organizations, first held in Brazil in 2001. The Forum has been organized to provide an open space for organizations and has been seen as an alternative to the World Economic Forum being held around the same time of year.

Its Forum in 2018 in Salvador, Bahia, in Brazil, reflected themes discussed in this chapter with its strapline being: 'To Resist is to Create, To Resist is to Transform'.

In addition to the world forum, regional and more thematic forums have also been established in Europe, America, Asia and the Middle East.[2] The Forum's Charter of Principles includes respecting every human right, encouraging mobilization for inclusive democracy practices and support for movements of people against dehumanizing processes. The principles reflect the movement's opposition to neoliberalism and calls for an inclusive globalization.

The significance of the World Social Forum has been threefold. Firstly, its success reflects the continued strength and support for civil society organizations and movements around the world. Secondly, it demonstrates the extent to which many civil society organizations see themselves as actors for change, challenging the dominant capitalist ideologies around the world. Finally, the Forum and its various regional and specialist initiatives demonstrate a form of engagement that is participative, open and democratic.

Forms of Engagement to Achieve Social Change

Within the debates around civil society and social change, there has to be some discussion and analysis of the role of the public in these processes. This poses the question about awareness-raising and learning. The next section will look specifically at the role of education but before doing so, there needs to be some discussion as to what is the knowledge and values base upon which these calls for social change from civil society bodies are based.

Gyoh (2015) addresses these questions in his research on how knowledge was constructed and applied in both international NGOs and grassroots-based youth-led organizations. He suggested that all too often NGOs saw the public as the 'troops' to follow their orders for lobbying policymakers. Whilst many organizations may have some public engagement in their campaigns, it tended to be on terms they determined.

Major NGOs have also tended to increasingly rely on public engagement to be based around forms of passive actions or what could be called 'clicktivism' (White 2010). Secondly, despite their aims of social justice and social change, many of the NGO communications to encourage public engagement have tended to reinforce more charitable and patronizing images.

This rather shallow form of engagement has been discussed in a number of studies (Darnton and Kirk 2011; Trewby 2014). Trewby's research, referred to in Chapter 10, on journeys to engagement, shows that there are often complex factors related to why and how an individual becomes involved in forms of social action. This can be related to family, culture or peer-group influences alongside their own personal experiences. Even when individual activists are encouraged to go beyond passive forms of engagement such as online petitions, it tends to be on an individualistic and consumerist basis related to changes in behaviour patterns regarding purchasing goods.

These points pose the question about the role of the individual or group within civil society and the extent to which their own voice is heard within any campaign or initiative for social change. Hogg (2011: 4) suggests that these people are seen as 'catalytic individuals' who can influence their peers to build public support for social change.

Gyoh suggests that what NGOs often tend to ignore and what could enhance their influence is to connect their campaign objectives to the 'self-transcendent values' of individuals. It is here that going beyond awareness-raising to processes of learning and connecting to identity formation and desire for change that campaigning can have a lasting impact.

It is therefore relevant to note that where NGOs today think more in terms of advocacy rather than direct campaigning, it has potentially a more transformative impact on those engaged. 'Advocacy' can be seen as a term that encourages and mobilizes its supporters for change, not as passive but as active agents for change. As Baillie Smith (2004: 741–9) notes, there is a need for NGOs to 'emphasise constituency building over providing information' through embracing more participatory approaches in the process of planning and designing activities aimed at promoting public engagement with global issues. This engagement of NGOs, as Yanacopoulos and Baillie Smith (2007: 300) suggest, should be based on a sense of cosmopolitanism, of global rights and a sense of solidarity.

Gyoh's research also raised the question of power in terms of the construction of knowledge in influencing and informing campaigns and advocacy strategies. He suggests, quoting Dogra (2012: 1), that 'we come to know the world through representations and that (NGO) representation does not simply represent facts but also constitute them'.

Referring to the work of Ollis (2008), Gyoh identified that an important element of understanding the engagement of activists for social change was the power of emotion. According to Ollis, 'adult activists act as agency and their learning is purposive and associated with emotions such as passion, anger, desire, compassion and a commitment to change' (ibid., 316). But, as Gyoh notes, there are different forms of emotion, and this is particularly relevant within the development context where it can be a sense of compassion but could equally be patronizing or even evoke negative reactions.

What Gyoh's research showed, influenced particularly by Castells' concept of the 'network society', is that NGOs no 'longer command the monopoly as social agents that can mobilise mass action. The advances in digital communication technology have enabled a diffusion of this process through the possibilities digital networks afford autonomous social actors and emphasise the counter power the Network Society brings to agency'.

From his analysis of organizational campaigning, Gyoh devised two forms of 'global campaigner', the first being the more passive awareness approach which is usually top-down and the catalytic individual which was more bottom-up and included a sense of 'critical consciousness' as well as local action.

These observations pose wider questions about the extent to which leading international NGOs can be seen as being leading advocates for social change. All too often, whilst promoting elements of campaigns for change, they retreat to more traditional humanitarian and development modes of engagement based around relief and aid, often due to fundraising pressures.

Gyoh's research challenged the view that campaigning can directly lead to forms of social change. Instead, he said, campaigners need to recognize and develop their role as catalysts for enhancing public understanding and to be clear about their own values and their relation to social justice.

Wilson (2010) asked how NGOs could move people from apathy to action by promoting active citizenship amongst populations in the North. She investigated approaches used by development and social change NGOs, examining the assumptions that 'experiences shape attitudes' and that 'changes in attitudes result in changes in behaviour' (Wilson 2010: 277). One project studied by Wilson was Oxfam Australia's Refugee Realities, an exhibition where participants went through simulated experiences. Wilson argued that this could establish emotional connections and activate feelings of empathy, and having this experience of injustice can make people more inclined to act (ibid., 277). Initial findings from participants who went through the exhibition suggested that 92 per cent felt that the exhibition 'would affect their future engagement with refugees in some way' (ibid., 277). Her results supported the idea that experiential learning can have a profound effect on attitudes and demonstrated the importance of emotional aspects of learning.

There are some potential dangers, however, with this emotive approach, as will be shown later in this chapter in the research by Tallon (2013). But as Hanley's (2020) research on global citizenship education in Kazakhstan demonstrated, an educational approach, an empathy-based pedagogy, can be a valuable way of starting a process of engaging teachers in global issues.

These approaches pose issues around where and how does education relate to the aims of the NGOs and civil society bodies more broadly. It is to that area that this chapter now turns.

Civil Society and the Role of Education and Learning

The engagement and support of young people for particular campaigns and organizational goals has often been seen by many NGOs as coming through educational activities.

As can be seen from the observations so far in this chapter, many civil society bodies have a goal of social change and influencing policymakers. What this however poses is: How does the organization see the role of building understanding and learning about the issue they wish to change amongst their own constituency and supporters and the public more widely? This means: What role does education play within the organization?

This has been particularly an issue within the debates around organizations concerned with global and sustainable development issues. This volume, in earlier chapters, outlined the importance of the central role of pedagogy and the learner coming to their own conclusions about the most appropriate forms of social action.

This is not necessarily how many civil society organizations have seen the purpose of education. Within a lot of the practices of development and environmental NGOs, there has been a tendency to see education as little more than a way to raise awareness and understanding and then seek support and involvement in seeking change. The independent voice of the learner and the need for them to critically reflect on the issues and come to their own conclusions has often been seen as an unnecessary luxury. As a result, within the discourses around development and global education, for example, there have been questions raised about the role of NGOs (see Weber 2012; Gyoh 2015; Tallon 2013).

For many NGOs, particularly international development organizations, learning about global and development issues has been seen as part of the process of building support for their activities but also in providing the knowledge, skills and values base to encourage social action for social change Krause (2010). summarizes these elements as follows:

- Inform and raise awareness of development issues
- Change attitudes and behaviours
- Enable understanding of causes and effects of global issues to mobilize citizens through informed action.

But as earlier chapters have identified, learning and social change cannot be reduced to some form of linear process. There are complex ideological and social forces that influence learning including in the case of global and development issues, the influences of colonialism and charitable attitudes.

A feature of some international NGOs has been to see their approach to education as related to building a global culture of solidarity with closer links to social movements. International NGOs, for example, have a unique ability to link different groups and communities around the world and offer a vehicle for citizens in wealthy countries to express their concerns and provide solidarity. Also, many NGOs have a strong values base. For a number within the development and global education sector, this is often based on a Christian philosophy of compassion and solidarity.

What NGOs can also provide are differing viewpoints and perspectives from that, say, of governments and curriculum bodies. Many of them would have links to Southern partners and this could enable voices of the dispossessed and marginalized to be included in any learning process.

These issues pose the different ways NGOs may see their relationship to processes of learning to be: Is it to provide information, is it to provide pathways to social action or is it to inform and enrich the education that is taking place?

Civil Society Organizations and Education for Social Change

From the evidence discussed earlier, it is clear that within the discourses around global citizenship and sustainable development education many civil society organizations see a linkage between their approaches and social change. Education is seen as the 'engine' for change, acting as the driver and facilitator and seeing a connection between what they are learning and the goal of a more just and sustainable world. Also, as this and other chapters have identified, 'transformative learning' could be said to summarize this linkage. But to what extent is this transformation about changes at a personal level, organizational, local, national or global?

A useful interpretation of the role of civil society organizations as agents for transformative change can be seen in a report by Fricke and Gathercole (2015) for a European network of development education NGOs. They identified three types of change:

- *Personal transformation* that includes respect for others, sense of social and environmental responsibility, sense of belonging, commitment to learning and action.
- *Education systems transformation* including enabling the learner to acquire interdisciplinary and holistic perspective, learners and educators as contributors to the education process and an 'education that enables learners to practice and improve action-orientated and decision-making skills'.

- *Community and societal transformation* resulting in eradication of poverty and inequality, realization of human rights, human development that is sustainable and systematic change in decision-making processes.

What Fricke and Gathercole also note, referring particularly to the work of Scott and Gough (2003), is that learning is complex and does not follow a linear process. They suggest instead, referring to the influence of Freire and the training materials published by Hope and Timmel (1989), of an approach rooted in popular and liberatory education which helps people 'become critical, creative, free, active and responsible members of society' (ibid., vol. 1.8).

Another useful model is that proposed in a report by Rene Susa for Bridge 47 using a framework developed by Naberhaus and Sheppard (2015). Whilst this approach is directed at how to secure social change, it suggests a particular role that could be directly relevant for civil society organizations (Susa: 2019). It proposes four different roles of 'systematic activism':

- *Acupuncturist*, who uses windows of opportunity in the political/economic system to target key leverage points that can help shift the system.
- *Questioner*, who supports deliberation on fundamental questions and can help create new discourse and a cultural shift.
- *Broker*, who creates meaningful connections and learning cycles around the question of system change between movements and networks at multiple geographical levels, including globally.
- *Gardener*, who helps the new system emerge by naming, connecting, nurturing and illuminating the pioneers of the new system (Susa 2019: 14–15).

Susa notes that whilst these roles had different functions, only by working 'together can they bring about the required social transformation' (ibid.). The model also suggests that change happens at three different levels:

- *Level of culture*, where dominant societal values and world views are and eventually shift.
- *Level of regimes*, where the dominant political, economic and social institutions are and where new or transformed institutions emerge.
- *Level of niches*, where pioneers experiment with ideas and seeds of new systems (ibid.).

This framework has relevance to the debates outlined in this chapter because it suggests a complex role for civil society organizations that moves beyond the role of being the transmitter of knowledge to being that of facilitator, enabler and critical engager with appropriate issues. What Susa further suggests is that his framework has value if the NGO recognizes that there are no simple solutions or predetermined outcomes.

What both of these frameworks suggest is that the role of civil society organizations in seeking social change is complex and should not be focused solely on guiding the learner towards a predetermined path. Change comes as a result of transformation at a number of different levels from the individual to the approaches towards education to wider global society. The models also suggest that any desire for seeking social change requires taking risks, trying out new and innovative ideas and recognizing that the mere processes of transformation may have unintended consequences on the individual, the organization and society as a whole.

Civil Society Organizations and Sustainable Development

There has been a lot of rhetoric around the importance of civil society as a key agent in securing social change. This can be seen through various international programmes such as progress on the Sustainable Development Goals (SDGs). For example, within the promotion of UN initiatives around global citizenship, civil society organizations have been seen as key players who can experiment with models of effective practice, test out new ideas and engage the wider public. However, a study on civil society organizations' engagement within the SDGs process showed that in many countries there were considerable weaknesses in terms of a multi-stakeholder process. What was significant was the lack of 'civic space' for NGOs to air their views and engage in an open democratic process (Fowler and Biekart 2020).

This reflects a wider issue of the extent to which the independent voices of civil society have been heard during the policy initiatives around sustainable development ever since the Rio Summit since 1992. Whilst there have been spaces for civil society within the various international initiatives since then, the extent to which their voice is seen as being linked to education and empowering communities to take action for change is perhaps more debatable (Tota 2014). As has been noted in other chapters, civil society organizations have often been used by policymakers as a means to promote and secure support for a specific initiative, to encourage changes in behaviour or to act as implementers of programmes.

An example that reflects these issues well has been the programmes on global citizenship in South Korea.

Role of NGOs as Global Citizenship Education Providers in South Korea

South Korea is an important country to consider within the debates around the role of civil society organizations for social change through global citizenship because its history and culture of engagement is rather different to most Western countries.

From the beginnings of the twenty-first century, there was evidence of a considerable number of NGOs engaging in promoting global citizenship themes within formal education. Whilst many of these programmes focused primarily on raising awareness of international development issues, there were some that took a more critical and social justice approach. Most however tended to emphasize a more moral and humanitarian approach (Sim 2016).

The South Korean government, influenced by having a former leading figure of the country as UN secretary general at the time, saw global citizenship as an important mechanism to equip learners with the knowledge and skills to live and work in the global economy of the twenty-first century. This led to a different model of global citizenship being promoted, one that framed engagement in learning about global issues in more neoliberal terms (Cho 2016; Cho and Mosselson 2018; Pak and Lee 2018).

Global citizenship education was formally introduced within the school curriculum in 2015. Since then, through a programme based around supporting lead teachers, professional development courses have been run to deliver global citizenship themes within the school classroom. This top-down process has had a number of consequences. NGOs were involved in the delivery of the programmes but on government terms; and secondly, teachers felt ill-equipped to deliver global citizenship.

Noh's (2019) study directly addresses this. Noh's research found that NGOs, because they were acting as subcontractors of government programmes, promoted global citizenship education in a neoliberal form, emphasizing learning other languages, cultural awareness, international volunteering and a charitable rather than social justice approach. Noh called on Korean development NGOs to change themselves first in order to be 'agents of change' and provide alternatives to the dominant state-driven approach.

Similar perspectives can be seen in Cho's (2016) study, which notes that he had found more than twenty-five NGOs offering global citizenship support to teachers. Many of these NGOs were interested in promoting different approaches but felt constrained by funding and by how global citizenship was being framed. Whilst similar themes and comments can be found about the role of NGOs in other countries (Biccum 2010), what is significant about the evidence from South Korea is that because the approach to global citizenship was seen as very top-down, the organizations felt disempowered and unable to promote their counter-hegemonic approaches.

Research on CSOs and Education for Social Change

An ongoing tension therefore within many NGOs has been the extent to which educational programmes are important in themselves in informing young people about global issues and an approach where the focus has been on supporting or delivering projects that have defined outcomes related to specific campaigns. There have been a number of doctoral research studies that have addressed these themes. The first to consider is Nadya Weber's (2012) research on the role of international NGOs. In her research on the educational programmes of the international NGO Save the Children in Canada and the United Kingdom, and influenced by the work of Barnett and Weiss, Weber suggested there were differing roles they could and did play. These included the ends justifying the means and a more long-term dialogical role (Barnett and Weiss 2008: 43–8).

Weber found that these positions covering fundraising, communications, specific campaigns and advocacy, and educational programmes presented inevitable challenges and contradictions. She found there was a challenge for Save the Children, as with other NGOs, of being able to both have short-term campaigning objectives and support 'collective, participatory and equitable dialogue' through educational programmes. These NGOs 'have the potential to facilitate the dialogical relationships that can open up possibilities for the collective and participatory communications that could lead to changes in the power structures and dynamics of the dichotomized world of North and South and rich and poor' (ibid., 48).

Unfortunately, since Weber conducted her research, due to financial constraints and changing policy priorities, Save the Children in the United Kingdom has cut virtually all of its educational programmes. However, her research is a reminder of the need to understand the complex challenges such organizations face in wanting to consider educational programmes.

Bullivant's (2020) research looked at the outlooks and perspectives of workers within grassroots development education organizations, called Development Education Centres (DECs) in England. Her research noted that central to their view of development education and global learning was the idea of change. She found that they articulated this change through three areas:

- Moral and political aims and values
- Processes of change and how change takes place
- Dimensions or scope of change (ibid., 81).

Looking at these three areas in turn, she identified a strong 'personal, moral and political endeavour, informed by values' from the people she interviewed. As one worker commented, 'all my working life I have been passionate about social justice issues'. Another was even more direct and said:

> fundamentally I'm an activist and I see education as a way of changing the world, so I'm not fundamentally an educator, you know, my end goal isn't you know making people more open minded and critical thinking, my end goal is you know the world is a better place. (ibid., 82)

Bullivant referred to Freire and publications such as *Training for Transformation*, mentioned earlier in this volume. She noted that the aim of social change was more implicit than explicit in the educational activities of these DEC workers. But what was evident was the sense that Freirean ideas related closely to their moral beliefs. There was also a sense of passion and personal commitment to their work:

> I do this because I really care about it, because it makes me angry and maybe it is the best thing to take any kind of emotion then out of it and go no OK we can use the participatory methods, we can use, sort of, encourage critical thinking and they will reach their own conclusions, but then that for some, surely, if I'm passionate and I work in it because of my own belief, feelings then my passion becomes diminished if I then have to remove that from the equation. (ibid., 83)

There was, however, a tension between the DEC workers' beliefs and their practices, the extent to which they could and should have a clear stance or whether they should promote themselves as neutral.

The second area Bullivant's research identified was a process-orientated approach to change. Reflecting similar debates in the work of Coelho, Caramelo and Menezes (2018), she suggested three distinct approaches:

- Awareness raising for the purpose of providing information
- 'Results-orientated' approaches aimed at behaviour change in individuals or wider institutions, whether through advocacy, campaigning or activism
- Constructivist and 'process-orientated approach', where the emphasis is on education and developing critical thinking and skills to live more responsibly and enact change, combining elements of 'personal and social transformation' (Coelho et al. 2018: 42; Bullivant 2020: 86).

Bullivant also found within these approaches a tendency towards a more open-ended and less prescriptive pedagogy. However, there was also still a distinct view that had transformational goals. This reflected wider debates between liberal and individualistic pedagogies and those with a more radical and collective focus.

This perceived distinction between what Bullivant called 'trusting the process' and wider aims of social justice (ibid., 93) reflects debates raised in this volume about different pedagogical approaches. Noting the work of Brown (2013) and Blackmore (2014), Bullivant (2020: 96) suggested that a way through this was to see the role of the educators as catalytic individuals or organic intellectuals.

Tallon's research on how NGOs in New Zealand promoted development and global issues within their educational programmes for schools reflects some of these complex questions through the ways they aim to engage learners. To Tallon, a key finding was the ways in which images were promoted by NGOs and how this related to their fundraising agenda. But what was even more concerning was the way some NGOs used emotion as a way of gaining support from young people:

> In 2007, I witnessed an NGO worker expressively use emotion to move a captive audience of high school students firstly, to a sense of horror, then pity and then guilt, which could be relieved if their proffered action was taken. The NGO's speaker was addressing a school assembly and although I was standing in the foyer I could see the photos of emaciated Asian children on the large screen and I could hear emotive music. The students were very quiet until the teachers and I heard something coming from the auditorium: *sniffing*. A number of the students had been emotionally moved to cry. This poignant moment was shattered by an outburst from the teacher standing next to me. She swore loudly, and then said in a very irritated voice '*Great, how am I supposed to teach them maths after this?*' (Tallon 2013: 51)

This example from Tallon shows the dangers of how NGOs can use their perceived 'expertise' to influence the outlook of the learner. This approach of the NGO worker engenders a sense of 'guilt and empathy' and a need to feel 'compassionate for the less fortunate, or made to feel guilty that they are wealthy and privileged' (Tallon 2003). Tallon notes, referring to the work of Chouliaraki (2010) and Andreotti (2011), that this approach reinforces the role of the learner as a moral agent, a saviour and ethnocentric.

There is however the danger of equating all NGOs with these criticisms, whereas if one looks at the educational work of organizations such as Oxfam, for example, there is much more of an emphasis on an open-ended approach to learning. Their curriculum for global citizenship education is based on a:

> framework to equip learners for critical and active engagement with the challenges and opportunities of life in a fast-changing and interdependent world. It is transformative, developing the knowledge and understanding, skills, values and attitudes that learners need both to participate fully in a globalised society and economy, and to secure a more just, secure and sustainable world than the one they have inherited. (Oxfam 2015: 5)

What this framework demonstrates is the central place of learning and the including of skills such as critical thinking. This is why their approach is based on 'learning, thinking and action'. The framework further stated:

> alongside a rigorous development of global understanding and multiple perspectives, an education for global citizenship should also include opportunities for young people to develop their skills as agents of change and to reflect critically on this role. (ibid.)

In bringing the evidence from research together on the role of civil society organizations, one of the most valuable has been the research by Tarozzi (2020) reviewing the influence of NGOs across Europe on global citizenship education. He found that NGOs play a pivotal role in the following three main areas of engagement and achievement:

- *Theory*, by developing the concepts being used around the field. (However, he found that the terms were still under-theorized and NGOs could do more in these areas through more partnerships with academic bodies.)
- *Practice*, by developing innovative approaches, they provide evidence of learning and bring in progressive and student-centred approaches. They promote innovative educational practices often with a clear values base.
- *Policy*, as they are often the bodies that governments turn to for advice on development of strategies. They are also the leading actors for lobbying for funding for global citizenship education (ibid.).

Tarozzi concluded that the role of NGOs was significant because:

- It brought in critical voices from below.
- They are more flexible and open to change than other bodies.
- They can merge the agendas of different political actors and various topics and bring groupings together.
- They bring in an innovative, values-based, transformative approach into school practice and teacher education programmes.
- Generally supportive of multi-stakeholder approaches.

Tarozzi did, however, note some of the criticisms of the practices of NGOs that have been mentioned earlier in this chapter. These include a tendency towards focusing on their own agendas which can often move into fundraising and campaigning priorities. Due to their needs to continually generate income, they have to constantly strive for visibility for the NGO. This relates to the theme raised at the beginning of the chapter about the tensions with their relationship to the state. This can often lead to NGOs 'softening their critical voices' (Tota 2014).

These examples of research demonstrate the difficult tightrope many civil society organizations have had to walk. The organizations want to have space to promote their own approaches to learning but this can all too easily become compromised by funding constraints. However, as these research studies also show, too many organizations put their own profile-raising above educational objectives. Tarozzi's conclusions suggest, on the other hand, that NGOs have potentially a very valuable role to play at theoretical, policy and practical levels. It is to practice that this chapter now turns.

Case Studies

There are civil society organizations around the world that demonstrate many of the issues discussed in this chapter. In the United States for example, organizations like the Asia Society play an important role in making available good-quality educational resources to teachers. Around Europe, there are similar organizations that have a clear social justice component, and these include organizations discussed elsewhere in this volume, including Bridge 47 discussed in Chapter 12. For the purposes of this chapter, three different types of organizations are reviewed, an international development NGO, a grassroots organization and a body that emerged out of social media and web-based initiatives.

CAFOD

Within the United Kingdom, one NGO that has consistently linked its education to broader social justice and change has been CAFOD, that is, Catholic Agency for Overseas Development. It relates its educational programme with schools and young people to broader Catholic social teaching, based on principles of dignity, solidarity, the common good, option for the poor, peace, care for creation and the dignity of work and participation (CAFOD, n.d.). Its pedagogical approach has been based on the four-part model: *see* (pupil-centred learning), *judge* (analysis), *action* (do something) and *celebrate* (share with others).

CAFOD produces a range of resources for schools and runs professional development programmes for teachers. Like many NGOs, they have been particularly active around climate change. To CAFOD, however, its support for education and campaigns around climate action must be seen as contributing to the 'common good', going beyond 'greening' for development, prioritizing the needs of the poorest and eradicating the inequalities that exist in the world. Furthermore, the engagement of young people in climate action needs to be done in an 'inclusive and participatory way' that can clearly be seen to empower all involved.

Another feature of their educational work is their youth leadership programme which aims to develop future leaders through engagement in forms of action within a school context that can then be replicated within wider society. An underlying theme of this programme is the promotion of a message of hope, that they themselves can influence social change. They see this programme as challenging young people 'to become aspiring leaders by reflecting on their responsibility towards others and the planet'. From this deepening of understanding global issues, 'young people will become empowered to run social action projects' (CAFOD 2020).

RISC

Within the United Kingdom, there are a number of grassroots organizations whose function is to promote and support learning about global and development issues within their locality. These organizations are called Development Education Centres, and have been in existence in different towns and cities for over thirty years and provide an important focal point for accessing resources, providing professional development opportunities and engaging in projects and initiatives that support social change.

One of the most effective and long lasting of these centres is Reading International Solidarity Centre (RISC). Like many other such centres, RISC runs training courses for teachers, and its educational projects have included ones on whole school change, understanding Islam and how to monitor changing attitudes by teachers and pupils. Central to their educational work is the promotion of global citizenship.

But what makes the Centre different from many similar ones in the United Kingdom is their close involvement and engagement with local community groups. They do this by running a Global Café, which provides rooms for hire and run one of the largest fair trade shops in the United Kingdom. One of their most innovative initiatives has been the development of a roof garden which has become an important educational resource for local schools and community groups.

This interest in food, gardens and the outdoors led RISC to develop a number of projects around this theme including Food4Families and Global Schools Gardens. These projects reflect their broader social change message of linking local to global issues to a wider public (Richards 2008, 2009). A feature also of their approach is the focus on 'individual power of agency' (Royant 2017: 116).

Another aspect of RISC's work is the interaction between educators and the wider public. As Royant's research on the work of the Centre notes:

> RISC's successful pedagogy has much to do with being able to support individuals and groups of people within society to re-present complex issues through simple actions. (ibid., 176)

To the workers at RISC, one of the ways they do this is through the use of visual images, particularly photographs, videos and the use made of their building.

Underpinning their work has been a distinctive pedagogical approach that has four interrelated categories:

- Widening access – providing a voice and reaching out.
- Being in solidarity with other people around the world and acknowledge existing diversity.
- Questioning and consciousness, including challenging assumptions, accepting difference and promoting values of such justice, tolerance, respect and sustainability and being global citizens.
- Social change, by making a difference, working towards a fairer society and changing the world through implementing alternative ways of living (ibid., 144).

RISC provides one of the best examples of the value of grassroots civil society organizations as actors for social change through their direct engagement with local communities and the role they see for themselves as enablers and facilitators.

Global Citizens Movement

One of the most internationally effective social media–focused organizations for social change is the Global Citizens movement. With considerable support from celebrities and well-known international figures, this movement has become an influential and important player in the promotion of social change.

Global Citizen has its headquarters in New York, with offices in Canada, South Africa, Australia, Germany and the United Kingdom. The organization was co-founded by Hugh Evans, Simon Moss and Wei Soo in 2008.

The work of the organization is primarily based around an online social platform that aims to encourage social action from people to combat global poverty and promote the Sustainable Development Goals.

This online platform provides information on a range of global issues and provides guidelines for actions individuals and organizations can take. Whilst most of the forms of action individuals can take consists of signing petitions or sending tweets, they do include learning opportunities based around quizzes on specific themes.

Their website makes reference to learning and its relation to change:

> If we learn more about why extreme poverty exists, make informed consumer decisions, and use our voices to advocate for change, we can ensure that the businesses, organizations and governments in our lives are contributing to a world without extreme poverty.
>
> Global Citizen encourages you to learn more and take action on a range of issues related to extreme poverty, helping to build the movement that will end extreme poverty. (Global Citizen 2020)

They have developed programmes with both corporate partners such as CISCO and DELTA, media bodies and a range of NGOs (Global Citizen n.d.). They have also introduced award programmes and supported fellowship and scholarship programmes.

What this movement demonstrates is the extent to which the term 'global citizen' has become popular and is touching many sectors of society. Through the internet and various forms of social media, the Global Citizen movement has become a valuable source of information and a potential inspirer to many thousands of young people about what forms of social action they could take.

The movement has focused primarily on using forms of social media, often online petitions to force policymakers to change direction. Through their campaigns they have influenced campaign policies on areas such as vaccines by health companies, clean water and family planning (McCarthy 2019).

The movement may perhaps come in for justifiable criticism in reinforcing some of the more consumerist and individualistic approaches towards global citizenship. The linkages with the corporate world do present some challenges and the extent to which it addresses some of the more power-related issues within societies and economies is perhaps open to question. But its appeal and influence cannot be ignored.

Conclusion

Civil society organizations have clearly played a leading role around the world in being agents for social change. In countries with undemocratic political structures, civil society is likely to be the place where dissent and calls for change can be most effectively heard.

But in countries where there has been a strong democratic tradition, civil society organizations, whilst being seen as signs of a healthy, informed and engaged citizenry, have in some instances become little more than an arm of the state, its soft underbelly that gives a human face to the delivery of government services. In a number of countries, particularly those with populist and far right governments, civil society organizations have suffered because of their independent positioning against the authoritarian state.

Whilst many civil society organizations have looked to education as a means of securing social change, this has all too often been framed within the extent to which it serves the agendas and needs of the NGO. This can be seen within the history and discussions around global citizenship, for example. Whilst there is no doubt that CSOs have been, in many countries, the leading players in promoting the inclusion of the term within education, the extent to which this has reflected a critical pedagogical perspective that recognizes participatory and open-ended forms of learning varies.

A second challenge for CSOs has been their relationship to the state. Over the past twenty years, any form of state resourcing for the work of NGOs has tended to be followed by caveats such as the extent to which the funding furthers state and national government agendas. Whilst themes such as global citizenship can in theory provide the opportunities for critical and more reflective approaches towards learning that might engender a desire for social change, there has been a countervailing tendency of furthering neoliberal agendas of economic competitiveness.

The example of South Korea discussed in this chapter highlights many of the contradictions and challenges civil society organizations face in supporting educational goals for social change. Whilst there can be a broad degree of consensus as to the value of global citizenship, the constraints on the funding of the NGO combined with a dominant view of the term by the state as furthering economic goals, means that it is much more challenging to promote a counter-hegemonic and independent educational strategy.

Thirdly, NGOs and civil society organizations will in many countries be faced with the challenges of the extent to which they have the opportunities and spaces for their approaches and resources to be used within formal education. To what extent should they relate what they produce to the needs of the curriculum and local or national state priorities, or should they consciously see their role as promoting a counter-hegemonic approach?

Fourthly, the ways in which people now learn and engage with society has been heavily influenced by the power of the internet and social media. This has had major repercussions for civil society organizations. Social media is now the dominant way in which they campaign and lobby for social change. The role the public, including young people, play in this process is one of continuing debate, as Gyoh's research has shown. What has been noticeable is that in the third decade of the twenty-first century the role of civil society organizations in terms of seeing education as a major vehicle of their work has considerably declined compared to, say, ten years ago. Some of this could be said to be due to decline in many countries of state funding but there has also been a drift towards seeing social media as the means to promote awareness and engagement in social and political campaigns. A consequence of this has been that within many organizations the deeper processes of learning have become marginalized.

This, it is suggested, is a major challenge if civil society organizations are to be seen as important stakeholders within education for social change. Social media is clearly here to stay. The question is, how can it be used in a way that encourages and supports critical thinking, looking at issues from different perspectives and recognizing that there is no one solution or even way forward in seeking change? Civil society organizations, because of their role, have potentially the greatest opportunity of all bodies in society to respond to these challenges. They have traditions of innovation, seeking alternative ways of delivering services and acting as voices for the marginalized. But it needs to be noted that this is not the case with all organizations. Some see their role as retaining the status quo in society. However, for those that have emerged from grassroots movements and in response to forms of injustice and inequality, civil society organizations, if reminded of their mission, can be leading players in seeking a more just world. As this and other chapters have suggested, recent social movements around climate change, racial and gender inequality could perhaps be the themes through which this transformation takes place.

Questions for Further Consideration

- What do civil society organizations bring to the discussions about education for social change? What could be said to be their distinctive features and contribution?
- What are the strengths and weaknesses of civil society organizations' engagement with global citizenship programmes?
- What does the example of South Korea tell us about the relationship of civil society to the state in delivering educational programmes?
- In what ways is social media changing the ways civil society organizations engage with initiatives for global social change?

Further Reading

Allen, C., D. McAdam and D. Pellow (2010), *What is the Role of Civil Society in Social Change?* Available online: http://chrisallan.info/wp-content/uploads/2010/04/Supporting-successful-movements-2.03.pdf

Cho, H. and J. Mosselson (2018), 'Neoliberal Practices Amidst Social Justice Orientations: Global Citizenship Education in South Korea', *Compare: A Journal of Comparative and International Education*, 48, no. 6: 861–78.

Cooper, R. (2018), *What is Civil Society, its Role and Value in 2018?*, K4D Falmer, University of Sussex-IDS.

Edwards, M. (2014), *When is Civil Society a Force for Social Transformation?* Available online: https://www.opendemocracy.net/en/transformation/when-is-civil-society-force-for-social-transformation/

Tarozzi, M. (2020), 'Role of NGOs in Global Citizenship Education', in D. Bourn (ed.) *Bloomsbury Handbook of Global Education and Learning*, 133–48, London: Bloomsbury.

12

International Organizations, UNESCO, Earth Charter and Putting the Sustainable Development Goals into Practice

Introduction

International organizations have played an important role in promoting education for social change. Most important of all have been United Nations bodies such as UNESCO and the body's initiatives promoting specific global goals. This chapter reviews the role these bodies have played in promoting education for social change particularly through the UN Millennium Development Goals (MDGs) and its successor programme, the Sustainable Development Goals (SDGs), and also the Decade on Education for Sustainable Development (ESD).

The impact of all these initiatives on calls for education for social change will be reviewed alongside the extent to which they framed the focus of international debates. The influence of UNESCO will be examined, and the nature of its work and influence will be looked at through its initiatives on education for sustainable development and global citizenship. Included also is the international initiative, Earth Charter, which, although not officially supported by UN bodies, has played an important educative function. In terms of research, two examples are considered, one looking at the impact of UNESCO on ESD in China and the second assessing the strengths and weaknesses of UNESCO's global citizenship programme. Finally, the chapter will address two international educational examples which have been heavily influenced by these initiatives, Bridge 47 and the World's Largest Lesson.

A theme throughout this chapter is that whilst these various international initiatives have enabled a range of policies and practices that promote social change to be introduced, they can also result in uncritical and more reformist and technical approaches.

From Rio Summit to the MDGs to the SDGs

A major factor influencing policies and research on education for social change has been a range of United Nations-led international agreements since the 1990s.

A major influence on education was the 1992 Rio Summit on Sustainable Development. The international agreement from the Summit and its commitment to raising awareness and understanding of environment and development issues within all aspects of education were a major stimulus for initiatives in many countries around the world. Although there were often major challenges with a lack of resources, the Summit created a common goal of education for sustainable development. The agreement encouraged the creation of a range of cross-disciplinary programmes and projects at all levels of education (Huckle and Sterling 1996). One of the features of the outcomes of the Summit was the creation of specific networks around Agenda 21 of the agreement and its emphasis on education (United Nations 1992).

The second was the Millennium Development Goals from 2000 to 2015. These eight goals, launched by the UN in 2000, related to reducing global poverty, improving health and education, furthering gender equality, promoting peace, human rights and environmental sustainability and the encouragement of global partnerships. The MDGs, as they became called, framed international development policies and programmes for the ensuing decade. Whilst there was some success in reducing global poverty, the goals became too instrumental and resourcing became too target-setting with insufficient attention to creative initiatives. There was also a tendency, in many of the programmes framed to deliver the MDGs, to give a sense of the Global North helping the Global South.

Both of these initiatives had an impact on education. Following the Rio Summit, there were numerous programmes, policies and initiatives that aimed to bring environmental and development themes more closely together (Bourn 2005). In the United Kingdom, for example, a special government advisory panel on Sustainable Development was created that had a considerable influence on including sustainability themes within the school curriculum between 2005 and 2010. With regard to the MDGs, they were also influential in shaping the programmes and funding priorities around development and global education. In the United Kingdom, the MDGs were used as the criteria for the Development Awareness Fund. Whilst funding for development awareness projects required that the projects had to have clear educational goals, they also had to demonstrate relevance to the MDGs and how the project would advance them. Many innovative projects were undertaken from this funding between

1998 and 2010, but many of them failed to demonstrate these linkages because it was impossible to show the connection between a project in a school or university or learning about specific development issues and combating global poverty (Dominy et al. 2009).

This example reflects an observation made by Hartmeyer (2004) that by framing educational programmes in this way, the emphasis came to be on solutions to predetermined goals and on public relations rather than what was the nature and impact of the learning that was undertaken.

Impact of the Decade on Education for Sustainable Development

Alongside the MDGs and prior to the establishment of the SDGs initiative, the United Nations in 2002 adopted a resolution calling for a Decade on Education for Sustainable Development, running from 2005 to 2014, and co-ordinated by UNESCO. A very significant initiative by both having UN support and running over a decade, it allowed policymakers and practitioners at all levels to develop strategies and long-term plans for embedding sustainable development within educational programmes. The Decade aimed to integrate the values inherent in sustainable development into all aspects of learning and to encourage changes in behaviour that allowed for a more sustainable and just society for all (UNESCO 2005).

The Decade sought to 'mobilise the educational resources of the world to help create a more sustainable future'. There was also an emphasis within the UNESCO materials around the Decade to encourage 'changes in behaviour that created a more sustainable future in terms of environmental integrity, economic viability and a just society for present and future generations' (UNESCO 2009).

UNESCO, as the lead agency for the Decade, worked to encourage new partnerships across all sectors of society, promote research, monitoring and evaluation, act as a forum for relevant stakeholders, share good practice and support member states to put ESD into appropriate curriculum and policies. An underlying principle of the Decade was to 'reorient education towards sustainability, which in turn had the potential to impact the way people think' (ibid.).

Ten years later, in their final report on the monitoring and evaluation of the Decade, UNESCO suggested that there had been major accomplishments during the ten years including a range of national policies and agreements as well as increased engagement in sustainable development from many schools, universities, community-based organisations, international NGOs and the private sector (UNESCO 2014a).

The launch of the UN Decade provided a new opportunity to ensure that education programmes and initiatives at all levels (local, national, regional, global) were, 'closely linked to understanding the world in which we live, the divisions between rich and poor and the need to engage people in working for a more just and equitable world' (Bourn 2005: 15). It was hoped that the Decade would emphasize the need for a balance between, and an integration of, the environmental, economic and social aspects of development, with attention also being paid to the cultural dimension.

However, a decade later, the evidence was much more patchy as to its impact. A major criticism of the Decade was its failure to bring into many of the debates at the time some of the underlying issues and tensions and potential different perspectives within some of the key UNESCO documents. There was very little reference to the divisions between rich and poor or the cause of overconsumption in many countries. Although UNESCO had itself recognized the need for changes in societies, there was also not sufficient attention given to the local realities in which many people were living (Firth and Smith 2013).

Huckle and Wals (2015), in reviewing the Decade, were even more critical, suggesting that the Decade represented no more than business as usual. To them, the Decade did not lead to policymakers challenging their own assumptions about ESD. In their review of case studies for policymakers and practitioners produced during the Decade, Huckle and Wals (ibid., 493) noted that whilst there were references to the empowerment of change agents, there was relatively little critical analysis of current social and political systems and how change could take place. They suggested that the Decade was about social adaptation rather than social change.

The extent to which these criticisms are justified is perhaps open to debate. UNESCO was clearly wanting the Decade to encourage a more transformative approach to learning but due to its structures and relationship with governments, a number of compromises were inevitably made. For example, during the Decade 'education for all', which has been a long-standing UN goal, became part of the targets and goals which ensured a connection to the MDGs. There was also a shift in priorities during the Decade from reorientating of formal curricula to one that focused on quality education and prioritizing climate change, biodiversity and disaster risk reduction (UNESCO 2014b: 17). As a consequence, it resulted in some of the more radical and transformative ideas such as eco-pedagogy and global citizenship for sustainable development growing outside of the orbit of the Decade.

But what the Decade did do is provide spaces and opportunities for creative and innovative initiatives at a local and a national level. This was particularly the case in the early years of the Decade where national governments supported committees and working groups with resources to promote education for sustainable development within all sectors of education (Chalkley, Haigh and Higgitt 2010; Summers and Cutting 2016; Gadsby and Bullivant 2010).

Sustainable Development Goals

Since 2015, the dominant international framework for educational programmes has been the Sustainable Development Goals, or Global Goals. Unlike the MDGs, these goals extend to all countries and regions of the world and cover a much broader canvas.

There are seventeen goals:

- No poverty
- Zero hunger
- Good health and well-being
- Quality education
- Gender equality
- Clean water and sanitation
- Affordable and clean energy
- Decent work and economic growth
- Industry, innovation and infrastructure
- Reduced inequalities
- Sustainable cities and communities
- Responsible consumption and production
- Climate action
- Life below water
- Life on land
- Peace, justice and strong institutions
- Partnerships for the goals.

Within these goals are a series of targets. Whilst they can provide a comprehensive overview of future international priorities, many of the recommendations are suggestions rather than commitments.

The goals are seen as a plan of action for 'peace, planet and prosperity'. The support of governments from around the world to this UN initiative is, however, impressive. Its ambitious nature can be seen in the Preamble to their Declaration:

> [The Goals] seek to strengthen universal peace in larger freedom. We recognise that eradicating poverty in all its forms and dimensions, including extreme poverty, is the greatest global challenge and an indispensable requirement for sustainable development. All countries and all stakeholders, acting in collaborative partnership, will implement this plan. We are resolved to free the human race from the tyranny of poverty and want to heal and secure our planet. We are determined to take the bold and transformative steps which are urgently needed to shift the world onto a sustainable and resilient path. (United Nations 2015: 1)

Critics of the goals suggest there is a lack of accountability and coherence, 'unequal power relations and depoliticisation' (Belda-Miguel, Boni and Calabuig 2019: 386). The SDGs:

> do not overcome the de-politicisation of aid discourses and policies as they still frame development problems as technical, managerial and measurable problems. For example, issues of power and key political issues such as redistribution are totally absent from the Agenda. (ibid., 387)

It could also be argued that there are contradictions within the goals by them calling for action on climate change yet having economic growth as a specific goal.

Whatever are the contradictions and weaknesses in the goals, they have become the framework and template for many initiatives on sustainable development. This can be seen in the range of educational initiatives that have used the goals as the basis for learning about global and sustainability issues. These include the *TeachSDGs*[1] initiative, the *Get Up and Goals Project* discussed in an earlier chapter and the *World's Largest Lesson,* which is discussed later in this chapter. All of these projects focus on providing resources, ideas for school lessons and online activities for school children and teachers.

Perspectives on the SDGs and Social Change

The discussions on the promotion of the SDGs within education pose questions about the extent to which initiatives such as this encourage or hinder a sense of social change. As noted earlier in this chapter, there have been criticisms of UN initiatives for either being too prescriptive or just reinforcing the status quo. As earlier chapters in this volume have suggested, if education for sustainable development is to have any real meaning, it has to include systematic change. This is what Sterling noted in his reflections on the Decade and in his initial interventions into framing the content of the SDGs. He noted in 2014 that most of the high-level sustainable development reports associated with the post-2015 development agenda almost invariably underplayed the role of education as a vehicle of social change (see Sterling 2014b). Sterling further commented that in outlining the means of implementation for the SDGs, the UN bodies failed to recognize the potential systematic change role of education. Education, he suggests, can foster creativity and enthusiasm; it could build lasting change because it is owned and affected by participating stakeholders and learners.

In answer to the criticism that SDGs, like other such UN initiatives, are too goal orientated, Sterling argues that if the approach taken is a learner-centred view alongside a goal-orientated approach, then different interpretations can emerge. He criticized the current focus of Goal 4 and its targets because of its mechanistic approach to education as an instrument of change. Sterling said, 'education can play a vital role in bringing about sustainable change if change is owned by affected and participating stakeholders' (Sterling 2015: 27).

Kioupi and Voulvoulis (2019), in their review of the literature around ESD and the SDGs, also emphasized the importance of systematic thinking. They noted:

> Systems thinking is widely recognised as an effective way to reframe the SDGs in order to highlight their integration and reflect on important directions towards building sustainable societies, compensating at the same time, for their shortcomings and limitations. It offers the potential of a richer view on the relationship between Education and Sustainability, with ESD playing an active role in delivering the transformative changes required for society to move towards a sustainability state. (ibid., 5)

Reflecting wider concerns already discussed in this chapter and elsewhere in this volume, they suggest that seeing sustainable development as an end state, as a goal, is problematic. Instead, their view on the promotion of the SDGs and a sustainable future is: 'a system state can only emerge as the result of complex interactions between system parameters and conditions with education guiding the transformational process for society reaching such a dynamic state.' This means that systematic change is more of a process than a product. Moreover, they suggest that 'a future of the UN 2030 Global Agenda should be localised to address the needs and requirements of local [communities] that society will aspire to reach, a vision of a world transformed by the SDGs' (ibid.).

A slightly different perspective is proposed by Brown and McCowan (2018), who suggest that the SDGs are unimaginative and ignore the need to rethink what is taught in the classroom. They suggest that a potential response to this challenge can be seen in *buen vivir,* 'a notion emerging from indigenous cultures and political movements in Latin America'. This approach is based on an alternative model to development and notions that economic growth is the answer. The concept of *buen vivir* has some similarities to concepts such as *Ubuntu* (Pieniazek 2020) in Africa, and other perspectives that relate personal growth to ecology and well-being, and notions of peace and harmony. These question the emphasis on the economic in development.

For Brown and McCowan, *buen vivir* more recently has been seen to mean 'good living', harmonious coexistence and living with nature in accordance with principles of reciprocity, complementarity, solidarity and relationality. In this respect, it relates closely to the emerging discourses around eco-pedagogy and the importance of breaking down the divisions between human and nature. The *buen vivir* approach challenges Western notions of progress and some form of linear development. It suggests, with regard to the SDGs, that there is also a need to question the emphasis on commodification and instead pose an alternative to the dominant narrative of modernity.

Finally, Brown and McCowan state that their approach poses major questions about the role and nature of education. Going beyond a human capital approach, *buen vivir* suggests that education should be following these principles:

- *Epistemological pluralism:* acknowledging and transiting between different forms of knowing.
- *Porosity of boundaries:* non-rigid classification of the educational space, education professionals and disciplines.
- *Holism of learning:* bringing together of the manual, practical, technical, abstract, aesthetic and spiritual.
- *Cooperativism:* avoidance of competition-based education and the consequent progressive filtering out of students from level to level.
- *Compassion and nonviolence:* recognition of the importance of peace in all aspects of life, including nonviolent communication.
- *Collectivism:* learning collectively within a web of relationships between people and with the non-human world.
- *Meaningful livelihoods:* a link with enriching forms of work (rather than alienating employability).

- *Living the present:* education as a state of being, not aimed at the exchange value of qualifications (Brown and McCowan 2018: 320).

Many of the principles Brown and McCowan raise can be seen elsewhere in this volume particularly in terms of forms of pedagogy. What they suggest is that these principles provide a philosophy of living with a greater ownership by communities of the nature and form of education being provided. They recognize the dangers of essentialism around this approach, of romanticizing perspectives of indigenous communities. But what is relevant is that within the international discourses around ESD and the SDGs, *buen vivir* is seen as a process of learning and living; it can pose important questions for all concerned with international policy formation and implementation.

UNESCO and Education for Sustainable Development

Following the Decade on ESD, UNESCO has retained its lead role within the UN in this area and developed a Global Action Plan from 2015 to 2019 which had five priority areas. These were to advance policy, transform learning and training environments, build the capacities of educators and trainers, empower and mobilize youth and accelerate sustainable solutions at a local level. A road map for taking forward these priorities was introduced that had two objectives:

1. to reorient education and learning so that everyone has the opportunity to acquire the knowledge, skills, values and attitudes that empower them to contribute to sustainable development.
2. to strengthen education and learning in all agendas, programmes and activities that promote sustainable development (UNESCO 2014c).

UNESCO also aimed to promote and share good practice from around the world, but it is evident that activities tended to become focused around specific issues such as climate change, biodiversity, disaster risk reduction, water, cultural diversity, sustainable urbanization and sustainable lifestyles. This reflected the growing focus on the influence of the SDGs in guiding policy implementation.

One of the strengths of UNESCO's work in ESD has been its ability to bring together key stakeholders from around the world, promote examples of good practice, organize appropriate international gatherings and outline specific learning objectives. Concerning this last point around learning objectives, UNESCO in 2017 published a booklet on this theme but reflecting the changing priorities within the body, the focus was on the relationship of ESD to a number of SDG targets. This publication did show, however, the continued support within UNESCO for relating ESD in its broadest sense to actions for social change. It noted that ESD can enable individuals to develop the skills to take action:

> ESD is holistic and transformational education that addresses learning content and outcomes, pedagogy and the learning environment. Thus, ESD does not only integrate contents such as climate change, poverty and sustainable consumption into the curriculum; it also creates interactive, learner-centred teaching and learning settings. What ESD requires is a shift from teaching to learning. It asks for an action-oriented, transformative pedagogy, which supports self-directed learning, participation and collaboration, problem-orientation, inter- and transdisciplinarity and the linking of formal and informal learning. (UNESCO 2017: 7)

To UNESCO, ESD remains an important element of its educational programme, and there is still a desire to relate the learning to forms of social action that are transformative.

UNESCO and Global Citizenship

UNESCO's engagement with global citizenship is more recent than that of sustainable development, and its importance has grown in part due to support from the South Korean government and the enthusiastic support of the former secretary general of the UN, Ban Ki-Moon. In a similar vein to that of ESD, global citizenship education has been seen in holistic and transformative terms but with a specific focus on a values-based approach.

UNESCO's work on global citizenship education has resulted in bringing together key stakeholders in the field through appropriate conferences and forums, producing a database of relevant material and examples of practice. However, the engagement in global citizenship could be said to have broadened its focus too much by including within its remit a range of international initiatives around the prevention of violent extremism[2] and education about the Holocaust and other genocides.[3] UNESCO's work on languages in education also became included within the programmes on global citizenship.[4] Another initiative that became included was a joint initiative with the United Nations Office on Drugs and Crime (UNODC) on Global Citizenship Education for the Rule of Law.

These examples perhaps suggest an approach to global citizenship education that is more about defending existing societies rather than seeking social change, however well intended the initiatives may be.

Yet, despite these question marks about their programme, UNESCO's work on global citizenship has clearly been very influential around the world. There is evidence now of engagement in the area in Africa, Latin America and Asia, which has meant that it can now be seen as a term that is more than a 'western construction'.

An influential document produced in 2016 on the *ABCs of Global Citizenship Education* summarizes well the thinking on what is meant by the term at that time. Produced through a series of questions and answers, the booklet, for example, suggested that global citizenship referred primarily to 'a sense of belonging to the global community and a common sense of humanity, with its presumed members experiencing solidarity and collective identity among themselves and collective responsibility at the global level'. The booklet further suggested that the goal of global citizenship education is 'to empower learners to engage and assume active roles both locally and globally, to face and resolve global challenges and ultimately to become proactive contributors to a more just, peaceful, tolerant, inclusive, secure and sustainable world'. Reflecting the debates about the relationship to ESD, peace education and education for international understanding, the booklet suggested that they are all part of a transformative and holistic pedagogy. The perspectives outlined suggest an approach that could be summarized as humanistic and cosmopolitan, that 'promotes respect for diversity and solidarity for humanity' (UNESCO n.d.).

Bringing ESD and Global Citizenship Together

UNESCO became increasingly conscious of the limitations of having two parallel initiatives, and in 2019, in Vietnam, a Forum on Education for Sustainable Development and Global Citizens was held. At this conference there were clearly attempts to show the synergies between the two areas and promote a more values-based and holistic approach. This meant emphasizing all three learning dimensions that need to be developed:

- Cognitive: To acquire knowledge, understanding and critical thinking about global, regional, national and local issues, the interconnectedness and interdependency of different countries and populations, as well as social, economic and environmental aspects of sustainable development.
- Social and emotional: To have a sense of belonging to a common humanity, sharing values and responsibilities, empathy, solidarity and respect for

differences and diversity, as well as feel and assume sense of responsibility for the future.
- Behavioural: To act effectively and responsibly at local, national and global levels for a more peaceful and sustainable world.[5]

Through this initiative and increased acceptance of the need to frame ESD and global citizenship initiatives within the SDGs framework, there is recognition within UNESCO of the need to bring these areas closer together.

This can now be seen in the organization's road map for ESD to 2030 which makes reference to competencies related to empathy, solidarity and action-taking that can further SDG 4 (UNESCO 2020).

Role of the Earth Charter

Finally, within the discussions on international initiatives that suggest education for global social change, it is important to consider the *Earth Charter*. The Charter grew out of the discussions around the Rio Summit in 1992, and two years later, Maurice Strong (secretary general of the Rio Earth Summit) and Mikhail Gorbachev, working through organizations they each founded (Earth Council and Green Cross International, respectively), launched an initiative (with support from the Dutch government) to develop an Earth Charter as a civil society initiative. The Charter was seen as a way of engaging wider society in many of the themes outlined in the Summit. Following a lengthy consultation process, a Charter was agreed in 2000. The Charter gained support from UNESCO and a wide range of international organizations including IUCN – The World Conservation Union.

The Charter has since then become a mechanism for engaging individuals, communities, local and regional authorities, businesses, trade unions and civil society organizations from throughout the world. It has been used to support peace negotiations, as a basis for educational textbooks, as a code of ethics and as a lobbying tool to governments and international bodies (see Corcoran, Vilela and Roerink 2005).

What the Charter aims to do is promote a vision that all peoples around the world can support and share. This can be summarized in its Preamble:

We stand at a critical moment in Earth's history, a time when humanity must choose its future. As the world becomes increasingly interdependent and fragile, the future at once holds great peril and great promise. To move forward we must recognize that in the midst of a magnificent diversity of cultures and life forms we are one human family and one Earth community with a common destiny. We must join together to bring forth a sustainable global society founded on respect for nature, universal human rights, economic justice, and a culture of peace. Towards this end, it is imperative that we, the peoples of Earth, declare our responsibility to one another, to the greater community of life, and to future generations. (Earth Charter n.d.: 1)

Underpinning the Charter are sixteen principles supported by four pillars: Respect and Care for the Community of Life, Ecological Integrity, Social and Economic Justice, and Democracy, Nonviolence, and Peace. It concludes with *The Way Forward*.

The Charter was particularly influential during the Decade on ESD within which it produced, in partnership with UNESCO, a publication of case studies telling stories of practice from around the world. The stories in this publication reflect the way the Charter has been used, as a tool for promoting a values-based approach to learning, that is transformative, encouraging interdisciplinary and participatory methodologies that can be adapted and applied to appropriate local and cultural contexts (Earth Charter and UNESCO 2007).

The relevance and importance of the Charter has been noted by Huckle and Wals (2015) because it brings in themes that have often been missing from many of the discourses and policy initiatives around ESD. For example, it brings in the ethical, cultural and political dimensions. Huckle and Wals also note that the Charter goes beyond a 'greening of the curriculum' approach. The Charter is important because it goes beyond the environment versus development agenda and brings in themes such as indigenous knowledges, human rights and cultural identity. Whilst the Charter could be criticized for being all things to all people and rather idealistic, it can on the other hand become a tool that enables communities and people from around the world to identify their own relationship to the environmental and global challenges of today.

As Newman has noted, the Charter can be seen as a transformational text, of 'seeing the world in a new way' (Newman 2009 :103).

Finally, an example of the way in which the Charter has been used as a vehicle for social change has been the Paulo Freire Institute in Brazil. It has developed the concept of eco-pedagogy. Using this approach, the Institute developed a range of training materials. To the Institute, the Charter has been seen both as a code of planetary ethics and as a call to action (Paulo Freire Institute n.d.).

The Charter then is an important example of bringing together several of the themes identified in this volume. However, there are dangers of it being interpreted as a model for some form of universal values system within education. For example, its potential quasi-religious language in some places has come in for some criticisms (Ferrari, 2002). But it is an approach that poses global ethical questions and puts centre stage to discussions on sustainable development, the importance of justice and a sense of moral responsibility (McGrady & Regan, 2008).

OECD

The Organization for Economic Co-operation and Development (OECD) is an important and influential international body that has had a considerable influence on education policies around the world. It is an organization of thirty-seven democratic countries that support free-market economies. Much of its educational work has been based around promoting research, gathering evidence and producing reports related to skills which was referred to in Chapter 6 of this volume. I have elsewhere (Bourn, 2018) written about the contribution of OECD to the promoting of softer skills and green skills. Much of its work over the past decade has reflected a dominant neoliberal agenda with economic success relying human capital(Vaccari and Gardinier, 2019). For OECD, therefore, many of the themes discussed in this volume would not be on their agenda. However, their vision publication of *The Future We Want* (OECD, 2018) does make some reference to themes from the international policy initiatives around sustainable development. For example, it calls for new solutions in a rapidly changing world and suggests that there are three challenges, environmental, economic and social. The report notes that 'education needs to aim to do more than prepare young people for the world of work; it needs to equip students with the skills they need to become active, responsible and engaged citizens' (Ibid. 4). Whilst there is some recognition of the wider environmental and social challenges in the report, it does not challenge dominant orthodoxies around the economy.

Within its PISA initiatives, OECD undertook in 2018 specific research on global competencies, and the outcomes of this were published in 2020 (OECD, 2020). This report and the material produced leading up to it demonstrated a focus within the organization on skills and competencies rather than active engagement in society, that is, global citizenship. Even within the references to values and attitudes, the emphasis was on respect for other cultures, there is no mention of questioning forces of power and causes of inequality. The implications of this approach are that social change through education comes through economic competition and a more skilled workforce rather than any promotion of a common humanity (Vaccari and Gardinier, 2019).

It has also been influential in encouraging international standard setting through its Programme for International Student Assessments (PISA).

Research

In identifying relevant research on the role of international organizations and education for social change, UNESCO, as this chapter has highlighted, is the most obvious example to focus on. The two studies discussed in the following paragraphs, however, come from very different standpoints and pose the role of UNESCO in very different ways. Han's (2019) study looks at the role of UNESCO and national state bodies on influencing Education for Sustainable Development (ESD) in China. For the purposes of this chapter, the focus is on the evidence emerging from Han's research on the influence of UNESCO.

Hatley's (2018) study, referred to also earlier in this volume, is more conceptual and critiques the organization's global citizenship programme.

Firstly, Han's research on how UNESCO has influenced China's ESD programmes identifies important questions regarding the interplay of global-national-local actors within the governance of the initiative. The research identified that UNESCO acts as an orchestrator 'that exercises indirect and soft governance'. This does not mean that there was no leadership and engagement from other bodies such as the state, NGOs, academics. Rather, as Han suggests, UNESCO's functions are '"to serve", *not* "to direct": set global norms and agendas, develop and broker knowledge and ideas, build capacity, and bring actors together for common goals' (Han 2019: 145).

This research highlights one example of the way international organizations can exercise governance of initiatives at a national or local level. Some might provide financial support, others technical expertise or political support. UNESCO's role, as this research shows, is more through an indirect approach.

Han identified that in a such a centralized state as China, the role of an international body such as UNESCO is always going to be played in a more indirect or 'soft' way. One of the most important ways UNESCO did this was by acting as a 'knowledge hub'. 'UNESCO convenes flows of ESD knowledge to the Chinese stakeholders while it also solicits local knowledge from the Chinese ESD stakeholders' (ibid., 148).

It also needs to be noted that the Chinese national government continues to take UNESCO seriously. It has a Permanent Delegation to UNESCO in Paris, and the National Committee for the organization is a very influential body within many sectors of education. Although a range of stakeholders have been involved in the ESD project in China, the national government remained the ultimate authority.

ESD has been recognized as an important part of Chinese educational policies since 2010, and UNESCO has resourced a range of initiatives and programmes on this topic for schools and teachers.

An important feature of Han's research was the role of 'knowledge workers' or international experts who have been particularly influential within UNESCO in implementing the ESD project. These experts acted as flows of knowledge on ESD ideas, and were an essential feature in the global educational governance (ibid.,148). As Han noted, 'The development of the ESD ideas in China is a process of UNESCO deepening its influence on Chinese education practice. The core expert team in China started with research and pilot projects on ESD and gradually transferred the UNESCO ideas into local practice' (ibid.).

Han also notes the challenges 'knowledge workers' had in China. Some of them translated ESD materials from other countries but their influence was constrained by 'their educational background, languages, and a western dominant history of the discursive development of ESD' (ibid., 158).

In the conclusion to the thesis, Han suggests that UNESCO should consider amplifying its soft mechanisms and continue to cultivate extensive networks to further mobilize its resources and orchestrate new ideas and policies across scales (ibid., 168).

The second research considered here is Jenny Hatley's thesis on *The Values of Global Citizenship Education and Implications for Social Justice* (2018). Aspects of Hatley's thesis are discussed elsewhere in this volume but here the focus is on the evidence from her research on reviewing UNESCO's initiatives on global citizenship in terms of the ideological role they have played within the international discourses, policies and practices in the field. Hatley suggests that UNESCO asserts a 'specific and controlled narrative around values' (p.163) in relation to global citizenship education. She further suggests that this promotes a perspective that these values are universal, resulting in encouraging policymakers and practitioners to follow their approach.

UNESCO's approach to global citizenship can therefore, as Hatley suggests, ignore specific social contexts. There appeared to be no recognition of difference. She further suggests this is because of a top-down model of global citizenship and the continued dominance of Western powers. UNESCO having a 'closed and fixed meaning of values' can result, as Hatley suggests, in the social practices of the organization adopting an inappropriate mindset in line with this perspective.

Hatley then looked at the way UNESCO uses its Associated Schools Project Network (ASPnet) to further this perspective. Their promotion and support for this Network consciously emphasizes calling on schools to integrate 'UNESCO's values and become role models in their community and beyond'. Schools should, moreover, develop and use educational materials based on these values (ibid.,170).

Whilst Hatley's research is important and has some validity, it does ignore the potential networking and stakeholder role that UNESCO can and does play. For example, the organization has supported the development of a database or 'clearing house'[6] of resources and materials on global citizenship education and thereby acts as a point of contact and opportunity for networking for all relevant stakeholders.

Both Hatley and Han's research studies do, however, show the influence of UNESCO, albeit as a form of 'soft power'. The extent to which the organization acts as an agent for change or as a preserver of dominant Western discourses and practices is likely to be an ongoing debate.

Case Studies

Bridge 47

This is a European Commission–funded initiative led by a network of civil society organizations that ran from 2017 to 2020. Its main function has been to facilitate networking and promoting examples of good practice around Target 4.7 of the SDGs. There has been a particular focus on global citizenship education. The project had four main elements:

- Networking – bringing people and organizations together to learn from each other through events and social media activities.
- Advocacy – calling for more and better global citizenship education.
- Partnership, particularly with organizations new to global citizenship education, including businesses, foundations, political bodies and universities.

- Identify and develop new and innovative forms of practice that can particularly build capacity of civil society organizations. This is to include a grants programme, training programmes, training the trainers seminars and conferences.

Target 4.7 of the Sustainable Development Goals created spaces and opportunities for a range of civil society organizations to develop new and creative approaches to building support for global citizenship and sustainable development themes within all sectors of education. An important element of Bridge 47 has been its ability to engage with a wide range of organizations including two global networks, three national development education networks, co-ordinating bodies for NGOs and civil society organizations with specific expertise in the field of global citizenship.

An example of the materials that the network produced was an Envision policy paper on transformative education. The paper noted:

> SDG Target 4.7 describes education as transformative when it is value-based and designed to promote global citizenship, sustainable development, human rights, gender equality, peace and appreciation of cultural diversity. This necessarily requires an action-oriented approach which bridges educator and learner through all the innovative forms of education leading to the notionof global citizenship. It inevitably builds a link between personal individual development and systemic change. (Bridge 47 2020a: 2)

This approach of seeing Target 4.7 as being an important engine for encouraging systematic and social change has been a major theme of the work of the network. It called for a European wide strategy for Target 4.7 that had transformative education as a key element, being part of competency frameworks, teacher training and school curriculum (Bridge 47 2020a).

This emphasis on transformative education has been seen by Bridge 47 as a way of bringing together the various elements of SDGs. Its road map policy of 2020 stated, for example:

> Target 4.7 reflects the transformative power of education by promoting global citizenship, sustainable development, human rights, gender equality, peace, and appreciation of cultural diversity. (Bridge 47 2020b)

World's Largest Lesson

The World's Largest Lesson[7] is an educational initiative managed by Project Everyone to engage children all over the world in learning about and taking action around the SDGs. Since its launch in September 2015, it has reached children and young people in over 130 countries and has produced a range of resources, suggested lesson plans and access to online courses for teachers. One of the features of the initiative has been its ability to gather support from international celebrities such as Emma Watson, Serena Williams and Malala Yousafzai. The initiative has had the support and involvement of UNICEF, and this has enabled the initiative to have an impact in many different countries.

Social change themes feature in a number of their activities. For example, one of the sample lesson plans is on community action. The objectives of the lesson are the following:

> To use the Global Goals as a catalyst for students in identifying a local community issue that they want to help solve, and create an action plan to get started. (World's Largest Lesson 2020)

Activities include participating in a community walk, identifying issues from interviews with local people and planning action. The outcomes of these activities to be shared with others (ibid.).

The programme has recognized that the promotion and use of the resources will need to be adapted to differing local and national conditions. One example that demonstrates this is in Nigeria, where learning about the SDGs has been promoted through an after-school club. From this learning about the goals, students became engaged in local community action. The evidence of the impact of these clubs on the children showed that students expressed much more interest in solving global problems and were more inspired to make positive social change after participating in the clubs.

Other evidence gained from the programme showed that the children wanted to 'try and make things better' when they observed a problem in their own environment and that teachers noted a clear shift in children expressing a desire to take action to solve wider global problems.

Around the world, schools are encouraged to engage with the activities promoted each year by the World's Largest Lesson and work towards a time during the year when this is brought together within the school as a whole.

Conclusion

This chapter has reviewed the role and influence of global initiatives and international organizations in determining the nature and focus of educational programmes around social change. From the Rio Summit in 1992 to the Sustainable Development Goals launched in 2015, education for social change can be seen within the various initiatives around sustainable development and global citizenship. However, as Hartmeyer noted, there is a danger that this approach to learning can lead to a methodology focused on predetermined goals rather than a more open and critical approach to specific campaigns. Whilst initiatives such as the World's Largest Lesson have been particularly successful and popular with many schools and teachers around the world, there is always the danger that the learning can be undertaken in an uncritical and reflective manner.

This chapter has shown that the dominant international organization has been UNESCO, which has played a major role in the promotion of educational programmes around the Sustainable Development Goals and, more recently, global citizenship. But as Hatley and Sterling have demonstrated, much of this engagement, despite good intentions, has tended to reproduce ideological messages that reinforce the status quo rather than questioning dominant social and political thinking.

What, however, could be argued, is that despite these criticisms, initiatives such as the Decade on ESD and the more recent programmes around the SDGs and more specifically on global citizenship have provided space and opportunities for more creative and critical approaches. It is clear that the Bridge 47 initiative tries to do this, and there is evidence that the Earth Charter also provides spaces for a more reflective and critical approach. But without resources, funding, training and support that encourage a more open-ended approach, many educationalists around the world will tend to follow what is provided for them. There is also the challenge, as Brown and McCowan suggest, that educational initiatives will not take into account local and cultural perspectives and approaches to learning. International bodies such as UNESCO are aware of these challenges but in the dominant neoliberal times of today, there is always the call for evidence, statistical data and models of learning that demonstrate impact of programmes in terms of changes in behaviour and development of skills and knowledge.

Global initiatives have become the dominant frame for taking forward education for social change in many countries. The SDGs have become the basis for many funding programmes at a national level. The extent to which they provide the basis for areas such as global social justice and transformative learning is one that perhaps needs further research and investigation.

Questions for Further Consideration

- In what ways has UNESCO framed international discussions on education for social change?
- What do you see as the significance of the SDGs in promoting social change?
- What are the main lessons that can be learnt from the various UN initiatives on ESD for promoting education for social change?
- What are the strengths and weaknesses of civil society organizations' initiatives in support of educational programmes to promote an understanding of the SDGs?

Further Reading

Brown, E. and T. McCowan (2018), 'Forum: *Buen vivir* – Reimagining Education and Shifting Paradigms', *Compare*, 48, no. 2: 317–23.

Corcoran, P. B., M. Vilela and M. Roerink (eds) (2005), *The Earth Charter in Action*, Amsterdam: KIT Publishers.

Huckle, J. and A. Wals (2015), 'The UN Decade of Education for Sustainable Development: Business as Usual in the End', *Environmental Education Research*, 21, no. 3: 491–505.

Kioupi, V. and N. Voulvoulis (2019), 'Education for Sustainable Development: A Systemic Framework for Connecting the SDGs to Educational Outcomes', *Sustainability*: 1–18.

UNESCO (2015), *Global Citizenship Education Topics And Learning Objectives*. Paris: UNESCO.

Conclusion

Introduction

This volume has aimed to show the ways in which education can be a vehicle for social change. It has identified the different historical and contemporary social and cultural traditions and discourses that have informed approaches to education for social change. Themes such as social justice, transformative learning and promoting distinctive participatory pedagogical practices have been identified. The volume has also shown the influence of international policy agreements and bodies such as UNESCO in framing educational practices that have a social change component.

The volume began by reviewing educational goals in relation to human rights and universal values. The strengths and weaknesses of such approaches were identified but what was noted as particularly important as a component of any social change agenda was the UN Convention on the Rights of the Child. This Convention provides an important framework for understanding the linkages between rights and social justice and, as noted through the work of organizations like UNICEF, provides a valuable pedagogical approach for education for social change.

The discussions on education for democracy, liberation and socialism showed the ways in which the terms had both a utopian and an empowering role. All of these themes had visions for a better and more engaged citizenry within society but what all of them have been faced with are the challenges of dominant economic and ideological forces. It is the extent to which these movements have provided openings and opportunities for counter-hegemonic practices that needs to be further considered.

The influence of global forces and what neoliberal globalization poses, both negatively and positively, for a social change agenda, have been discussed. In many countries around the world, this neoliberal form of globalization has had a disproportionately negative effect on poorer communities whilst increasing the wealth of the richest. What is also evident is that globalization has posed major questions about the role, nature and contribution of education to society. Global movements and forms of technology have created new democratic spaces for marginalized people to have a greater voice. It is clear that social media is going to have an increasingly dominant influence on how social change takes place in the coming decades.

Social Justice and Transformative Learning

Social justice, alongside transformative learning, emerges as the most common theme from reviewing the literature and practices around social change. As noted earlier in this volume, social justice provides the glue to having a vision for social change. Whilst the term 'social justice' may be open to many interpretations, there is a degree of consensus within the proponents of a social justice educational approach that relates change to combating inequalities and oppression in all sectors of societies and calls for approaches to learning that value freedom and democratic practices, and recognize a plurality of perspectives.

This means that a pedagogy for global social justice is suggested as being key to promoting education for social change. Included in this approach is an understanding of power and inequality, the development of knowledge and skills in order to make a difference and, from this, to work towards a more equitable and just world. It includes posing questions rather than seeking solutions, to open up debate and encourage critical thinking. This also means a close relationship to critical pedagogy and Freirean ideas such as *conscientizacáo or* critical consciousness development.

A second and related key element of education for social change is transformative learning. As Mezirow suggests, this approach to learning includes a process of self-reflection and changes in world views by the learner as well as forms of social action.

Education for Sustainable Development and Global Citizenship

Most of the chapters make reference to existing literature and debates around education for sustainable development and global citizenship. These areas are suggested as being important discourses around education for social change and have had considerable international influence due to their promotion by bodies such as UNESCO and their inclusion in the United Nations' Sustainable Development Goals. Both areas have also been interpreted in a variety of ways, even if there is a degree of commonality in definitions about the importance of social change. There is ongoing debate about the extent to which both sustainable development and global citizenship imply changes in individual behaviour or more systematic change.

What is evident from research, particularly from recent doctoral studies, is that both education for sustainable development and global citizenship are academic, policy and practice discourses that resonate closely with social justice education. However, there is a need for these linkages to be developed further, and perhaps one of the few that is directly addressing this is Misiaszek's (2021) work on *Ecopedagogy*, which, through a Freirean lens, connects environmental and sustainable development concerns to planetary social justice.

Examples of Practice

From Chapter 6 onwards, this volume has aimed to demonstrate examples of practice from around the world that bring to life themes identified from the literature and the research. These examples cover specific national initiatives, primarily from the United Kingdom and North America, but also international initiatives such as the World's Largest Lesson, the Global Citizen programme and student climate campaigns.

What many of these examples show is that learning about global and sustainable issues poses questions about forms of social engagement and action. They also show that this engagement needs to be based on deep knowledge and appropriate skills. References are made throughout the volume to the dangers of social action being seen as just an emotional response to an issue or a request to support a major campaign.

This is why the role of civil society organizations needs to be explored in terms of their role and contribution. These organizations are an important part of any society, providing the space for voices that are independent from the state. But their role needs careful consideration, as Chapter 12 in this volume demonstrated. To play an effective role, civil society organizations need to give greater consideration to their potential educative function, what this means and how it can inform the wider public. The role and influence that global citizenship and sustainable development areas now have within many societies is in large part due to the voices and practices of civil society organizations.

Innovation and Creative Practice

A theme throughout this volume, and one that is particularly relevant in the chapters on sectors of education, is the extent to which there are opportunities and openings for innovative and creative practices. Social change agendas often challenge dominant orthodoxies and ideologies within societies. Education can have a major role in providing alternative voices and counter-hegemonic perspectives. This area is particularly discussed within the chapters on the role of teachers and academics. Whilst many teachers around the world may be constrained by the relevant national curriculum, in most schools there are usually still opportunities for their particular pedagogical approaches to be introduced. What often constrains this creativity are the lack of resources, confidence and opportunities for professional development to enable them to explore further the approaches they may wish to take in the classroom. Within higher education, as Chapter 9 noted, there are more opportunities for academics to bring in a social justice and change agenda. This however needs to be framed within a pedagogical approach that opens up the minds of the student to consider differing voices and perspectives, to question their assumptions and to provide them with possible pathways if they wish to take this learning further.

Young people are recognized throughout this volume as becoming important players in calls for social change in many countries around the world. They have been the leading force behind the climate emergency movements and have been active around both the Black Lives Matters and MeToo campaigns. What the evidence of young people's engagement in these areas demonstrates is the way in which their calls for social action have been informed by and, in many cases, have come out of their learning and experience. They have also been able, particularly through their use of social media, to capture the imagination of many of their peers and also successfully gain the ear of policymakers.

Learning for a Sustainable Future

One theme that had not been fully explored in this volume but that needs to be recognized in this concluding chapter is that of 'futures'. A pedagogy of hope also implies a sense of thinking about the future. There has been over the past two decades an emerging educational field around 'futures' with Dave Hicks, a leading UK proponent of global education, being one of its champions. He states that Futures education:

- Enables pupils to understand the links between their own lives in the present and those of others in the past and future.
- Increases understanding of the economic, social, political and cultural influences which shape people's perceptions of personal, local and global futures.
- Works towards achieving a more just and sustainable future in which the welfare of both people and planet are of equal importance (Hicks n.d.).

This approach implies a strong social change component, and he suggests that an important element of education has to include a knowledge and understanding of global problems, their impact upon our lives and the actions needed to address them. Hicks, however, goes further and suggests that in an increasingly uncertain world learners need to be aware of different views of the future and identify and consider a range of alternatives. He further notes that 'hopes and fears for the future often influence decision-making in the present' and suggests, reflecting themes mentioned earlier in this chapter, that 'hopes for the future can enhance motivation in the present and thus positive action for change' (Hicks 2012: 6–7).

Finally, in his important publication *Education for Hope in Troubled Times: Climate Change and the Transition to a Post-Carbon Future*, Hicks (2014), as the title suggests, relates futures and hope to a more sustainable world. A theme of this volume is 'education for transition', how educators can learn from the Transition Networks around the world about how to put sustainability into practice through positive visions of the future, systems thinking, building resilience and building up practice from local experience.

These publications of Hicks bring in an important final dimension to the discussions on education for social change by linking together hope and futures within a context of a learning for a sustainable world. They provide a valuable contribution that encourages learners to look forward to ways in which social change can be addressed and what form of future we should be working towards.

Pedagogy of Hope

Hope has to be part of a futures approach. An ongoing influence throughout this volume has been the work of Paulo Freire. One of his last publications was *Pedagogy of Hope* (1994), which brings many of his ideas into one volume. Freire stated that one of the tasks of the progressive educator is to unveil opportunities for hope (ibid., 9). He went further and stated that hope, however, is not enough. There is a need for critical hope and a kind of education in hope. In this volume, Freire reminds the reader of key themes that have been reflected in all of his writings. These include the need to engage in dialogue, to listen to others and understand their perspectives. The volume includes a number of observations and engagements with political struggles and the need to learn from them, particularly the continued influence of colonial forces. He also reminds the reader of the important role of the university both in its teaching function and in its role in research. Finally, Freire reminds the reader of the complexities of the processes of learning even for the oppressed:

> The oppressed must learn that hope born in the creative unrest of the battle, will continue to have meaning when, and only when, it can in its own turn give birth to new struggles on other levels. (ibid., 198)

This belief in a pedagogy of hope, that change is possible, is not only an important comment from Freire, it has to underpin all endeavours within education that seek a better and more just world.

Concluding Comments

Hope has to underpin all approaches to education for social change. Educators have a responsibility in encouraging a sense of a positive future, that change for the better is possible. Never has this been more important than it is in the third decade of the twenty-first century. The future of the planet depends on the extent to which the human race decides to tackle the impact of climate change. The fragile nature of people's lives has been further thrown into stark relief by the global pandemic.

This volume was written under the restrictions of this pandemic. Covid-19, although it affects everyone, has shown the many inequalities that exist in the world. It has been the most oppressed and most marginal in society that have suffered the worst. Around the world, however, communities and social movements have responded, often where the state has fallen short on its responsibilities, to support these peoples. Change in societies comes primarily through forms of collective action, through a hope and belief that anyone can make a difference. There is a need for international solidarity, if we are to achieve a more just and sustainable world.

These forms of action, however, need to come from an understanding of the issues, the skills in knowing where and how to make a difference, and a belief in a better society for the good of all.

This volume began by quoting well-known phrases of leading international figures from the past and the present. These phrases have been used to motivate and inspire many millions of people around the world. It has shown that despite the obstacles that may exist in societies, the continuing dominant influence of neoliberalism, the extent to which the state can work against creativity and innovation, and the injustices that exist, change will come. Hope and belief in social change has to be a priority for all educators.

Questions for Further Consideration

- What are the main things you have gained from reading this volume?
- To what extent do you agree that social justice and transformative learning should be central to any approach of education for social change?
- How can we ensure that the issues raised in this volume become part of the learning within many courses in universities and part of the training of teachers and other educators?
- What do you see as the most important question to consider when seeking to engage your peers in a process of social change?

Further Reading

Freire, P. (1994), *Pedagogy of Hope*, London: Bloomsbury.

Hicks, D. (2012), 'The Future Only Arrives When Things Look Dangerous: Reflections on Futures Education in the UK', *Futures*, 44, no. 1: 4–13.

Hicks, D. (n.d.), *Future Perspectives*. Available online: https://teaching4abetterworld.co .uk/future.html (accessed 11 November 2020).

Hicks, D. (2014), *Education for Hope in Troubled Times: Climate Change and the Transition to a Post-Carbon Future*, London: Trentham/IOE Press.

Misiaszek, G. W. (2021), *Ecopedagogy*, London: Bloomsbury.

Notes

Introduction

1 https://www.youtube.com/watch?v=TKsK-BoEafc
2 These models are explained in https://change.walkme.com/theories-of-change-management/#:~:text=3%20of%20the%20Best%20Theories%20of%20Change%20Management.,for%20Change.%203%203.%20Prosci's%20ADKAR%20Model.%20

Chapter 1

1 See, for example, the Convention against Discrimination in Education, 1960; the International Covenant on Economic, Social and Cultural Rights, 1966; the Convention on the Elimination of All Forms of Discrimination Against Women, 1979; and the Convention on the Rights of the Child, 1989 .
2 The ideas of Osler in relation to children's rights specifically is discussed in more detail in Chapter 7.

Chapter 2

1 Derby Labour Party local election leaflet, 1925.
2 (https://www.democraticeducation.co.uk/index.php/directory/list-view/78-phoenix-education-trust)

Chapter 3

1 See : http://shikshantar.org/library/library-articles/pedagogy-liberation-liberation-pedagogy; 'Paulo Freire and informal education', *The encyclopedia of pedagogy and informal education*. [https://infed.org/mobi/paulo-freire-dialogue-praxis-and-education/
2 http://www.educatorsforsocialjustice.org/rethinking-schools-article.html

3 https://08a3a74a-dec5-426e-8385-bdc09490d921.filesusr.com/ugd/38199c_75fb38
   6a758c4c21834dce207d917a4c.pdf
4 https://www.edliberation.org

Chapter 4

1 Further information about the current activities of the Center can be found at:
   https://highlandercenter.org/#programs
2 https://phm.org.uk

Chapter 5

1 http://inspiraleducation.com

Chapter 6

1 See https://www.tes.com/news/what-is-pedagogy-definition
2 https://www.globaljustice.org.uk
3 Outright is a specific UNICEF campaign around climate change and is discussed in
   more detail in Chapter 10.
4 https://chicagofreedomschool.org/programs/project-healus/
5 https://chicagofreedomschool.org/programs/freedom-fellowship
6 https://www.paulofreireschool.org/about/mission/
7 https://en.everybodywiki.com/Tyree_Scott_Freedom_School

Chapter 7

1 The evidence for this section is based on material published in Blum and Bourn
   (2019).
2 https://edu-africa.com/changing-lives/transformative-learning-global-citizenship/

Chapter 8

1 An earlier version of some of the themes and arguments outlined in this chapter first
   appeared in Bourn (2016) Teachers as Agents of Social Change, *International Journal
   of Development Education and Global Learning,* 7, no. 3: 63–77.

2 https://www.youtube.com/watch?v=sPUxeY8FWqc

3 See http://marygrosser.co.za/uploads/presentations/2008%20Grosser%20De%20W aal%20UJ%20Conference.pdf

4 These themes are developed further in Chapter 12.

5 https://www.pearson.com/uk/about-us/news-and-policy/reports-and-campaigns/g lobal-learning-programme.html

Chapter 9

1 https://studentsforglobalhealth.org/vision-mission/

2 https://sustainus.org

Chapter 11

1 This clarity of organization has been helped by observations from Massimiliano Tarozzi.

2 See wsf2018.org

Chapter 12

1 http://www.teachsdgs.org

2 https://en.unesco.org/preventingviolentextremismthrougheducation

3 https://en.unesco.org/themes/holocaust-genocide-education

4 https://en.unesco.org/themes/gced/languages

5 For further details on this conference, go to: https://bankimooncentre.org/bkmc-at tends-unesco-conference-esd-gced and https://www.rcenetwork.org/portal/unesco -forum-esd-and-gce-2019-gap-partner-network-meeting

6 https://www.gcedclearinghouse.org

7 https://worldslargestlesson.globalgoals.org

References

Adams, M., L. A. Bell and P. Griffin (1997), *Teaching for Diversity and Social Justice*, New York: Routledge.

Adams, P. (2014), 'Young People and Development: The Role of Global Youth Work in Engagement and Learning', In: S. McCloskey (ed) *Development Education in Policy and Practice*, 83–101, Hampshire: Palgrave Macmillan UK.

African Development Bank (AfDB) (2012), *Framework for Enhanced Engagement with Civil Society Organisations*, Washington, DC: AfDB. Available online: https://www .afdb.org/fileadmin/uploads/afdb/Documents/Policy-Documents/Framework%20fo r%20Enhanced%20Engagement%20with%20Civil%20Society%20Organizations.pdf (accessed 14 December 2020).

Alexander, N. (1990), *Education and the Struggle for National Liberation in South Africa*, Braamfontein: Skotaville.

Alexander, R. (2004), 'Still No Pedagogy? Principle, Pragmatism and Compliance in Primary Education', *Cambridge Journal of Education*, 34(1): 7–33.

Ali, U. N. (2015), 'Developing Agents of Change: A Case Study on Preservice Teacher Leaders' Conceptualizations of Social Justice Teacher Leadership', Unpublished PhD thesis, University of Missouri-Columbia.

Allen, C. D. (2016), 'Social Justice in Secondary Social Studies: Exploring How Teachers Enact Social Justice in the Classroom', Unpublished PhD thesis, The University of Texas at San Antonio.

Allen, C., D. McAdam and D. Pellow (2010), *What Is the Role of Civil Society in Social Change?* Available online: http://chrisallan.info/wp-content/uploads/2010/04/Suppo rting-successful-movements-2.03.pdf (accessed 20 November 2020).

Allman, P. and J. Wallis (1997), 'Commentary: Paulo Freire and the Future of the Radical Tradition', *Studies in the Education of Adults*, 29(2): 113–120.

Althusser, L. (1971), *Lenin and Philosophy and Other Essays*, London: NLB.

Anderson, P. H., L. Lawton, R. J. Rexeisen and A. C. Hubbard (2006), 'Short-Term Study Abroad and Intercultural Sensitivity: A Pilot Study', *International Journal of Intercultural Relations*, 30(4): 457–469.

Andreotti, V. (2006), 'Soft versus Critical Global Citizenship Education', *Policy and Practice—a Development Education Review*, 3: 40–51.

Andreotti, V. (2011), 'The Political Economy of Global Citizenship Education', *Globalisation, Societies and Education*, 9(3–4): 307–310.

Apple, M. (1982), *Education and Power*, New York: Routledge.

Apple, M. (2005), 'Are Markets in Education Democratic?' In: M. Apple, J. Kenway and M. Singh (eds), *Globalizing Education*, 209–230, New York: Peter Lang.

Apple, M. (2013), *Can Education Change Society?*, New York: Routledge.

Apple, M. (2014), *Official Knowledge—Democratic Education in a Conservative Age*, New York: Routledge.

Apple, M. and J. A. Bean (1999), *Democratic Schools*, Buckingham: Open University Press.

Arches, J. and J. Fleming (2006), 'Young People and Social Action: Youth Participation in the United Kingdom and United States', *New Directions for Youth Development*, 2006(111): 81–90.

Arkoun, M. (2004), 'For a Subversive Genesis of Values', In: J. Bindé (ed) *The Future of Values*, 47–54, Paris: Berghahn Books.

Aronowitz, S. and H. Giroux (1993), *Education Still Under Siege*, Westport, CT: Bergin and Garvey Press.

Asbrand, B. (2004), 'Competencies to Deal with Complexity: Fair Trade as a Learning Possibility in Global Education', *The Development Education Journal*, 11(1): 15–17.

Asbrand, B. and A. Scheunpflug (2006), 'Global Education and Education for Sustainability', *Environmental Education Research*, 12(1): 33–46.

Ashwin, P. (2019), 'Transforming University Teaching', *Centre for Global Higher Education Working Paper Series No. 49*.

Association of Education for Citizenship (1939), *Education for Citizenship in Elementary Schools*, London: Oxford University Press.

Atkinson, K. (2012), 'Education for Liberation: A Precursor to Youth Activism for Social Justice', Unpublished PhD thesis, San Francisco State University.

Austin, R. (1999), 'Popular History and Popular Education: El Consejo de Educación de Adultos de América Latina', *Latin American Perspectives*, 26(4): 39–68.

Ayers, W., T. Quinn and D. Stovall (eds) (2009), *Handbook of Social Justice in Education*, New York: Routledge.

Baillie Smith, M. (2004), 'Contradiction and Change? NGOs, Schools and the Public Faces of Development', *Journal of International Development*, 16(5): 741–749.

Balarin, M. (2011), 'Global Citizenship and Marginalisation: Contributions towards a Political Economy of Global Citizenship', *Globalisation, Societies and Education*, 9(3–4): 355–366.

Bamber, P. (2016), *Transformative Education Through International Service Learning*, Abingdon: Routledge.

Bamber, P., A. Bullivant and D. Stead (2014), 'Measuring Attitudes Towards Global Learning Among Future Educators in England', *International Journal of Development Education and Global Learning*, 5(3): 5–27.

Banks, J. A. (2008), 'Diversity, Group Identity and Citizenship Education in a Global Age', *Educational Researcher*, 37(3): 129–139.

Barnett, M. and T. G. Weiss (eds) (2008), *Humanitarianism in Question: Politics, Power, Ethics*, Ithaca, NY: Cornell University.

Barteau, H. L. and C. L. Webb (2019), 'Incorporating Socialist Educational Practices within a Democratic Society: A Comparison of the United States and Cuba's

Education Systems', *Review of Education, Pedagogy, and Cultural Studies*, 41(2): 99–114.

Bartiaux, F. (2009), 'Between School, Family and Media: Do Children Carry Energy-Saving Messages and Practices?', Paper presented at the European Council for an Energy Efficient Economy (ECEEE), La Colle sur Loup, France.

Bateson, G. (1987), *Steps to an Ecology of Mind: Collected Essays in Anthropology, Psychiatry, Evolution, and Epistemology*, Northvale, NJ: Jason Aronson.

Bayliss, J. and S. Smith (eds) (1999), *The Globalisation of World Politics—An Introduction to International Relations*, Oxford: Oxford University Press.

Beck, U. (2000), *What Is Globalization?*, Cambridge: Polity Press.

Belda-Miquel, S., A. Boni and C. Calabuig (2019), 'SDG Localisation and Decentralised Development Aid: Exploring Opposing Discourses and Practices in Valencia's Aid Sector', *Journal of Human Development and Capabilities* 20: 386–402.

Begum, N. and R. Saini (2019), 'Decolonising the Curriculum,' *Political Studies Review*, 17(2): 196–201.

Bell, D. V. J. (2016), 'Twenty-First Century Education: Transformative Education for Sustainability and Responsible Citizenship', *Journal of Teacher Education for Sustainability*, 18(1): 48–56.

Belle, C. (2019), 'What Is Social Justice Education Anyway?', *Education Week*, 23 January. Available online: https://www.edweek.org/ew/articles/2019/01/23/what-is-social-justice-education-anyway.html (accessed 18 November 2020).

Benhabib, S. (2002), *The Claims of Culture: Equality and Diversity in the Global Era*, Princeton, NJ: Princeton.

Benhayoun, J. (2020), 'The New Global University in the Post-COVID-19 World', *University World News*, 4 July. Available online: https://www.universityworldnews.com/post.php?story=20200704092348232 (accessed 13 December 2020).

Bentall, C. (2020), 'Continuing Professional Development of Teachers of Global Learning: What Works?' In: D. Bourn (ed), *The Bloomsbury Handbook of Global Education and Learning*, 356–368, London: Bloomsbury.

Bentall, C., N. Blum and D. Bourn (2010), *Returned Volunteers and Engagement with Development*, Final Report for VSO Longitudinal Study. Available online: https://discovery.ucl.ac.uk/id/eprint/1474867/1/VSO%20Research%20Final%20Report.pdf (accessed 8 November 2020).

Bettez, S. C. (2008), 'Social Justice Activist Teaching in the University Classroom', In: J. Deim and R. J. Helfenbein (eds), *Unsettling Beliefs: Teaching Theory to Teachers*, 279–296, Charlotte, NC: Information Age Publishing.

Bhambra, G. K., D.Gebrial, and K. Nisancioglu (2018), *Decolonising the University*, London: Pluto Press.

Biccum, A. (2010), *Global Citizenship and the Legacy of Empire*, Abingdon: Routledge.

Biesta, G. (2011), *Learning Democracy in School and Society*, Rotterdam: Sense Publishers.

Biesta, G. and N. Burbules (2003), *Pragmatism and Educational Research*, Boulder, CO: Rowman and Littlefield.

Biesta, G. and R. Lawy (2006), 'Citizenship-as-Practice: The Educational Implications of an Inclusive and Relational Understanding of Citizenship', *British Journal of Educational Studies*, 54(1): 34–50.

Biesta, G., M. Priestley and S. Robinson (2015), 'The Role of Beliefs in Teacher Agency', *Teachers and Teaching*, 21(6): 624–640.

Bigelow, B., L. Christensen, S. Karp, B. Miner and B. Peterson (eds) (1994), *Rethinking Our Classrooms: Teaching for Equity and Justice*, Milwaukee, WI: Rethinking Schools, Ltd.

Birdwell, J. and M. Bani (2014), *Introducing Generation Citizen*, London: Demos.

Birdwell, J., R. Birnie and R. Mehan (2013), *The State of the Service Nation—Youth Social Action in the UK*, London: Demos.

Blackmore, C. (2014), 'The Opportunities and Challenges for a Critical Global Citizenship Education in One English Secondary School', Unpublished PhD thesis, University of Bath, Department of Education.

Blum, D. (2011), *Cuban Youth and Revolutionary Values: Educating the New Socialist Citizen*, Austin, TX: University of Texas Press.

Blum, N. and D. Bourn (2019), 'Study Abroad and Student Mobility: Stories of Global Citizenship', *Development Education Research Centre Research Paper No. 21*, London: UCL-IOE.

Boal, A. (2008), *Theatre of the Oppressed*, London: Pluto Press.

Bosio, E. (2020), 'Implementing Principles of Global Citizenship Education into University Curricula', Unpublished PhD thesis, University College London.

Boston University (n.d.), *A Global Boston University*. Available online: http://www.bu.edu/global/ (accessed 11 December 2020).

Boughton, B. (2013), 'Popular Education and the "Party Line"', *Globalisation, Societies and Education*, 11(2): 239–257.

Bourdieu, P. (1973), 'Cultural Reproduction and Social Reproduction', In: R. Brown (ed), *Knowledge, Education and Cultural Change*, 71–112, London: Tavistock.

Bourdieu, P. (1990), *In Other Words: Essays Towards a Reflective Sociology*, Oxford: Blackwell.

Bourn, D. (1978), 'The Development of Labour Party Ideas on Education', Unpublished PhD thesis, Keele University.

Bourn, D. (2005), 'Education for Sustainable Development and Global Citizenship— The UK Perspective', *Applied Environmental Education and Communication*, 4(3): 233–237.

Bourn, D. (2008), 'Development Education: Towards a Re-Conceptualisation', *International Journal of Development Education and Global Learning*, 1(1): 5–22.

Bourn, D. (2009), 'Students as Global Citizens', In: E. Jones (ed), *Internationalisation: The Student Voice*, 28–29, Abingdon: Routledge.

Bourn, D. (2012), *Evaluation of Act Global Project*, London: DERC.

Bourn, D. (2014), *School Linking and Global Learning—Teachers' Reflections*, DERC Research Report No. 12, London: IOE/DERC.

Bourn, D. (2015), *The Theory and Practice of Development Education*, Abingdon: Routledge.

Bourn, D. (2016), *Global Citizenship and Youth Participation in Europe, S F Youth Project*, London: Oxfam GB and UCL Institute of Education.

Bourn, D. (2018a), *Fairtrade and Global Learning*, DERC Research Report No. 18, London: UCL-IOE and Fairtrade Foundation.

Bourn, D. (2018b), *Understanding Global Skills for 21st Century Professions*, London: Palgrave.

Bourn, D. and K. Brown (2011), 'Young People and International Development: Engagement and Learning', *DERC Research Paper No. 2*, London: IOE.

Bourn, D. and F. Hunt (2011), 'Global Dimension in Secondary Schools', *DERC Research Paper No. 1*, London: IOE.

Bourn, D. and A. McCollum (1995), *A World of Difference*, London: DEA.

Bourn, D. and A. Morgan (2010), 'Development Education, Sustainable Development, Global Citizenship and Higher Education: Towards a Transformative Approach to Learning', In: E. Unterhalter and V. Carpentier (eds), *Global Inequalities and Higher Education: Whose Interest Are We Serving?*, 268–286, Basingstoke: Palgrave Macmillan.

Bourn, D., A. McKenzie and C. Shiel (eds) (2006), *The Global University: The Role of the Curriculum*, London: DEA.

Bourn, D. and A. Pasha (2020), 'International Perspectives on Global Learning', In: C. Tweedale and J. Staufenberg (eds), *Developing Effective Learning in Nepal: Insights into School Leadership, Teaching Methods and Curriculum*, 26–42, Kathmandu, Nepal: British Council Nepal.

Bourn, D. and C. Shiel (2009), 'Global Perspectives: Aligning Agendas?', *Environmental Education Research*, 15(6): 661–677.

Bowles, S. and H. Gintis (2002), 'Schooling in Capitalist America Revisited', *Sociology of Education*, 75(1): 1–18.

Bowles, S. and H. Gintis (2011), *Schooling in Capitalist America*, London: Haymarket Books.

Boyles, D., T. Carusi and D. Attick (2009), 'Historical and Critical Interpretations of Social Justice', In: A. Ayers, T. Quinn and D. Stovall (eds), *Handbook of Social Justice in Education*, 30–42, New York: Routledge.

Bragg, S. (2007), '"Student Voice" and Governmentality: The Production of Enterprising Subjects??', *Discourse: Studies in the Cultural Politics of Education*, 28(3): 343–358.

Braster, S., F. Simon and I. Grosvenor (ed), *A History of Popular Education*, Abingdon: Routledge.

Braskamp, L. A., D. C. Braskamp and K. Merrill (2009), 'Assessing Progress in Global Learning and Development of Students with Education Abroad Experiences', *The Interdisciplinary Journal of Study Abroad*, 18: 101–118.

Breidlid, A. (2007), 'Education in Cuba—An Alternative Educational Discourse: Lessons to Be Learned?', *Compare: A Journal of Comparative and International Education*, 37(5): 617–634.

Brennan, J. (2008), 'Higher Education and Social Change Higher Education and the Future of Higher Education Research', *Higher Education*, 56(3): 381–393.

Bridge (2020a), *Transformative Education*. Available online: https://www.bridge47.org/sites/default/files/2020-09/bridge47_policy_paper-_transformative_education_v1_1 90820_5.pdf (accessed 20 November 2020), 47.

Bridge (2020b), *Envision 4.7 Road Map*. Available online: https://www.bridge47.org/sites/default/files/2020-01/envision_4.7_roadmap_0.pdf (accessed 20 November 2020), 47.

British Youth Council (BYC) (2020), *Review of Environment and Climate, Policy*. Available online: https://2u6szgq3e9x2hmfuy16guf8q-wpengine.netdna-ssl.com/wp-content/uploads/2020/07/Youth-Steering-Group-Climate-Change-Review-2020.pdf (accessed 19 October 2020).

Brock, G. (2009), *Global Justice—A Cosmopolitan Account*, Oxford: Oxford University Press.

Brookfield, S. (2000), 'Transformative Learning as Ideology Critique', In: J. Mezirow and Associates (ed), *Learning as Transformation: Critical Perspectives on a Theory in Progress*, 125–48, San Francisco, CA: Jossey-Bass.

Brown, E. (2013), 'Transformative Learning Through Development Education NGOs: A Comparative Study of Britain and Spain', Unpublished PhD thesis, University of Nottingham.

Brown, E. and T. McCowan (2018), 'FORUM: Buen vivir—Reimagining education and shifting paradigms', *Compare: A Journal of Comparative and International Education*, 48(2): 317–323.

Brown, P. and H. Lauder (1991), 'Education, Economy and Social Change', *International Studies in Sociology of Education*, 1(1–2): 3–23.

Bryan, A. (2012), 'Band-Aid Pedagogy, Celebrity Humanitarianism, and Cosmopolitan Provincialism: A Critical Analysis of Global Citizenship Education', In: C. Wankel and S. Malleck (eds), *Ethical Models and Applications of Globalization: Cultural, Socio-Political and Economic Perspectives*, 262–286, Hershey, PA: Business Science Reference.

Bullies Out (2019), *The Positives and Negatives of Young People Using Social Media*. Available online: https://bulliesout.com/latest-blogs/the-positives-and-negatives-of-young-people-using-social-media/ (accessed 16 October 2020).

Bullivant, A. (2020), 'From Development Education to Global Learning: Exploring Conceptualisations of Theory and Practice Amongst Practitioners in DECs in England', Unpublished PhD, Lancaster University.

Burbules, N. and C. Torres (eds) (2000), *Globalisation and Education: Critical Perspectives*, New York: Routledge.

CAFOD (n.d.), *Social Teaching*. Available online: https://cafod.org.uk/Pray/Catholic-social-teaching#dignity (accessed 10 December 2020).

CAFOD (2020), *Youth Leadership for Global Justice*. Available online: https://cafod.org.uk/Education/For-teachers/Connecting-Classrooms-CPD/Young-leadership (accessed 10 December 2020).

Camicia, S. and B. Franklin (2011), 'What Type of Global Community and Citizenship? Tangled Discourses of Neoliberalism and Critical Democracy in Curriculum and Its Reform', *Globalisation, Societies and Education*, 9(3–4): 311–322.

Cappy, C. L. (2016), 'Shifting The Future? Teachers as Agents of Social Change in South African Secondary Schools', *University of South Africa Education As Change*, 20(3): 119–140.

Case, K. (ed) (2017), *Intersectional Pedagogy: Complicating Identity and Social Justice*, New York, NY: Routledge.

Castells, M. (1996), *The Rise of the Network Society*, Oxford: Blackwell.

Castells, M. (2001), *The Internet Galaxy*, Oxford: Oxford University Press.

Castells, M. (2009), *Communication, Power*, Oxford: Oxford University Press.

Castles, S. and W. Wustenburg (1979), *The Education of the Future: An Introduction to the Theory and Practice of Socialist Education*, London: Pluto Press.

Centre for Alternative Technology (CAT) (2020), *Talking to Young People About Climate Change*. Available online: https://www.cat.org.uk/past-webinars/talking-to-young-people-about-climate-change/ (accessed 19 October 2020).

Chalkley, B., M. Haigh and D. Higgitt (eds) (2010), *Education for Sustainable Development: Papers in Honour of the United Nations Decade on Education for Sustainable Development (2005–2014)*, Abingdon: Routledge.

Chan, J. (2009), 'The Alternative Globalisation Movement, Social Justice and Education', In: W. Ayers, T. Quinn and D. Stovall (eds), *Handbook of Social Justice in Education*, 554–564, New York: Routledge.

Charon-Cardona, E. (2013), 'Socialism and Education in Cuba and Soviet Uzbekistan', *Globalisation, Societies and Education*, 11(2): 296–313.

Chicago Freedom Schools (n.d.), *Our Approach*. Available online: https://chicagofreedomschool.org/about-us/approach/ (accessed 19 October 2020).

Cho, H. S. (2016), 'The Gaps between Values and Practices of Global Citizenship Education: A Critical Analysis of Global Citizenship Education in South Korea', Unpublished PhD thesis, University of Massachusetts, Amherst.

Cho, H. S. and J. Mosselson (2018), 'Neoliberal Practices Amidst Social Justice Orientations: Global Citizenship Education in South Korea', *Compare: A Journal of Comparative and International Education*, 48(6): 861–878.

Cho, S. (2013), *Critical Pedagogy and Social Change*, New York: Routledge.

Chouliaraki, L. (2010), 'Post-Humanitarianism: Humanitarian Communication beyond a Politics of Pity', *International Journal of Cultural Studies*, 13(2): 107–126.

Christie, B. and K. Miller (2016), 'Academics' Opinions and Practices of Education for Sustainable Development: Reflections on a Nation-Wide, Mixed Methods Multidisciplinary Study.' In: M. Barth, G. Michelsen, M. Rieckmann and I. Thomas (eds), *Routledge Handbook of Higher Education for Sustainable Development*, 396–410, Abingdon: Routledge.

Clifford, V. and M. Haigh (2018), 'Internationalisation of the Curriculum Comes of Age', *University World News*, 23 November. Available online: https://www.universi tyworldnews.com/post.php?story=20181120132725749 (accessed 20 November 2020).

Coelho, D., J. Caramelo and I. Menezes (2018), 'Why Words Matter: Deconstructing the Discourses of Development Education Practitioners in Development NGOs in Portugal', *International Journal of Development Education and Global Learning*, 10(1): 39–58.

Cohen, J. and R. M. W. Travers (eds) (1939), *Educating for Democracy*, London: MacMillan.

Cohen, R. and S. Rai (2000), *Global Social Movements*, London: Athlone Press.

Coll, J. and C. Zalaquett (2007), 'The Relationship of Worldviews of Advisors and Students and Satisfaction with Advising: A Case of Homogenous Group Impact', *Journal of College Student Retention: Research, Theory and Practice*, 9(3): 273–281.

Collard, S. and M. Law (1989), 'The Limits of Perspective Transformation: A Critique of Mezirow's Theory', *Adult Education Quarterly*, 39(2): 99–107.

Cooper, R. (2018), *What Is Civil Society, Its Role and Value in 2018?—K4D*, Falmer: University of Sussex-IDS.

Corcoran, P. B., M. Vilela and M. Roerink (eds) (2005), *The Earth Charter in Action*, Amsterdam: KIT Publishers.

Coventry University (n.d.), *A Global University*. Available online: https://www.coventry .ac.uk/the-university/about-coventry-university/our-corporate-plan/a-global-univ ersity/ (accessed 29 October 2020).

Cox, H. (2011), 'What Factors Enable and Hinder Leadership for Sustainability in Hertfordshire Secondary Schools?' Unpublished MSc dissertation, London: London South Bank University.

Cranton, P. (2006), *Understanding and Promoting Transformative Learning: A Guide for Educators of Adults*, San Francisco: Jossey-Bass.

Crowther, J., V. Galloway and I. Martin (eds) (2005), *Popular Education: Engaging the Academy*, Leicester: NIACE.

Crowther, J. (2013), *The International Popular Education Network: Its Purpose and Contribution, Rizoma Freireano • N. 14 • Instituto Paulo Freire de España*. Available online: http://www.rizoma-freireano.org/the-international-popular-education- network (accessed 22 March 2021).

Curry-Stevens, A. (2007), 'New Forms of Transformative Education "Pedagogy for the Privileged"', *Journal of Transformative Education*, 5(1): 33–58.

Dalby, T. (2017), 'Space for a Change? An Exploration of Power, Privilege and Transformative Pedagogy in a Gap Year Education Programme in South America', Unpublished PhD thesis, University of East Anglia.

Darder, A. (2015), *Freire and Education*, New York: Routledge.

Darder, A., M. Baltodano and R. D. Torres (eds) (2003), *The Critical Pedagogy Reader*, New York: Routledge/Falmer.

Darder, A. M. and R. D. Torres (2004), *After Race: Racism after Multiculturalism*, New York: New York University Press.

Darnton, A. and M. Kirk (2011), *Finding Frames: New Ways to Engage the Public in Global Poverty*, London: BOND.

Da Silva, A. B. (2011), 'FRETILIN Popular Education 1973–78 and Its Relevance to Timor-Leste Today', Unpublished PhD thesis, Armidale, Australia: University of New England.

David, M. E. (2012), 'Feminism, Gender and Global Higher Education: Women's Learning Lives', *Higher Education Research and Development*, 31(5): 679–687.

Davison, J. (2012), 'Social Class and Education', In: J. Arthur and A. Petersen (eds), *The Routledge Companion to Education*, 236–246, Abingdon: Routledge.

Dawley-Carr, J. R. (2015), 'Citizenship Education in Cuba: Ideals, Contradictions, and Convivencia', Unpublished PhD thesis, Madison: University of Wisconsin.

Day, C. (1999), *Developing Teachers: The Challenges of Lifelong Learning*, London: Falmer.

De Angelis, R. (2020), 'Social, Transformative and Sustainable Learning: A Study of a Jamaican School and Community', Unpublished PhD thesis, University College London.

Delanty, G. (2003), *Community: Key Ideas*, London: Routledge.

Dell'Angelo, T. (2014), 'Creating Classrooms for Social Justice', *Edutopia*. Available online: https://www.edutopia.org/blog/creating-classrooms-for-social-justice-tabitha -dellangelo (accessed 15 October 2020).

Della Porta, D. and M. Diani (1999), *Social Movements: An Introduction*, Oxford: Blackwell.

Delors, J. (1996), *Learning, the Treasure Within: Report to UNESCO of the International Commission*, Paris: UNESCO.

Dewey, J. (1937), 'Education and Social Change', *Bulletin of the American Association of University Professors (1915–1955)*, 23(6): 472–474.

Dill, J. S. (2013), *The Longings and Limits of Global Citizenship Education: The Moral Pedagogy of Schooling in a Cosmopolitan Age*, Abingdon: Routledge.

Dirkx, J. M., J. Mezirow and P. Cranton (2006), 'Musings and Reflections on the Meaning, Context, and Process of Transformative Learning: A Dialogue between John M. Dirkx and Jack Mezirow', *Journal of Transformative Education*, 4(2): 123–139.

Dogra, N. (2012), *Representations of Global Poverty: Aid, Development and INGOs*, London: IB Tauris.

Doherty, B. and L. Taplin (2008), *Combining Consumer Education and Global Citizenship Education in Developing Consumer Citizenship in Young People: A Case Study of the Papapaa Fair Trade Teaching Initiative and the Dubble Fairtrade Chocolate Bar*. Paper presented at CRRC 2008, Queen's University Belfast. Available online: https://crrconference.org/Previous_conferences/downloads/2006dohertytaplin.pdf (accessed 15 October 2020).

Dolby, N. and F. Rizvi (2008), *Youth Moves—Identities and Education in Global Perspectives*, New York: Routledge.

Dominy, G., R. Goel, S. Larkins and H. Pring (2009), 'Review of Using Aid Funds in the UK to Promote Awareness of Global Poverty', Prepared for DFID, London, Central Office of Information.

Doring, A. (2002), 'Challenges to the Academic Role of Change Agent', *Journal of Further and Higher Education*, 26(2): 139–148).

Drury, J. and S. Reicher (2009), 'Collective Psychological Empowerment as a Model of Social Change: Researching Crowds and Power', *Journal of Social Issues*, 65(4): 707–725.

Dunhill, A. (2018), 'Does Teaching Children about Human Rights, Encourage Them to Practice, Protect and Promote the Rights of Others?', *Education 3–13*, 46(1): 16–26.

Durkheim, E. (1977), *The Division of Labour in Society*, New York: Free Press.

Durrant, J. and G. Holden (2006), *Teachers Leading Change*, London: Paul Chapman Publishing.

Earth Charter (n.d.), *Preamble*. Available online: https://earthcharter.org/read-the-earth-charter/preamble/ (accessed 1 December 2020).

Earth Charter and UNESCO (2007), *Good Practice Using the Earth Charter*, San Jose, Costa Rica and Paris: Earth Charter International and UNESCO.

Edge, K., K. Frayman and S. B. Jaafar (2008), *North South School Partnerships: Learning from Schools in the UK, Africa and Asia, Research Report*, London: IOE, UKOWLA and Cambridge Education.

EDU-Africa (n.d.), *Our Transforming Learning Journeys*. Available online: https://edu-africa.com/changing-lives/our-transformative-learning-journeys/ (accessed 29 October 2020).

Education For Liberation Network (2020), *Our Mission and Values*. Available online: https://www.edliberation.org/about-us/our-vision/ (accessed 24 December 2020).

Edwards, M. (2011), 'Introduction: Civil Society and the Geometry of Human Relations', In: M. Edwards (ed), *The Oxford Handbook of Civil Society*, 3–14, Oxford and New York: Oxford University Press.

Edwards, M. (2014), *When Is Civil Society a Force for Social Transformation?* Available online: https://www.opendemocracy.net/en/transformation/when-is-civil-society-force-for-social-transformation/ (accessed 23 November 2020).

Egan, A. (2012), 'The Elephant in the Room: Towards a Discourse on Development Education and Corporate Power', *Policy and Practice*, 14: 45–63.

Elliott, G., C. Fourali and S. Issler (eds) (2012), *Education and Social Change*, London: Continuum.

Ellis, M. (2013), 'The Personal and Professional Development of the Critical Global Educator', Unpublished PhD thesis, London: Institute of Education.

Ellis, M. (2016), *The Critical Global Educator*, Abingdon: Routledge.

Esposito, S. (2020), 'Youth Organization Sues Over Chicago Police 'Raid', Order to Not Feed Hungry Protesters—Lawyers for Chicago Freedom School in the South Loop Filed a Lawsuit Thursday in Federal Court', *Chicago Sun, Times*. Available online: https://chicago.suntimes.com/2020/6/25/21303132/chicaog-freedom-school-laws uit-police-department-raid-injunction-feed-protesters (accessed 15 October 2020), 25 June.

European Democratic Education Community (EUDEC) (n.d.), *What Is Democratic Education?* Available online: https://eudec.org/democratic-education/what-is-dem ocratic-education/ (accessed 13 October 2020).

European Union (n.d.), *Civil Society Organisations, Glossary of Summaries*. Available online: https://eur-lex.europa.eu/summary/glossary/civil_society_organisation.html (accessed 23 December 2020).

Farber, B. (1991), *Crisis in Education*, San Francisco: Jossey-Bass.

Ferrari, J. (2002), *Ark of Hope: The UN's Quest for World Religion, Catholic Insight*, November 1.

Findlay, A., R. King, A. Stam and E. Ruiz-Gelices (2006), 'Ever Reluctant Europeans: The Changing Geographies of UK Students Studying and Working Abroad', *European Urban and Regional Studies*, 13(4): 291–318.

Firth, R. and M. Smith (2013), 'As the un Decade of Education for Sustainable Development Comes to an End: What Has It Achieved and What Are the Ways Forward?', *Curriculum Journal*, 24(2): 169–180.

Fisher, S. (2001), 'Making Hope Practical and Despair Unconvincing; Some Thoughts on Transformative Education', *Appalachian Journal*, 29(1–2): 90–97.

Flaherty, C. (2020), *Scholars on Strike*. Available online: https://www.insidehighered.com/news/2020/09/09/scholars-strike-racial-justice (accessed 25 March 2021).

Florence, N. (1998), *Bell Hooks' Engaged Pedagogy*, Westport, CT: Bergin and Garvey.

Fowler, A. and K. Biekart (2020), 'Activating Civic Space for Sustainable Development', *Helping and Hindering Factors for Effective CSO Engagement in the SDGS*, Amsterdam: International Institute Of Social Studies (ISS).

Fraser, N. (2003), 'Social Justice in the Age of Identity Politics', In: G. Henderson and M. Waterston (eds), *Geographic Thought: A Praxis Perspective*, 72–91, London: Routledge.

Freire, P. (1972), *Pedagogy of the Oppressed*, London: Penguin.

Freire, P. (1984), 'Education, Liberation and the Church', *Religious Education*, 79(4), 524–545.

Freire, P. (1985), *Politics of Education: Culture, Power and Liberation*, London: MacMillan.

Freire, P. (1994), *Pedagogy of Hope*, London: Bloomsbury.

Freire, P. (2004), *Pedagogy of Indignation*, Boulder, CO; London: Paradigm.

Freire, P. (2005), *Teachers as Cultural Workers*, Cambridge, MA: Westview.

Freire, P. and I. Shor (1987), *A Pedagogy for Liberation*, London: MacMillan.

Fricke, H. J. and C. Gathercole (2015), *Monitoring Education for Global Citizenship: A Contribution to Debate, DEEEP Report 5*, Brussels: CONCORD.

Fullan, M. (1993), 'Why Teachers Must Become Change Agents', *Educational Leadership*, 50(6): 1–13.

Furlong, A. and F. Cartmel (2007), *Young People and Social Change*, 2nd edn, Oxford: OUP/McGraw Hill.

Fuss, D. (1989), *Essentially Speaking*, New York: Routledge.

Gadsby, H. and A. Bullivant (eds) (2010), *Global Learning and Sustainable Development*, Abingdon: Routledge.

Gallwey, S. (2009), 'Teaching About Fairtrade', *Policy and Practice: a Development Education Review* 9: 59–66.

Gasperini, L. (2000), 'The Cuban Education System: Lessons and Dilemmas', *Country Studies Education Reform and Management Publication Series*, 1(5): 1–36.

Gaudelli, W. (2016), *Global Citizenship Education: Everyday Transcendence*, New York, NY: Routledge.

Gerrard, J. (2011), 'Gender, Community and Education: Cultures of Resistance in Socialist Sunday Schools and Black Supplementary Schools', *Gender and Education*, 23(6): 711–727.

Get Up and Goals Project (n.d.), *The Project*. Available online: https://www.getupandgoals.eu/project (accessed 29 October 2020).

Gewirtz, S. (2006), 'Towards a Contextualized Analysis of Social Justice in Education', *Educational Philosophy and Theory*, 38(1): 69–81.

Gibson, J. (2008), 'The Myth of the Multitude: The Endogenous Demise of Alter-Globalist Politics', *Global Society*, 22(2): 253–275.

Giddens, A. (1991), *Modernity and Self-Identity: Self and Society in the Late Modern Age*, Cambridge: Polity Press.

Gilbert, C. and D. Heller (2010), *The Truman Commission and Its Impact on Federal Higher Education Policy from 1947 to 2010, Working Paper No. 9*. The Pennsylvania State University. Available online: https://ed.psu.edu/cshe/working-papers/wp-9 (accessed 12 December 2020).

Gillborn, D. and D. Youdell (2009), 'Critical Perspectives on Race and Schooling', In J. Banks (ed) *The Routledge International Companion to Multicultural Education*, 173–185, New York: Routledge.

Ginwright, S. and J. Cammarota (2002), 'New Terrain in Youth Development: The Promise of a Social Justice Approach', *Social Justice*, 29(4): 82–95.

Ginwright, S. and J. Cammarota (2007), 'Youth Activism in the Urban Community: Learning Critical Civic Praxis within Community Organizations', *International Journal of Qualitative Studies in Education*, 20(6): 693–710.

Ginwright, S. and T. James (2002), 'From Assets to Agents of Change: Social Justice, Organizing, and Youth Development', *New Directions for Youth Development*, 96(96): 27–46.

Giroux, H. (1981), *Ideology, Culture and the Process of Schooling*, Philadelphia: Temple University Press.

Giroux, H. (2003), 'Selling Out Higher Education', *Policy Futures in Education*, 1(1): 179–200.

Giroux, H. (2005), *Border Crossing*, 2nd edn, New York: Routledge.

Giroux, H. (2006), *The Giroux Reader*, Boulder, CO: Paradigm.

Giroux, H. (2010), 'Lessons to Be Learned From Paulo Freire as Education Is Being Taken Over by the Mega Rich', *Truthout*, 23 November. Available online: https://tr uthout.org/articles/lessons-to-be-learned-from-paulo-freire-as-education-is-being -taken-over-by-the-mega-rich/ (accessed 27 October 2020).

Giroux, H. (2011), *On Critical Pedagogy*, New York: Continuum.

Giroux, H. and E. Bosio (2021), 'Critical Pedagogy and Global Citizenship Education', In: E. Bosio (ed) *Conversations on Global Citizenship Education*, 3–12, New York: Routledge.

Global Citizen (n.d.), *Meet The Global Citizen NGO Partners*. Available online: https://ww w.globalcitizen.org/en/content/meet-our-ngo-partners/ (accessed 29 October 2020).

Global Citizen (2020), *Taking Action*. Available online: https://www.globalcitizen.org/en /take-action/ (accessed 29 October 2020).

Global Justice Now (2020), *About Us*. Available online: https://www.globaljustice.org.uk /about-us (accessed on 14 October 2020).

Goren, H. and M. Yemini (2017), 'The Global Citizenship Education Gap: Teacher Perceptions of the Relationship between Global Citizenship Education and Students' Socio-Economic Status', *Teaching and Teacher Education*, 67: 9–22.

Gramsci, A. (1971), *Selection from the Prison Notebooks*, London: Lawrence and Wishart.

Grant, C. A. (2009), 'Bottom-Up Struggle for Social Justice: Where Are the Teachers?' In: W. Ayers, T. Quinn and D. Stovall (eds), *Handbook of Social Justice in Education*, 654–656, New York: Routledge.

Griffiths, T. G. and Z. Millei (2013), 'Education In/for Socialism: Historical, Current and Future Perspectives', *Globalisation, Societies and Education*, 11(2): 161–169.

Grunsell, A. (2007), 'Social Justice', In D. Hicks and C. Holden (eds), *Teaching the Global Dimension*, 82–91, Abingdon: Routledge.

Gyoh, S. (2015), 'Exploring the Knowledge Dimension of NGO Campaigning on Global Poverty and Inequality: A Network Society Perspective', Unpublished PhD thesis, UCL-Institute of Education.

Hackman, H. (2005), 'Five Essential Components for Social Justice Education', *Equity and Excellence in Education*, 38(2): 103–109.

Hakken, D. (1983), 'Impacts of Liberation Pedagogy: The Case of Workers' Education', *Journal of Education*, 165(1): 113–129.

Hall, B. L. and J. R. Kidd (eds) (1978), *Adult Learning: A Design for Action*, London: Pergamon Press.

Hammond, C. D. and A. Keating (2018), 'Global Citizens or Global Workers? Comparing University Programmes for Global Citizenship Education in Japan and the UK', *Compare: a Journal of Comparative and International Education*, 48(6): 915–934.

Han, Q. (2019), 'Global Educational Governance in Practice: The UNESCO Education for Sustainable Development Project in China', Unpublished PhD thesis, Indiana University.

Hana-Meksem, K. (2014), 'Teachers Have to Be Role Models', *Education Ghana*, 27 April. Available online: https://educationgh.wordpress.com/2014/04/27/teachers -have-to-be-role-models/ (accessed 16 October 2020).

Hanley, N. (2020), 'Empathy-Based Pedagogical Approach to Global Citizenship Education: Kazakhstani Secondary Schools Context', Unpublished PhD thesis, University College London-Institute of Education.

Hansen, D. (2011), *The Teacher and the World*, Abingdon: Routledge.

Harbour, C. P. (2015), *John Dewey and the Future of Community College Education*, London: Bloomsbury.

Harnecker, C. P. (2013), 'Cuba's New Socialism: Different Visions Shaping Current Changes', *Latin American Perspectives*, 40(3), Latin America's Radical Left In Power: Complexities and Challenges in the Twenty-First Century, 107–125.

Hartmeyer, H. (2004), 'Global Education under Pressure. Do the Millennium Development Goals Set the Tone?', *ZEP: Zeitschrift für Internationale Bildungsforschung und Entwicklungspädagogik*, 27(2): 2–6. Available at: https://www .pedocs.de/volltexte/2013/6143/pdf/ZEP_2_2004_Hartmeyer_Global_Education.pdf.

Hartmeyer, H., J. McAuley and L. Wegimont (2019), *Global Education in Estonia*, Dublin: GENE.

Harvey, D. (1989), *The Condition of Postmodernity*, Oxford: Blackwell.

Harvey, D. (2003), *Young People in a Globalizing World, World Youth Report*, New York: United Nations.

Harvey, D. (2005), *A Brief History of Neoliberalism*, Oxford: Oxford University Press.

Hatley, J. (2018), 'The Values of Global Citizenship Education and Implications for Social Justice', Unpublished PhD thesis, Lancaster University.

Hatley, J. (2019), 'Universal Values as a Barrier to the Effectiveness of Global Citizenship Education: A Multimodal Critical Discourse Analysis', *International Journal of Development Education and Global Learning*, 11(1): 87–102.

Have, S. T., J. Rijsman, W. Have and J. Westhof (2018), *The Social Psychology of Change Management*, Abingdon: Routledge.

Heifetz, R. A. (1994), *Leadership Without Easy Answers*, Cambridge, MA: Belknap Press of Harvard University Press.

Heifetz, R., M. Linsky and A. Grashow (2009), *The Practice of Adaptive Leadership. Tools and Tactics for Changing Your Organization and the World*, Cambridge, MA: Harvard Business School Press.

Held, D. and A. McGrew (eds) (2000), *The Global Transformation Reader*, Cambridge: Polity Press.

Hobson, K. (2013), 'On the Making of the Environmental Citizen', *Environmental Politics*, 22(1): 56–72.

Hicks, D. (n.d.), *Future Perspectives*. Available online: https://teaching4abetterworld.co .uk/future.html (accessed 11 November 2020).

Hicks, D. (2012), 'The Future Only Arrives When Things Look Dangerous: Reflections on Futures Education in the UK', *Futures*, 44(1): 4–13.

Hicks, D. (2014), *Education for Hope in Troubled Times: Climate Change and the Transition to a Post-Carbon Future*, London: Trentham/IOE Press.

Hicks, D. and C. Holden (eds) (2007), *Teaching the Global Dimension*, Abingdon: Routledge.

Hogg, M. (2011), *Do We Need a Deeper, More Complex Conversation with the Public about Global Issues? A Review of the Literature*, London: Think Global, DEA.

Holden, C. (2007), 'Young People's Concerns', In: C. Holden and D. Hicks (eds), *Teaching the Global Dimension*, 31–42, Abingdon: Routledge.

Holst, J. D. (1999), 'The Affinities of Lenin & Gramsci: Implications for Radical Adult Education Theory and Practice', *International Journal of Lifelong Education*, 18(5): 407–421.

Holst, J. D. (2009), 'The Pedagogy of Ernesto Che Guevara', *International Journal of Lifelong Education*, 28(2): 149–173.

hooks, b. (1994), *Teaching to Transgress*, New York: Routledge.

Hooper, A. (2018), 'Factors Critical to the Success of School Links: A Kenyan Perspective', Unpublished masters dissertation, UCL Institute of Education.

Hope, A. and S. Timmel (1989), *Training for Transformation*, vols. 1–3, Gweru, Zimbabwe: Mambo Press.

Horton, M. and P. Freire (1990), *We Make the Road by Walking-Conversations on Education and Social Change*, Philadelphia: Temple University Press.

Huckle, J. and S. Sterling (1996), *Education for Sustainability*, London: Earthscan.

Huckle, J. and A. Wals (2015), 'The UN Decade of Education for Sustainable Development: Business As Usual in the End', *Environmental Education Research*, 21(3): 491–505.

Hudson, D. and J. van Heerde-Hudson (2012), '"A Mile Wide and an Inch Deep": Surveys of Public Attitudes Towards Development Aid', *International Journal of Development Education and Global Learning*, 4(1): 5–23.

Hunt, F. (2007), 'Schooling Citizens: A Study of Policy in Practice in South Africa', Unpublished PhD thesis, University of Sussex.

Hunt, F. (2012), *Global Learning in Primary Schools, DERC Research Paper no. 9*, London: IOE.

Hunt, F. (2014), 'Learner Councils in South African Schools: Adult Involvement and Learners' Rights', *Education, Citizenship and Social Justice*, 9(3): 268–285.

Hunt, F. and R. King (2015), *Supporting Whole School Approaches to Global Learning: Focusing Learning and Mapping Impact, DERC Research Report 13*, London: UCL-IOE.

Illeris, K. (2014), *Transformative Learning and Identity*, Abingdon: Routledge.

International Labour Organization (ILO) (n.d.), *Teachers, Educators and Their Organizations as Agents of Social Change*. Available online: https://www.ilo.org/ipec/Partners/Teachers/Teacherseducatorsandtheirorganizationsasagentsofsocialchange/lang--en/index.htm (accessed 16 October 2020).

Jalonen, F. and R. Chaudry (2016), *Youth Workers as Agents for Change*. Available online: https://educationaltoolsportal.eu/en/tools-for-learning/youth-workers-agents-change (accessed 29 October 2020).

Jansen, J. (1997), 'Why Outcomes-Based Education Will Fail: An Elaboration', In: J. Jansen and P. Christie (eds) (1999), *Changing Curriculum: Studies on Outcomes-Based Education in South Africa*, 145–156, Johannesburg: Juta.

Jennings, L. B., D. M. Parra-Medina, D. K. Hilfinger-Messias and K. McLoughlin (2006), 'Toward a Critical Social Theory of Youth Empowerment', *Journal of Community Practice*, 14(1–2): 31–55.

Jones, C. (2009), 'Moral Leadership: An Investigation of Global Dimension Leadership in UK Schools', Unpublished masters dissertation, Middlesex University.

Jooste, N. and S. Heleta (2017), 'Global Citizenship versus Globally Competent Graduates', *Journal of Studies in International Education*, 21(1): 39–51.

Jorgenson, S. (2010), 'De-Centering and Re-Visioning Global Citizenship Education Abroad Programs', *International Journal of Development Education and Global Learning*, 3(1): 23–38.

Jorgenson, S. and L. Shultz (2012), 'Global Citizenship Education (GCE) in Post-Secondary Institutions: What Is Protected and What Is Hidden under the Umbrella of GCE', *Journal of Global Citizenship and Equity Education*, 2(1): 1–22.

Kenway, J. and E. Bullen (2008), 'The Global Corporate Curriculum and the Young Cyberflaneur as Global Citizen', In: N. Dolby and F. Rizvi (eds), *Youth Moves—Identities and Education in Global Perspectives*, 17–32, New York: Routledge.

Killick, D. (2006), 'The Internationalized Curriculum: Making UK HE Fit for Purpose', *Academy Exchange: Supporting the Student Learning Experience, Issue*, 5(Winter): 13–15.

Killick, D. (2011), 'Students as Global Citizens: Being and Becoming Through the Lived Experience of International Mobility', Unpublished PhD thesis, Leeds Metropolitan University.

Killick, D. (2018), 'Graduates In/For a Multicultural and Globalising World', *On the Horizon*, 26(2), 72–78.

Kincheloe, J. L. (2004), *Critical Pedagogy Primer*, New York: Peter Lang.

Kioupi, V. and N. Voulvoulis (2019), 'Education for Sustainable Development: A Systemic Framework for Connecting the SDGs to Educational Outcomes', *Sustainability* 11(21): 1–18.

Kirkwood-Tucker, T. F., J. D. Morris and M. Lieberman (2011), 'What Kind of Teachers Will Teach Our Children? The Worldmindedness of Undergraduate Elementary and Secondary Social Studies Teacher Candidates at Five Florida Public Universities', *International Journal of Development Education and Global Learning*, 3(3): 5–28.

Kirshner, B. (2008), 'Guided Participation in Three Youth Activism Organizations: Facilitation, Apprenticeship, and Joint Work', *Journal of the Learning Sciences*, 17(1): 60–101.

Kirshner, B. (2009), '"Power in Numbers": Youth Organizing as a Context for Exploring Civic Identity', *Journal of Research on Adolescence*, 19(3): 414–440.

Knibbs, S., C. Mollidor, B. Stack and J. Stevens (2018), *National Youth Action Survey 2018*, London: Ipsos Mori and I Will.

Kollmuss, A. and J. Agyeman (2002), 'Mind the Gap: Why Do People Act Environmentally and What Are the Barriers to Pro-Environmental Behavior?', *Environmental Education Research*, 8(3): 239–260.

Korten, D. C. (1990), *Getting to the 21st Century: Voluntary Action and the Global Agenda*, Hartford: Kumarian Press.

Kraska, M., D. Bourn and N. Blum (2018), 'From Internationalization to Global Citizenship: Dialogues in International Higher Education', In: J. Davies and N. Pachler (eds), *Teaching and Learning in Higher Education: Perspectives from UCL*, 85–98, London: UCL IOE Press.

Krause, J. (2010), *The European Development Education Monitoring Report— Development Education Watch*, Brussels: DEEEP.

Kreienkamp, J. (2017), *Responding to the Global Crackdown on Civil Society, Policy Brief*, Washington, DC: Global Governance Institute.

Kuleta-Hulboj, M. (2020), 'Global Education in Poland', In: D. Bourn (ed), *The Bloomsbury Handbook of Global Education and Learning*, 121–132, London: Bloomsbury.

Kunkel-Pottebaum, H. E. (2013), 'Mission Possible: Teachers Serving as Agents of Social Change', Unpublished PhD thesis, MN: University of St Thomas.

Ladson-Billings, G. (1995), 'Toward a Theory of Culturally Relevant Pedagogy', *American Educational Research Journal*, 32(3): 465–491.

Ladson-Billings, G. and W. Tate (1995), 'Towards a Critical Race Theory of Education', *Teacher College Record*, 97(1): 47–68.

Lang, S. (2013), *NGOs, Civil Society, and the Public Sphere*, New York: Cambridge University Press.

Lanier, K. (2001), 'The Teaching Philosophy of bell hooks: The Classroom as a Site for Passionate Interrogation', Paper presented at the Annual Meeting of the American Educational Research Association, Seattle, WA.

Larkin, A. (2018), 'Seeking Global Citizenship Through International Experience/ Service Learning and Global Citizenship Education: Challenges of Power, Knowledge and Difference for Practitioners', In: I. Davies, L. C. Ho, D. Kiwan, C.

L. Peck, A. Peterson, E. Sant and Y. Waghid (eds), *The Palgrave Handbook of Global Citizenship and Education*, 557–572, London: Palgrave Macmillan.

Laski, H. (1923), 'Knowledge as a Civic Discipline', In: O. Stanley (ed), *The Way Out*, 48–49, Oxford: Oxford University Press.

Leeds, D. E. C. (2013), *World Class Teaching*. Available online: http://leedsdec.org.uk/projects.php (accessed 28 October 2020).

Leicht, A., J. Heiss and W. J. Byun (eds) (2018), *Issues and Trends in Education for Sustainable Development (Issue 1)*. Available online: https://unesdoc.unesco.org/ark:/48223/pf0000261445 (accessed 11 November 2020).

Laurence, J. (2020), 'City Settles Chicago Freedom School Lawsuit', Chicago: Block Club, 4 July. Available online: https://blockclubchicago.org/2020/07/04/city-settles-chicago-freedom-school-lawsuit-after-group-was-cited-for-offering-food-to-pro testers-trapped-downtown/ (accessed 15 October 2020).

Leighton, R. (2012), 'Sociology of Education', In: J. Arthur and A. Petersen (eds), *The Routledge Companion to Education*, 58–65, Abingdon: Routledge.

Leonard, A. (2014), 'School Linking: Southern Perspectives on the South/North Educational Linking Process: From Ghana, Uganda and Tanzania', Unpublished PhD thesis, London Institute of Education.

Leopold, D. (2011), 'Education and Utopia: Robert Owen and Charles Fourier', *Oxford Review of Education*, 37(5): 619–635.

Lissovoy, N. (2008), *Power, Crisis and Education for Liberation*, New York: Palgrave.

Llanes, À. and C. Muñoz (2009), 'A Short Stay Abroad: Does It Make a Difference?', *System*, 37(3): 353–365.

Lovett, W. (1876), *The Life and Struggles of William Lovett*, London: Trubner.

Lundy, L. (2007), '"Voice" is Not Enough: Conceptualising Article 12 of the United Nations Convention on the Rights of the Child', *British Educational Research Journal*, 33(6): 827–942.

Lupinacci, J. and A. Happel-Parkins (2015), 'Recognize, Resist, and Reconstitute: An Ecocritical Framework in Teacher Education', *The SoJo Journal: Educational Foundations and Social Justice Education*, 1(1): 45–61.

Lynn, M. and M. E. Jennings (2009), 'Power, Politics, and Critical Race Pedagogy: A Critical Race Analysis of Black Male Teachers' Pedagogy', *Race Ethnicity and Education*, 12(2): 173–196.

MacDonald, R. (1920), *Parliament and Democracy*, London: National Labour Press.

Macintyre, S. (1980), *A Proletarian Science: Marxism in Britain, 1917–1933*, Cambridge: Cambridge University Press.

MacTavish, J. (1916), *What Labour Wants From Education*, London: Workers Education Association.

Makarenko, A. (1973), *The Road to Life*, 2 vols., Moscow: Progress Publishers.

Mannings, N. and K. Edwards (2014), 'Does Civic Education for Young People Increase Political Participation? A Systematic Review', *Educational Review*, 66(1): 1–21.

Marginson, S. (2016), *Higher Education and the Common Good*, Manchester: MUP.

Marquand, D. (1977), *Ramsay MacDonald*, London: Jonathan Cape.

Marshall, H. (2007), 'Global Education in Perspective: Fostering a Global Dimension in an English Secondary School', *Cambridge Journal of Education*, 37(3): 355–374.

Marshall, H. (2011), 'Instrumentalism, Ideals and Imaginaries: Theorising the Contested Space of Global Citizenship Education in Schools', *Globalisation, Societies and Education*, 9(3–4): 411–426.

Martin, F. and H. Griffiths (2012), 'Power and Representation: A Postcolonial Reading of Global Partnerships and Teacher Development through North–South Study Visits', *British Educational Research Journal*, 38(6): 907–927.

Mayo, P. (2017), 'Gramsci, Hegemony and Educational Politics', In: N. Pizzolato and J. D. Holst (eds), *Antonio Gramsci—A Pedagogy to Change the World*, 35–48, Cham, Switzerland: Springer.

McBriar, A. M. (1962), *Fabian Socialism and English Politics, 1884–1918*, Cambridge: Cambridge University Press.

McCarthy, J. (2019), 'What Exactly Is the Global Citizens Movement', *Global Citizen*, 26 September. Available online: https://www.globalcitizen.org/en/media/activate/?subPage=/en/content/what-is-a-global-citizen (accessed 12 December 2020).

McCloskey, S. (ed) (2014), *Development Education in Policy and Practice*, London: Palgrave.

McCowan, T. (2012), 'Opening Spaces for Citizenship in Higher Education: Three Initiatives in English Universities', *Studies in Higher Education*, 37:, 1–17.

McCowan, T. (2019), *Higher Education for and Beyond the Sustainable Development Goals*, London: Palgrave, 481–494.

McDermott, C. (2007), *Design: The Key Concepts*, Abingdon: Routledge.

McDonald, K. (2006), *Global Movements: Action and Culture*, Oxford: Blackwell.

McDonald, M. and K. Zeichner (2009), 'Social Justice Teacher Education', In: W. Ayers, T. Quinn and D. Stovall (eds), *Handbook of Social Justice in Education*, 611–624, New York: Routledge.

McGrady, A. G. and E. Regan (2008), 'Ethics in a Global World: The Earth Charter and Religious Education', *British Journal of Religious Education*, 30(2): 165–170.

McLaren, P. (1998), *Life in Schools: An Introduction to Critical Pedagogy in the Foundations of Education*, 3rd edn, New York: Longman.

McLaren, P. (2003), 'Critical Pedagogy: A Look at the Major Concepts', In: A. Darder, M. Baltodano and R. D. Torres (eds), *The Critical Pedagogy Reader*, 69–96, New York: Routledge/Falmer.

McLaren, P. and P. Leonard (1993), *Paulo Freire: A Critical Encounter*, New York: Routledge.

Merryfield, M. (2009), 'Moving the Center of Global Education: From Imperial Worldviews That Divide the World to Double Consciousness, Contrapuntal Pedagogy, Hybridity, and Cross-Cultural Competence', In: T. F. Kirkwood-Tucker (ed), *Visions in Global Education*, 215–239, New York: Peter Lang.

Mezirow, J. (2000), 'Learning to Think Like an Adult. Core Concepts of Transformation Theory', In: J. Mezirow and Associates (eds), *Learning as Transformation. Critical Perspectives on a Theory in Progress*, 3–33, San Francisco, CA: Jossey-Bass.

Mezirow, J. (2009), 'Transformative Learning Theory', In: J. Mezirow and E. W. Taylor (eds), *Transformative Learning in Practice: Insights from Community, Workplace, and Higher Education*, 18–32, San Francisco: Jossey-Bass.

Mezirow, J. (2012), 'Learning to Think Like an Adult: Core Concepts of Transformation Theory', In: E. Taylor and P. Cranton (eds), *The Handbook of Transformative Learning: Theory, Research and Practice*, 73–95, San Francisco: Jossey-Bass.

Middlemiss, L. (2014), 'Individualised or Participatory? Exploring Late-Modern Identity and Sustainable Development', *Environmental Politics*, 23(6): 929–946.

Miller, G., E. Bowes, D. Bourn and J. M. Castro (2012), *Learning about Development at A-Level. A Study of the Impact of the World Development A-Level on Young People's Understanding of International Development*, DERC Research paper no. 7, London: IOE.

Ministry of Education (MoE) (2001), *Manifesto on Values, Education and Democracy*, Pretoria: Government Printer.

Misiaszek, G. W. (2015), 'Ecopedagogy and Citizenship in the Age of Globalisation: S. Connections between Environmental and Global Citizenship Education to Save the Planet', *European Journal of Education*, 50(3): 280–292.

Misiaszek, G. W. (2021), *Ecopedagogy*, London: Bloomsbury.

Moore, J. (2005), 'Is Higher Education Ready for Transformative Learning?: A Question Explored in the Study of Sustainability', *Journal of Transformative Education*, 3(1): 76–91.

Moraes, S. (2014), 'Global Citizenship as a Floating Signifier: Lessons from UK Universities', *International Journal of Development Education and Global Learning*, 6(2): 27–42.

Morgan, A. (2007), 'Minding the World: Integral Transformative Learning for Geographical and Environmental Wisdom', Unpublished PhD thesis, Institute of Education, University of London.

Morgan, K. (1975), *Keir Hardie: Radical and Socialist*, London: Weidenfeld and Nicolson.

Morton, A. L. (ed) (1973), *Political Writings of William Morris*, London: Lawrence and Wishart.

Mravcová, A. (2016), 'Practical Implementation of Global Citizenship Education at the Slovak University of Agriculture', *International Journal of Development Education and Global Learning*, 8(1): 57–77.

Mulenga, D. C. (2001), 'Mwalimu Julius Nyerere: A Critical Review of His Contributions to Adult Education and Postcolonialism', *International Journal of Lifelong Education*, 20(6): 446–470.

Mullahey, R., Y. Susskind and B. Checkoway (1999), *Youth Participation in Community Planning*, Chicago: American Planning Association.

Naberhaus, M. and A. Sheppard (2015), *Re.Imagining Activism: A Practical Guide for the Great Transition*, Brussels: Smart CSOs Lab / Michael Naberhaus. Available online: http://www.smart-csos.org/tools-publications/toolkit-for-civil-society-activists (accessed 20/11/2020).

Nambinga, S. M. (n.d.), 'Teachers as Agents of Change in Society', *SWAPO Party*. Available online: http://www.swapoparty.org/teachers_as_agents_of_change_in_so ciety.html (accessed 16 October 2020).

NAS, UWT and Equaliteach (n.d.), *Universal Values*, London: NAS/UWT. Available online: https://www.nasuwt.org.uk/uploads/assets/uploaded/b49175fd-4bf6-4f2d-a c5b2759c03015be.pdf (accessed 20 November 2020).

National Youth Agency (n.d.), *Young People and Social Action*. Available online: https ://nya.org.uk/work-with-us/young-people-social-action/ (accessed 16 October 2020).

National Youth Agency (2018), *#iwill, Social Action and Youth Work*. Available online: https://nya.org.uk/2018/11/iwill-social-action-and-youth-work/ (accessed 16 October 2020).

Newman, J. (2009), 'Value Reflection and the Earth Charter', In: A. Stibbe (ed), *The Handbook of Sustainable Literacy*, 99–104, Dartington: Green Books.

Nicholson, J. H. (1936), *Education and Modern Needs*, London: Nicholson and Watson.

Nickel, J. (2007), *Making Sense of Human Rights*, 2nd edn, Malden, MA: Blackwell Publishing.

Noh, J.-E. (2019), 'The Legitimacy of Development Nongovernmental Organizations as Global Citizenship Education Providers in Korea', *Education, Citizenship and Social Justice*, 14(3): 241–259.

North Eastern University (n.d.), *The Global University*. Available online: https://www .northeastern.edu/academic-plan/strategic-themes/the-global-university/ (accessed 29 October 2020).

Novak, M. (2000), 'Defining Social Justice', *First Things*. Available online: https://www.fir stthings.com/article/2000/12/defining-social-justice (accessed 15 October 2020).

NSVRC (2014), *Sexual Awareness Month—Becoming an Agent of Social Change*. Available online: https://nsvrc.org/sites/default/files/saam_2014_becoming-an-agent -of-social-change_0.pdf (accessed 18 October 2020).

Nussbaum, M. (2002), 'Education for Citizenship in an Era of Global Connection', *Studies in Philosophy and Education*, 21(4/5): 289–303.

Nussbaum, M. (2006), *Frontiers of Justice*, Cambridge, MA: Harvard University Press.

Nyerere, J. K. (1976), 'Education and Liberation', *Africa Development / Afrique et Développement*, 1(3): 5–12.

Nyerere, J. K. (1978), 'Development Is for Man, by Man and of Man: The Declaration of Dar-es-Salaam', In: B. L. Hall and J. R. Kidd (eds) *Adult Learning: A Design for Action*, 27–36, Oxford: Pergamon Press.

O'Connor, K. and K. Zeichner (2011), 'Preparing US Teachers for Critical Global Education', *Globalisation, Societies and Education*, 9(3–4): 521–536.

Odora Hoppers, C. (2009), 'Education, Culture and Society in a Globalizing World: Implications for Comparative and International Education', *Compare: A Journal of Comparative and International Education*, 39(5): 601–614.

OECD (2011), *Towards an OECD Skills Strategy*, Paris: OECD.

OECD (2015), *Skills for Social Progress, the Power of Social and Emotional Skills*, Paris: OECD.

OECD (2016), *Getting Skills Right: Assessing and Anticipating Changing Skill Needs*, Paris: OECD.

OECD (2017), *Getting Skills Right: So, Set 3, Skills for Job Indicators*, Paris: OECD.

OECD (2018), *The Future We Want*, Paris: OECD.

OECD (2020), *PISA 2018 Results (Volume VI) Are Students Ready To Thrive In An Interconnected World*, Paris: OECD.

Ollis, T. (2008), 'The Accidental Activist: Learning Embodiment and Action', *Australian Journal of Adult Education*, 48(2): 317–335.

Orr, D. W. (1992), *Ecological Literacy: Education and the Transition to a Postmodern World*, Albany, NY: State University of New York Press.

O'Sullivan, E. (1999), *Transformative Learning: Educational Vision for the 21ˢᵗ Century*, London: Zed Books.

O'Sullivan, E., A. Morrell and M. A. O'Connor (eds) (2002), *Expanding the Boundaries of Transformative Learning*, New York: Palgrave.

Osler, A. (2016), *Human Rights and Schooling*, New York: Teachers College Press.

Osler, A. and H. Starkey (2010), *Teachers and Human Rights Education*, Stoke-on-Trent: Trentham Books.

Otunnu, O. (2015), 'Mwalimu Julius Kambarage Nyerere's Philosophy, Contribution, and Legacies', *African Identities*, 13(1): 18–33.

Oxfam (2015), *Education for Global Citizenship—A Curriculum Guide for Schools*, Oxford: Oxfam.

Oxley, L. and P. Morris (2013), 'Global Citizenship: A Typology for Distinguishing Its Multiple Conceptions', *British Journal of Educational Studies*, 61(3): 301–325.

Paige, R. M., G. W. Fry, E. M. Stallman, J. Josić and J. Jon (2009), 'Study Abroad for Global Engagement: The Long-Term Impact of Mobility Experiences', *Intercultural Education*, 20(sup1): S29–S44.

Pak, S.-Y. and M. Lee (2018), '"Hit the Ground Running": Delineating the Problems and Potentials in State-Led Global Citizenship Education (GCE) through Teacher Practices in South Korea', *British Journal of Educational Studies*, 66(4): 515–535.

Palser, R. (2020), *Education for Social Change*, London: Amazon.

Pantić, N. (2015), 'A Model for Study of Teacher Agency for Social Justice', *Teachers and Teaching*, 21(6): 759–778.

Parker, L. and D. O. Stovall (2004), 'Actions Following Words: Critical Race Theory Connects to Critical Pedagogy', *Educational Philosophy and Theory*, 36(2): 167–182.

Partners Training for Transformation (n.d.), *How We Do It*. Available online: http://www .trainingfortransformation.ie/index.php/how-we-do-it (accessed 15 October 2010).

Pashby, K. (2011), 'Cultivating Global Citizens: Planting New Seeds or Pruning the Perennials? Looking for the Citizen-Subject in Global Citizenship Education Theory', *Globalisation, Societies and Education*, 9(3–4): 427–442.

Pashby, K., M. da Costa, S. Stein and V. Andreotti (2020), 'A Meta-Review of Typologies of Global Citizenship Education', *Comparative Education*, 56(2): 144–164.

Paulo Freire Institute (n.d.), *Earth Charter and Education for Social Change*. Available online: https://earthcharter.org/wp-content/assets/virtual-library2/images/uploads/X-%20The%20Earth%20Charter%20and%20Education%20for%20Social%20Cha nge.pdf (accessed 20 November 2020).

Payne, C. M. (2003), 'More Than A Symbol of Freedom: Education for Liberation and Democracy', *Phi Delta Kappan*, 85(1): 22–28.

Percy-Smith, B. and D. Burns (2013), 'Exploring the Role of Children and Young People as Agents of Change in Sustainable Community Development', *Local Environment*, 18(3): 323–339.

Phillips, A. and T. Putnam (1980), 'Education for Emancipation: The Movement for Independent Working Class Education 1908–1928', *Capital and Class*. Available online: https://www.cseweb.org.uk/pdfs/010/010_018.pdf#:~:text=EDUCA TION%20FOR%20EMANCIPATION%3A%20THE%20MOVEMENT%20FOR %20INDEPENDENT%20WORKING,which%20are%20imparting%20instruct ion%20in%20false%20economics.%22%5B1%20%5D (accessed 20 November 2020).

Pieniazek, M. A. (2020), 'Ubuntu: Constructing Spaces of Dialogue in the Theory and Practice of Global Education', In: D. Bourn (ed), *The Bloomsbury Handbook of Global Education and Learning*, 76–89, London: Bloomsbury.

Pizzolato, N. and J. D. Holst (eds) (2017), *Antonio Gramsci—A Pedagogy to Change the World*, Cham, Switzerland: Springer.

Pontis Foundation (n.d.), *Our Vision*. Available online: https://www.nadaciapontis.sk/en /our-vision/ (accessed 13 October 2020).

Postman, N. and C. Weingartner (1971), *Teaching as a Subversive Activity*, London: Penguin.

President's Commission on Higher Education (1947), *Higher Education for American Democracy*, New York, NY: Harper & Brothers Publishers.

Pring, B. (1937), *Education: Capitalist and Socialist*, London: Methuen.

Pugh, K. (2016), 'To What Extent Does Participation in Social Action Projects Enable Development of Global Skills in Young People in Brazil and England?', Unpublished masters dissertation, Institute of Education.

Pyarelal (1997), *Mahatma Gandhi Volume IX Book 1 the Last Phase*, Ahmedabad: Navajivan Publishing House.

Quin, J. (2009), 'Growing Social Justice Educators: A Pedagogical Framework for Social Justice Education', *Intercultural Education*, 20(2): 109–125.

Radiukiewicz, A. and I. Grabowska-Lusinska (2007), 'Education for Democratic Citizenship in Poland', *Journal of Social Science Education*, 6(2): 21–28.

Raina, S. (2007), 'Role of a Teacher in Society', *Ezine@rticles*, 23 September. Available online: https://ezinearticles.com/?Role-of-a-Teacher-in-Society&id=746217 (accessed 16 October 2020).

Ramsden, P. (1998), 'Managing the Effective University', *Higher Education Research and Development*, 17(3): 347–370.

Rawls, J. (1971), *A Theory of Justice*, revised edn, Cambridge: Belknap Press of Harvard University Press.

Rawls, J. (1993), *Political Liberalism*, New York: Columbia University Press.

Ray, L. (2007), *Globalisation and Everyday Life*, Abingdon: Routledge.

Reid, F. (1966), 'Socialist Sunday Schools in Britain, 1892–1939', *International Review of Social History*, 11(1): 18–47.

Reilly Carlisle, L., B. W. Jackson and A. George (2006), 'Principles of Social Justice Education: The Social Justice Education in Schools Project', *Equity and Excellence in Education*, 39(1): 55–64.

Rhoads, R. A. and K. Szelényi (2011), *Global Citizenship and the University: Advancing Social Life and Relations in an Interdependent World*, Stanford, CA: Stanford University Press.

Richards, D. (2008), *Edible Boardrooms and Allotments in the Sky*. Available online: https://www.risc.org.uk/images/gardens/roof-garden/roof-garden-edible-board rooms.pdf (accessed 20 October 2020).

Richards, D. (2009), 'Pushing the Boundaries', *Rizoma Freireano*, 5: 1–10.

Right to Education (n.d.), *Understanding Education as a Right*. Available online: https ://www.right-to-education.org/page/understanding-education-right (accessed 23 November 2020).

Ritzer, G. (2000), *The McDonaldisation of Society*, London: Sage.

Rizvi, F. (1998), 'Some Thoughts on Contemporary Theories of Social Justice', In: B. Atweh, S. Kemmis and P. Weeks (eds), *Action Research in Practice: Partnerships for Social Justice in Education*, 47–56, London: Routledge.

Robinson, A. A. and L. Levac (2018), 'Transformative Learning in Developing as an Engaged Global Citizen', *Journal of Transformative Education*, 16(2): 108–129.

Robinson, C. (2017), 'Translating Human Rights Principles into Classroom Practices: Inequities in Educating about Human Rights', *The Curriculum Journal*, 28(1): 123–136.

Robinson, C., L. Phillips and A. Quennerstedt (2020), 'Human Rights Education: Developing a Theoretical Understanding of Teachers' Responsibilities', *Educational Review*, 72(2): 220–241.

Robertson, S. E. (2008), 'Teaching for Social Justice: A Case Study of One Elementary Teacher's Experience with Implementing Social Justice Education in the Social Studies', Unpublished PhD thesis, The University of Texas at Austin.

Rosen, M. (n.d.), *Education for Liberation*. Available online: https://www.michaelrosen. co.uk/education-for-liberation/ (accessed 13 October 2020).

Rouse, J. E. (2011), 'Social Justice Development: Creating Social Change Agents in Academic Systems', Unpublished PhD thesis, University of North Carolina at Greensboro.

Rowan, L. (2019), *Higher Education and Social Justice*, London: Palgrave.

Royant, L. (2017), 'Global Citizenship Education: A Case Study of the UK-Based Non-Governmental Organisation Reading International Solidarity Centre', Unpublished PhD thesis, University of Reading.

Rubagiza, J., J. Umutoni and A. Kaleeba (2016), 'Teachers as Agents of Change: Promoting Peacebuilding and Social Cohesion in Schools in Rwanda', *Education As Change*, 20(3): 202–224.

Rutzen, D. (2015.), 'Aid Barriers and the Rise of Philanthropic Perfectionism', *International Journal of Not-For-Profit Law*, 17(1): 1–42.

Ryan, A. (2011), 'Conscientization: The Art of Learning', In: A. O'Shea and M. O'Brien (eds), *Pedagogy, Oppression and Transformation in a 'Post-Critical' Climate*, 86–101, London: Bloomsbury.

Sallah, M. (2009), 'Conceptual and Pedagogical Approaches to the Global Dimension of Youth Work in British Higher Education Institutions', *The International Journal of Development Education and Global Learning*, 1(3): 39–55.

Sallah, M. (2014), *Global Youth Work: Provoking Consciousness and Taking Action*, Lyme Regis, UK: Russell House Publishing.

Sallah, M. (2020a), 'Towards the Second Duality of Global Youth Work: The Environment and Disruptive Action', *Policy and Practice: A Development Education Review*, 30: 115–129.

Sallah, M. (2020b), 'A Scholar-Activist's Heretic Attempts to "Eradicate Poverty" from a Southern Perspective, through Disruptive Global Youth Work', *Revista Sinergias*, 10: 13–28.

Sant, E. (2019), 'Democratic Education: A Theoretical Review (2006–2017)', *Review of Educational Research*, 89(5): 655–696.

Sant, E., S. Lewis, S. Delgado and E. W. Ross (2018), 'Justice and Global Citizenship Education', In: I. Davies, L.-C. Ho, D. Kiwan, C. Peck, A. Peterson, E. Sant and Y. Waghid (eds), *The Palgrave Handbook of Global Citizenship and Education*, 227–244, London: Palgrave.

Sarabhai, K. V. (2013), 'ESD and Global Citizenship Education', *Journal of Education for Sustainable Development*, 7(2): 137–139.

Sayed, Y. (2016), 'Teachers Have a Crucial Role to Play in Building Social Cohesion', *The Conversation*, 29 August. Available online: https://theconversation.com/teachers-have-a-crucial-role-to-play-in-building-social-cohesion-60823 (accessed 20 November 2020).

Scharmer, C. O. (2018), *The Essentials of Theory U: Core Principles and Applications*, Oakland, CA: Berrett-Koehler Publishing.

Schattle, H. (2008), *The Practices of Global Citizenship*, Lanham, MD: Rowman and Littlefield.

Schecter, A. (2016), *Student Sues Walden University*. Available online: https://www.nbcnews.com/news/us-news/student-sues-walden-university-i- wasted-six-years-my-life-n690706 (accessed 25 March 2021).

Scheunpflug, A. (2011), 'Global Education and Cross-Cultural Learning: A Challenge for a Research-Based Approach to International Teacher Education', *International Journal of Development Education and Global Learning*, 3(3): 29–44.

Schugurensky, D. (2014), *Paulo Freire*, London: Bloomsbury.

Scott, P. (2015), 'Universities Are Losing Their Sense of Public Responsibility and Social Purpose', *The Guardian*, 6 January. Available online: https://www.theguardian.com /education/2015/jan/06/public-universities-becoming-corporate-losing-social-pu rpose (accessed 20 November 2020).

Scott, W. and S. Gough (2003), *Sustainable Development and Learning—Framing the Issues*, Abingdon: Routledge.

Sen, A. (2010), *The Idea of Justice*, London: Penguin.

Send My Friend (2016), *Local to Global Fact Sheet*. Available online: https://sendmyf riend.org/wp-content/uploads/2016/03/Local-to-global-fact-sheet-2016.pdf (accessed 14 October 2020).

Shah, S. (2011), 'Building Transformative Youth Leadership: Data on the Impacts of Youth Organizing', *Funders Collaborative on Youth Organizing, New York*. Available online: http://fcyo.org/media/docs/2525_Paper_11_CompleteWeb.pdf (accessed 28 October 2020).

Sharma, N. (2008), *Makiguchi and Gandhi: Their Educational Relevance for the 21ˢᵗ Century*, MD: University Press of America.

Sharma, N. (2020), *Value-Creating Global Citizenship Education for Sustainable Development: Strategies and Approaches*, Cham, Switzerland: Palgrave.

Sharma, R. and S. Monteiro (2016), 'Creating Social Change: The Ultimate Goal of Education for Sustainability', *International Journal of Social Science and Humanity*, 6(1): 72–76.

Shiel, C. (2007), 'Developing and Embedding Global Perspectives across the University', In: S. Marshall (ed), *Strategic Leadership of Change in Higher Education*, 158–173, London and New York: Routledge.

Shiel, C. (2013), 'Developing Global Perspectives: Global Citizenship and Sustainable Development within Higher Education', Unpublished PhD thesis, Bournemouth University.

Shor, I. (1990), 'Liberation Education: An Interview with Ira Shor', *Language Arts*, 67(4), 342–352.

Shor, I. (1992), *Empowering Education: Critical Teaching for Social Change*, Chicago: The University of Chicago Press.

Shove, E., M. Pantzar and M. Watson (2012), *The Dynamics of Social Practice: Everyday Life and How It Changes*, London: Sage.

Shultz, L. (2007), 'Educating for Global Citizenship: Conflicting Agendas and Understandings', *Alberta Journal of Educational Research*, 53(3): 248.

Shultz, L. (2010), 'Conflict, Dialogue and Justice: Exploring Global Citizenship Education as a Generative Social Justice Project', *Journal of Contemporary Issues in Education*, 4(2): 3–15.

Shultz, L. (2011a), 'Decolonising Social Justice Education', In: A. A. Abdi (ed), *Decolonizing Philosophies of Education*, 29–42, Rotterdam: Sense Publishing.

Shultz, L. (2011b), 'What Do We Ask of Global Citizenship Education? A Study of GC Education in a Canadian University', *International Journal of Development Education and Global Learning*, 3(1): 5–22.

Shultz, L. (2018), 'Global Citizenship and Equity: Cracking the Code and Finding Decolonial Possibility', In: I. Davies, L.-C. Ho, D. Kiwan, C. L. Peck, A. Peterson, E. Sant and Y. Waghid (eds), *The Palgrave Handbook of Global Citizenship and Education*, 245–256, London: Palgrave.

Shultz, L., A. A. Abdi and G. H. Richardson (eds) (2011), *Global Citizenship Education in Post-Secondary Institutions*, New York, NY: Peter Lang.

Shultz, L. and S. Jorgenseon, 'Global Citizenship Education (GCE) in Post-secondary Institutions: What Is Protected and What Is Hidden under the Umbrella of GCE', *Journal of Global Citizenship & Equity Education*, 2(1): 1–22.

Silver, H. (1975), *English Education and the Radicals 1750–1850*, London: Routledge Kegan Paul.

Sim, H.-J. R. (2016), 'Global Citizenship Education in South Korea through Civil Society Organizations: Its Status and Limitations', *Asian Journal of Education*, 17(S): 107–129.

Simon, B. (1965), *Education and the Labour Movement*, London: Lawrence and Wishart.

Simon, B. (1994), *The State and Educational Change*, London: Lawrence and Wishart.

Singh, M. (2011), 'The Place of Social Justice in Higher Education and Social Change Discourses', *Compare: A Journal of Comparative and International Education*, 41(4): 481–494.

Singleton, J. (2015), 'Head, Heart and Hands Model for Transformative Learning: Place as Context for Changing Sustainability Values—Transforming Eco-Paradigms for Sustainable Values', *Journal of Sustainability Education*, 9(March): 1–16.

Sipos, Y., B. Battisti and K. Grimm (2008), 'Achieving Transformative Sustainability Learning: Engaging Head, Hands and Heart', *International Journal of Sustainability in Higher Education*, 9: 68–86.

Sizemore, B. A. (1973), 'The Future of Education for Black Americans', *The School Review*, 81(3): 389–404.

Skatkin, M. and G. Cov'janov (1994), 'Nadezhda Krupskaya', *Prospects, The Quarterly Review of Comparative Education*, XXIV(1/2): 49–60. Available online: nhttp:/ /www.ibe.unesco.org/sites/default/files/krupskae.pdf#:~:text=education%2C% 20eradication%20of%20illiteracy%2C%20and%20children's%20and%20youth,ma in%20organizers%20of%20the%20socialist%20system%20of%20educatio (accessed 20 November 2020).

Slavkova, L. and N. Korte (2019), *Challenges of Transition in Eastern Europe: Lessons for Civic Education*, Berlin: D.R.A.E.V.

Stanford University (2017), *Stanford's Mission*. Available online: http://exploredegrees .stanford.edu/stanfordsmission/ (accessed 20 November 2020).

Starkey, H. (2017), 'Globalisation and Education for Cosmopolitan Citizenship', In: J. Banks (ed), *Citizenship Education and Global Migration*, 41–62, Washington, DC: American Education Research Association.

Steiner, M. (ed) (1993), *Developing the Global Teacher*, Stoke-On-Trent: Trentham.

Stein, S. (2020), 'Pluralizing Possibilities for Global Learning in Western Higher Education', In: D. Bourn (ed), *The Bloomsbury Handbook of Global Education and Learning*, 63–75, London: Bloomsbury.

Stein, S. and V. Andreotti (2016), 'Postcolonial Insights for Engaging Difference in Educational Approaches to Social Justice and Citizenship', In: A. Petersen, R. Hattam, M. Zembylas and J. Arthur (eds), *The Palgrave International Handbook of Education for Citizenship and Social Justice*, 229–245, London: Palgrave.

Stephens, J. C., M. E. Hernandez, M. Román, A. C. Graham and R. W. Scholz (2008), 'Higher Education as a Change Agent for Sustainability in Different Cultures and Contexts', *International Journal of Sustainability in Higher Education*, 9(3): 317–338.

Sterling, S. (2003), 'Whole Systems Thinking as a Basis for Paradigm Change in Education: Explorations in the Context of Sustainability', Unpublished PhD thesis, University of Bath.

Sterling, S. (2010), 'Transformative Learning and Sustainability: Sketching the Conceptual Ground', *Learning and Teaching in Higher Education*, 5: 17–33.

Sterling, S. (2014a), 'Contradiction or Complement: Can Higher Education Be Deeper Education?', In: P. B. Corcoran and B. Hollingshead (eds), *Intergenerational Learning and Transformative Leadership for Sustainable Futures*, Wageningen, the Netherlands: Wageningen Academic Publishers.

Sterling, S. (2014b), 'Separate Tracks or Real Synergy? Achieving a Closer Relationship between Education and SD, Post-2015', *Journal of Education for Sustainable Development*, 8(2): 89–112.

Sterling, S. (2015), 'Commentary on "Goal 4: Education"', In: J. Mengel, D. Young, G. Gisbert and C. Symon (eds), *International Council for Science (ICSU) & International Social Science Council (ISSC) Review of the Sustainable Development Goals: The Science Perspective*, 27–30, Paris: ICSU.

Sterling, S., L. Maxey and H. Luna (eds) (2013), *The Sustainable University: Progress and Prospects*, Abingdon: Routledge, Earthscan.

Stibbe, A. (ed) (2009), *The Handbook of Sustainable Literacy*, Dartington: Green Books.

Stromquist, N. P. and K. Monkmann (eds) (2000), *Globalisation and Education*, Oxford: Rowman and Littlefield.

Struve, A. (2019), 'Anti-Oppressive Education With A "Different Kind of Rigor": Teachers' and Administrators' Perspectives of A Social Justice Education Program at an Affluent Public High School', Unpublished Doctorate in Education, University of San Francisco.

Summers, D. and R. Cutting (eds) (2016), *Education for Sustainable Development in Further Education*, London: Palgrave.

Sundaram, V. (2018), 'Gender, Sexuality and Global Citizenship Education: Addressing the Role of Higher Education in Tackling Sexual Harassment and Violence', In: I. Davies, L. C. Ho, D. Kiwan, C. L. Peck, A. Peterson, E. Sant and Y. Waghid (eds), *The Palgrave Handbook of Global Citizenship and Education*, 409–424, London: Palgrave Macmillan.

Susa, R. (2019), *Global Citizenship Education (GCE) for Unknown Futures—Mapping Past and Current Experiments and Debates*, Helsinki: Bridge, 47.

SustainUs (2020a), *About Us*. Available online: https://sustainus.org/about/ (accessed 19 October 2020).

SustainUs (2020b), *Sustaining Our Resistance*. Available online: https://sustainus.org/training/ (accessed 19 October 2020).

Sutherland, A., R. Susa and V. Andreotti (2020), 'Gesturing Towards New Horizons of North-South Community-Engaged Learning', In: D. Bourn (ed), *The Bloomsbury Handbook of Global Education and Learning*, 385–401, London: Bloomsbury.

Svitačová, E. and A. Mravcová (2014), 'Implementation of Global Development Education into the Curriculum at the Faculty of Economics and Management, Slovak University of Agriculture', *International Journal of Development Education and Global Learning*, 6(2): 43–61.

Szucs, E. U. (2009), 'The Role of Teachers in the 21st Century', *Sens Public*, 22 October. Available online: http://www.sens-public.org/articles/667/?lang=fr (accessed 16 October 2020).

Tan, L. (2009), 'The F E's of Emancipatory Pedagogy: The Rehumanisation Approach to Inner City Youth', In: W. Ayers, T. Quinn and D. Stovall (eds), *Handbook of Social Justice in Education*, 485–496, New York: Routledge.

Tallon, R. (2013), 'What Do Young People Think of Development? An Exploration into the Meanings Young People Make from NGO Media', Unpublished PhD thesis, Victoria University of Wellington.

Tarlau, R. (2017), 'Gramsci as Theory, Pedagogy and Strategy: Educational Lessons from the Brazilian Landless Workers Movement', In: N. Pizzolato and J. D. Holst (eds), *Antonio Gramsci—A Pedagogy to Change the World*, 107–126, Cham, Switzerland: Springer.

Tarozzi, M. (2020), 'Role of NGOs in Global Citizenship Education', In: D. Bourn (ed), *Bloomsbury Handbook of Global Education and Learning*, 133–148, London: Bloomsbury.

Tarozzi, M. and C. Torres (2016), *Global Citizenship Education and the Crisis of Multiculturalism*, London: Bloomsbury.

Tarrow, S. (2005), 'The Dualities of Transnational Contention: "Two Activist Solitudes" or a New World Altogether?', *Mobilization: An International Quarterly*, 10(1): 53–72.

Tawney, R. H. (1924), *Education: The Socialist Policy*, London: Independent Labour Party.

Taylor, E. (2009), 'Fostering Transformative Learning', In: J. Mezirow and E. W. Taylor (eds), *Transformative Learning in Practice: Insights from Community, Workplace, and Higher Education*, 3–17, San Francisco: Jossey-Bass.

Teitelbaum, K. (1993), *Schooling for "Good Rebels": Socialist Education for Children in the United States, 1900–1920*, Philadelphia, PA: Temple University Press.

Teitelbaum, K. and W. Reese (1983), 'American Socialist Pedagogy and Experimentation in the Progressive Era: The Socialist Sunday School', *History of Education Quarterly*, 23(4): 429–454.

Terrill, R. (1974), *R. H. Tawney and His Times: Socialism as Fellowship*, London: Andre Deutsch.

Thomas, I. (2016), 'Challenges for Implementation of Education for Sustainable Development', In: M. Barth, G. Michelsen, M. Rieckmann and I. Thomas (eds), *Routledge Handbook of Higher Education for Sustainable Development*, 56–71, Abingdon: Routledge.

Thomas, O., W. Davidson and H. McAdoo (2008), 'An Evaluation Study of the Young Empowered Sisters (YES!) Program: Promoting Cultural Assets among African American Adolescent Girls through a Culturally Relevant School-Based Intervention', *Journal of Black Psychology*, 34(3): 281–308.

Tibbitts, F. and P. G. Kirchschlaeger (2010), 'Perspectives of Research on Human Rights Education', *Journal of Human Rights Education*, 2(1): 8–29.

Tikly, L. and A. M. Barret (eds) (2013), *Education Quality and Social Justice in the Global South*, Abingdon: Routledge.

Torres, C. A. (2017), *Theoretical and Empirical Foundations of Critical Global Citizenship Education*, New York: Routledge.

Torres, C. A. and T. R. Mitchell (1998), *Sociology of Education: Emerging Perspectives*, New York: State University of New York Press.

Tota, P. M. (2014), 'Filling the Gaps: The Role and Impact of International Non-Governmental Organisations in 'Education for All'', *Globalisation, Societies and Education*, 12(1): 92–109.

Trades Union Council (1937), *Education for Democracy*, London: TUC.

Trewby, J. (2014), 'Journeys to Engagement with the UK Global Justice Movement: Life Stories of Activist-Educators', Unpublished PhD thesis, Institute of Education.

Tyson, C. A. and S. C. Park (2008), 'Civic Education, Social Justice and Critical Race Theory', In: J. Arthur, I. Davies and C. Hahn (eds), *Education for Citizenship and Democracy*, 29–39, London: SAGE.

UKSCN (2020a), *Our Demands*. Available online: https://ukscn.org/our-demands/ (accessed 19 October 2020).

UKSCN (2020b), *Accountability Agreement*. Available online: https://ukscn.org/account ability-agreement (accessed 19 October 2020).

UKSCN (2020c), *How I Went From Shy Kid to School Striker*. Available online: https:// ukscn.org/blog/2020/02/12/how-i-went-from-shy-kid-to-school-striker/ (accessed 19 October 2020).

United Nations (1948), *Universal Declaration of Human Rights*. Available online: https:// www.ohchr.org/EN/UDHR/Documents/UDHR_Translations/eng.pdf (accessed 27 October 2020).

United Nations (1992), Agenda 21, United Nations Conference on Environment & Development Rio de Janeiro, Brazil, 3 to 14 June 1992. Available online: https://sustainabledevelopment.un.org/content/documents/Agenda21.pdf (accessed 20 November 2020).

United Nations Human Rights Office (1999), *The Right to Education*. Available online: https://www.ohchr.org/EN/Issues/Education/Training/Compilation/Pages/d)GeneralCommentNo13Therighttoeducation(article13)(1999).aspx (accessed 23 December 2020).

United Nations (2003), 'Universal Values—Peace, Freedom, Social Progress, Equal Rights, Human Dignity—Acutely Needed, Secretary-General Says at Tübingen University, Germany', *UN Press Release*. Available online: https://www.un.org/press/en/2003/sgsm9076.doc (accessed 11 October 2020).

United Nations (2015), Transforming our World: The 2030 Agenda for Sustainable Development. Available online: https://sdgs.un.org/2030agenda (accessed 20 November 2020).

United Nations (2016a), *Sustainable Development Goals—Quality Education*. Available online: https://sdgs.un.org/goals/goal4 (accessed 27 October 2020).

United Nations (2016b), *United Nations Uses NGOs to Promote 'Global Citizenship' for 2030 Agenda*. Available online: https://technocracy.news/united-nations-uses-ngos-promote-global-citizenship-2030-agenda/ (accessed 29 October 2020).

United Nations (2020), *Young People Take Action for Social Change: International Youth Day 2020*. Available online: https://www.un.org/development/desa/en/news/social/young-people-take-action-for-global-change.html (accessed 16 October 2020).

UNESCO (n.d.), *Teachers*. Available online: https://en.unesco.org/themes/teachers (accessed 16 October 2020).

UNESCO (n.d.), *The ABCs of Global Citizenship Education*, Paris: UNESCO. Available online: http://unesdoc.unesco.org/images/0024/002482/248232E.pdf (accessed 1 December 2020).

UNESCO International Institute for Educational Planning (IIEP) (n.d.), *Brief No.3 Effective and Appropriate Pedagogy*. Available online: https://learningportal.iiep.unesco.org/en/issue-briefs/improve-learning/teachers-and-pedagogy/effective-and-appropriate-pedagogy (accessed 28 December 2020).

UNESCO International Bureau of Education (n.d.), *Intolerance and Extremism Through Universal Values in the Curricula*, Paris: UNESCO.

UNESCO (2005), *The DESD at a Glance*, Paris: UNESCO. Available online: http://unesdoc.unesco.org/images/0014/001416/141629e.pdf (accessed 20 November 2020).

UNESCO (2009), *Review of Contexts and Structures for Education for Sustainable Development 2009*, Paris: UNESCO.

UNESCO (2012), '*Youth and Skills—Putting Education to Work*', *EFA Global Monitoring Report*, 2012, Paris: UNESCO.

UNESCO (2014a), *Teaching and Learning: Achieving Quality for All, EFA Global Monitoring Report 2013/14*, Paris: UNESCO.

UNESCO (2014b), *Shaping the Future We Want: Un Decade of Education for Sustainable Development,—2005–2014—Final Report*, Paris: UNESCO.

UNESCO (2014c), *Roadmap for Implementing the Global Action Programme on Education for Sustainable Development*, Paris: UNESCO.

UNESCO (2015), *Rethinking Education*, Paris: UNESCO.

UNESCO (2016a), *Global Citizenship | United Nations Educational, Scientific and Cultural Organization*, Paris: UNESCO.

UNESCO (2016b), *Global Education Monitoring Report: Education for People and Planet. Creating Sustainable Futures for All*, Paris: UNESCO.

UNESCO (2017), *Education for Sustainable Development—Learning Objectives*, Paris: UNESCO.

UNESCO-IICBA (2017), *Transformative Pedagogy for Peace Building—A Guide for Teachers*, Addis Ababa: UNESCO-IICBA.

UNESCO (2018), *Higher Education as a Common Good*. Available online: http://www.iiep.unesco.org/en/higher-education-global-common-good-4444 (accessed 20 November 2020).

UNESCO (2019), *Right to Education Handbook*, Paris: UNESCO. Available online: https://www.right-to-education.org/sites/right-to-education.org/files/resource-attachments/RTE-UNESCO_Right%20to%20education%20handbook_2019_En.pdf (accessed 21 November 2020).

UNESCO (2020), *Education for Sustainable Development—A Road Map—ESD for 2030*, Paris: UNESCO.

UNICEF (n.d.), *Youth for Climate Action*. Available online: https://www.unicef.org/environment-and-climate-change/youth-action#raisingyouth (accessed 29 October 2020).

UNICEF and UNESCO (2007), *A Human Rights Based Approach to Education for All*, New York: UNICEF. Available online: https://www.unicef.org/publications/files/A_Human_Rights_Based_Approach_to_Education_for_All.pdf (accessed 20 November 2020).

UNICEF (2008), *Our Climate, Our Children, Our Responsibility: The Implications of Climate Change for the World's Children*, London: UNICEF.

UNICEF UK (n.d.), *What Is a Rights Respecting School?* Available online: https://www.unicef.org.uk/rights-respecting-schools/the-rrsa/what-is-a-rights-respecting-school (accessed 15 October 2020).

UNICEF UK (2018a), *Rights and Respecting Schools Impact Report*. Available online: https://www.unicef.org.uk/rights-respecting-schools/wp-content/uploads/sites/4/2019/07/Impact-Report-2018_Final-170719.pdf (accessed 15 October 2020).

UNICEF UK (2018b), *Theory of Change Evidence*. Available online: https://www.unicef.org.uk/rights-respecting-schools/wp-content/uploads/sites/4/2018/01/RRSA-Theory-of-Change-Evidence-Booklet.pdf (accessed 15 October 2020).

UNICEF UK (2020a), *Outright Campaign Introduction—Learning Activities*. Available online: https://www.unicef.org.uk/rights-respecting-schools/wp-content/uploads/sites/4/2020/09/Campaign-Introduction-for-Facilitators-working-with-children-under-12.pdf (accessed 19 October 2020).

UNICEF UK (2020b), *Youth Advocacy Toolkit*, London: UNICEF UK.

Vaccari, V. and M. Gardinier (2019), 'Towards One World or Many? A Comparative Analysis of OECD and UNESCO Global Education Policy Documents', *International Journal of Development Education and Global Learning*, 11(1): 68–86.

Values Based Education (n.d.), *What Is Values Based Education?* Available online: https://www.valuesbasededucation.com/aboutus/what-is-vbe (accessed 11 October 2020).

Van Der Heijden, H. R. M., J. J. M. Geldens, D. Beijaard and H. L. Popeijus (2015), 'Characteristics of Teachers as Change Agents', *Teachers and Teaching: Theory and Practice*, 21(6): 681–699.

Van Dyck, C. (2017), *Concept and Definition of Civil Society Sustainability*, Washington, DC: Centre for Strategic and International Studies. Available online: http://csis-website-prod.s3.amazonaws.com/s3fs-public/publication/170630_VanDyck_CivilSocietySustainability_Web.pdf (accessed 29 October 2020).

Van Poeck, K., L. Östman and J. Öhman (eds) (2019), *Sustainable Development Teaching*, London: Routledge.

Vare, P. and W. Scott (2007), 'Learning for a Change: Exploring the Relationship between Education and Sustainable Development', *Journal of Education for Sustainable Development*, 1(2): 191–198.

Vaughan, R. P. and M. Walker (2012), 'Capabilities, Values and Education Policy', *Journal of Human Development and Capabilities*, 13(3): 495–512.

Verma, R. (ed) (2010), *Be the Change: Teacher, Activist, Global Citizen*, New York: Peter Lang Publishing.

Vincent, C. and M. Hunter-Henin (2018), 'The Problem with Teaching 'British Values' in School', *The Conversation*, 6 February. Available online: https://theconversation.com/the-problem-with-teaching-british-values-in-school-83688 (accessed 15 December 2020).

Vogel, I. (2012), *Review of the Use of 'Theory of Change' in International Development—Review Report*, London: DFID.

Wade, R. C. (2004), 'Citizenship for Social Justice', *Kappa Delta Pi Record*, 40(2): 64–68.

Wade, R. C. (2007), *Social Studies for Social Justice: Teaching Strategies for the Elementary Classroom*, New York: Teachers College Press.

Wahr, F., J. Underwood, L. Adams and V. Prideaux (2013), 'Three Academics' Narratives in Transforming Curriculum for Education for Sustainable Development', *Australian Journal of Environmental Education*, 29(1): 97–116.

Walden University (2017), *Faculty Handbook, 2014–2015*, Available online: https://www.waldenu.edu/–/media/Walden/files/about–walden/walden–university–2017–social–change–report–final–v–2.pdf?la=en) (accessed 20 November 2020).

Walden University (2020), *Academic Guide*. Available online: https://academicguides. waldenu.edu/social-change/mission#:~:text=Walden%20University%27s%20Miss ion%20is%20to%20provide%20a%20diverse,of%20individuals%2C%20communitie s%2C%20organizations%2C%20institutions%2C%20cultures%2C%20and%20societ ies (accessed 20 November 2020).

Walker, C. (2016), 'Environment and Children's Everyday Lives in India and England: Experiences, Understandings and Practices', Unpublished PhD thesis, UCL Institute of Education.

Walker, C. (2017), 'Tomorrow's Leaders and Today's Agents of Change? Children, Sustainability Education and Environmental Governance', *Children and Society*, 31(1): 72–83.

Wals, A., C. Valentina, P. Tassone, P. Hampson and J. Reams (2016), 'Learning for Walking the Change', In: M. Barth, G. Michelsen, M. Rieckmann and I. Thomas (eds), *Routledge Handbook of Higher Education for Sustainable Development*, 25–39, Abingdon: Routledge.

Watts, R. and C. Flanagan (2007), 'Pushing the Envelope on Youth Civic Engagement: A Developmental and Liberatory Psychology Perspective', *Journal of Community Psychology*, 35(6): 779–792.

Weaver, H. N. (2000), 'Balancing Culture and Professional Education: American Indians/Alaska Natives and the Helping Professions', *Journal of American Indian Education*, 39: 1–18.

Weber, N. (2012), 'A Comparative Study of the Shifting Nature of International Nongovernment Organisation Global Education Programming in Canada and the United Kingdom', Unpublished PhD thesis, University of Toronto.

White, M. (2010), *Activism after Clicktivism*. Available online: http://micahmwhite.com/ clicktivism-articles/activism-after-clicktivism (accessed 20 November 2020).

Williams, S. and J. Edleston (eds) (2010), *Connect, Challenge, Change: A Practical Guide to Global Youth Work*, London: Think Global.

Wilson, E. K. (2010), 'From Apathy to Action: Promoting Active Citizenship and Global Responsibility amongst Populations in the Global North', *Global Society*, 24(2): 275–296.

Wierenga, A., J. R. Guevera and S. Beadle (2013), 'Youth Led Learning', In: A. Wierenga and J. R. Guevera (eds), *Education for Global Citizenship: A Youth-Led Approach to Learning Through International Partnerships*, Carlton, Victoria: Melbourne University Press.

Woodcraft Folk (n.d.), *About Us*. Available online: https://woodcraft.org.uk/about (accessed 18 October 2020).

Woodcraft Folk (2013), *Educational Aims and Principles*. Available online: https:// woodcraft.org.uk/sites/default/files/WcF%20APP-January%202013_0.pdf (accessed 18 October 2020).

Woodcraft Folk (2020), *What Is Social Action?* Available online: https://woodcraft. org.uk/sites/default/files/What%20is%20social%20action%20session%20.pdf (accessed 18 October 2020).

Woodin, T. (2015), *Co-Operation, Learning and Co-Operative Values*, Abingdon: Routledge.

Woodin, T. (2019), 'Co-Operative Schools: Democratic Values, Networks and Leadership', *International Journal of Inclusive Education*, 23(11): 1164–1179.

World Bank (n.d.), *Civil Society*. Available online: https://www.worldbank.org/en/a bout/partners/civil-society/overview (accessed 29 October 2020).

World's Largest Lesson (2020), *Turning Learning Into Action*. Available online: https:// worldslargestlesson.globalgoals.org/wp-content/uploads/2020/08/Turning -Learning-Into-Action-Community-Mapping-For-The-Global-Goals-1.pdf (accessed 20 November 2020).

Wright, A. (1987), *R. H. Tawney*, Manchester: Manchester University Press.

Wright, C. (2011), 'Postcolonial Cosmopolitanisms', In: V. Andreotti and L. M. de Souza (eds), *Postcolonial Perspectives on Global Citizenship Education*, 47–67, London: Routledge.

Wyness, M. (2009), 'Adult's Involvement in Children's Participation: Juggling Children's Places and Spaces', *Children and Society*, 23(6): 395–406.

Yanacopoulos, H. and M. Baillie Smith (2007), 'The Ambivalent Cosmopolitanism of International NGOs', In: A. Bebbington, S. Hickey and D. Mitlin (eds) *Can NGOs Make a Difference? The Challenge of Development Alternatives*, 298–315, London: Zed Books.

Yob, I. M. (2018), 'Conceptual Framework for a Curriculum in Social Change', *Journal of Social Change*, 10(1): 71–80.

Yob, I. M., S. Danver, S. Kristensen, W. Schulz, K. Simmons, H. M. Brashen, R. Sidler Krysiak, L. Kiltz, L. Gatlin, S. Wesson and D. R. Penland (2016), 'Curriculum Alignment with a Mission of Social Change in Higher Education', *Innovative Higher Education*, New York: Springer, 41(3): 203–219.

Young, I. M. (1990), *Justice and the Politics of Difference*, Princeton, NJ: Princeton University Press.

Zemach-Bersin, T. (2012), 'Entitled to the World: The Rhetoric of U.S. Global Citizenship Education and Study Abroad', In: V. Andreotti and L. M. de Souza (eds), *Postcolonial Perspectives on Global Citizenship Education*, 87–104, New York: Routledge.

Zollers, N. J., L. R. Albert and M. Cochran-Smith (2000), 'In Pursuit of Social Justice: Collaborative Research and Practice in Teacher Education', *Action in Teacher Education*, 22(2): 1–14.

Index